THE ROUGH GUIDE TO

Money Online

There are more than one hundred and fifty Rough Guide travel, phrasebook, and music titles, covering destinations from Amsterdam to Zimbabwe, languages from Czech to Vietnamese, and musics from World to Opera and Jazz

www.roughguides.com

Rough Guide Credits

Text editor: Mark Ellingham; **Assistant Editor**: Jessica Gill
Production: Michelle Draycott, Julia Bovis,
Helen Ostick and Margaret Doyle

Publishing Information

This first edition published October 2000 by
Rough Guides Ltd, 375 Hudson Street, New York 10014, USA

Distributed by the Penguin Group

Penguin Putnam, Inc., 375 Hudson Street, New York 10014, USA
Penguin Books Canada Ltd, 10 Alcorn Avenue, Toronto,
Ontario, Canada M4V 1E4

Typeset in Bembo and Helvetica to an original design by Henry Iles.
Printed in Canada by Webcom.

A catalogue record for this book is available from the British Library.
ISBN 1-85828-676-X

THE ROUGH GUIDE TO

Money Online

by John Scalzi

ROUGH GUIDES

Rough Guides

We set out to do something different when the first Rough Guide was published in 1982. Mark Ellingham, just out of university, was traveling in Greece. He brought along the popular guides of the day, but found they were all lacking in some way. They were either strong on ruins and museums but went on for pages without mentioning a beach or taverna. Or they were so conscious of the need to save money that they lost sight of Greece's cultural and historical significance. Also, none of the books told him anything about Greece's contemporary life – its politics, its culture, its people, and how they lived.

So with no job in prospect, Mark decided to write his own guidebook, one which aimed to provide practical information that was second to none, detailing the best beaches and the hottest clubs and restaurants, while also giving hard-hitting accounts of every sight, both famous and obscure, and providing up-to-the-minute information on contemporary culture. It was a guide that encouraged independent travelers to find the best of Greece, and was a great success, getting shortlisted for the Thomas Cook travel guide award, and encouraging Mark, along with three friends, to expand the series.

The Rough Guide list grew rapidly and the letters flooded in, indicating a much broader readership than had been anticipated, but one which uniformly appreciated the Rough Guide mix of practical detail and humor, irreverence and enthusiasm. Things haven't changed. The same four friends who began the series are still the caretakers of the Rough Guide mission today: to provide the most reliable, up-to-date, and entertaining information to independent-minded travelers of all ages, on all budgets.

We now publish more than 150 titles and have offices in London and New York. The travel guides are written and researched by a dedicated team of more than 100 authors, based in Britain, Europe, the USA and Australia. We have also created a unique series of phrasebooks to accompany the travel series, along with an acclaimed series of music guides, and a best-selling pocket guide to the Internet and World Wide Web. We also publish comprehensive travel information on our Web site: www.roughguides.com

Acknowledgments

Every smart writer acknowledges his or her agent first of all, and I'll do it too: Thank you Robert Shepard. This is an appropriate book for us, since Robert and I met online. Robert is a good and dedicated agent who knows how to calm writers in panicky moods—and he's also a genuinely good human being (which apparently isn't always a requirement for being a good agent). At Rough Guides, Mark Ellingham has been a great editor for this book—and I would say that even if he weren't also the publisher. Thanks also to Jean Marie Kelly and Simon Carloss, for walking me through what all the rest of being published is about. There's something slightly surreal about being told that little piggy banks are being sent out to drum up support for your book, but it's a good sort of surreal.

Friends have acted as frontline editors and sounding boards for ideas, and helped me depressurize during the writing process. Specific thanks go to Regan Avery, Shelley Skinner, and Stephen Bennett for reading rough drafts and giving me excellent critical comments. *Green* magazine editor and pal Ken Kurson gave me general clarifications on particular subjects, and also paid me some money to write stuff for him. Thanks, Ken. Thanks also: Cian Chang, Christy Gaitten, Ann Merzi, John Anderson, Erin Barbee, Nora Yannuzzi, Troy and Kerry Parkins, Brooke Patterson, Deven Desai, Kevin Stampfl, Natasha Kordus, Joy Rosenthal, Mykal Burns, Shara Zoll, Stephanie Lynn, and Daniel Mainz. Additional thanks to Norm Sattler, Sam Harsh, Brian Wilson, and Rob Cooper.

I got my start writing finance articles for America Online, and still contribute there thanks to some excellent folks, past and present, in the Personal Finance channel. Thanks go out to Rob Shenk (who owns Yosemite Sam), Steve Gaitten, Steve "Smob" Mobley, and to all the folks who edit my stuff, which currently includes Vicki Passmore, Coates Bateman, and Mimi Shea. Other AOLers to thank: Heather Perram, Bonnie Witlin, Thomas Kriese, Miriam Bookey, and Tracy Bromley.

John Scalzi
Sterling, VA, October 2000

Dedicated to Keith Johnson, Lawrence McMillan, and Jacqueline Kahn, teachers and friends all, and to Kristine and Athena, my wife and child.

Contents

Part One

Part One

The Guide

1

Money, the Net, and You

READ THIS FIRST

When people think of the Internet and the Web, they think of money. And who can blame them? In the short time that the Internet and the Web have existed as an economic force, they've received more financial coverage, influenced more business decisions, precipitated more frenzied investing, and made more instant millionaires than any other single phenomenon in world history. Twenty years ago, no one in their right mind would have dreamed that something born out of the mere connections between computers could possibly have as much financial influence as, say, the oil industry. Or banks. Or automobiles. But it has—for sure.

However, underneath the Internet IPOs and the browser wars, behind the multibillion-dollar mergers and the 23-year-old computer programmers worth more than their parents, grandparents, and great-grandparents put together, an even more remarkable financial revolution is taking place on the Net. It's more remarkable because, long after the dotcom financial bubble bursts and the sages get tired of comparing Net investors to tulip speculators of the seventeenth century, this "other" revolution will have changed the way the world does its business. This financial revolution is the revolution of online banking, stock trading, and financial planning.

Why is it so significant? Well, for the first time in the history of the world, the mechanics of world business are becoming truly democratized. You have more control over your money than any of your ancestors ever did. Ever.

Think about it. Five years ago, if you wanted to invest $10,000, you pretty much had to place it into the hands of strangers: stockbrokers who were nominally beholden to you but who had their own agenda (or at the very least, a desire to take long lunches at almost exactly the time you wanted to get hold of them). Every stock move you made had to go through them and they took a nice big bite of your money every time they called in an order. But what could you do? You didn't have access to real-time quotes or to the system that allowed orders to be placed. Just because it was your money didn't mean you got respect.

Flash forward. Today, you place that $10,000 in an Internet brokerage account from the Web or from AOL. You watch the stock prices of the companies in your portfolio jitter like nervous birds, thanks to a ticker in real-time. You double-click on one of those stocks and look at a historical chart, showing its movement over the last year. You read the latest *Associated Press* story on the company, so fresh off the wire that a copy editor missed a typo. You examine the most recent earnings estimates from the analysts. And, armed to your eyebrows with all this financial intelligence, you make the trade. For a fraction of the cost a stockbroker would ding you for.

And you're just one of millions, using the Net for all manner of financial transactions. Your paycheck is almost certainly electronically deposited into your checking account—and you can go online at 3am to transfer funds into savings, or pay your bills over your computer. If on April 15 (at 11:37pm), you discover you are missing that 1099-MISC form you so desperately need to finish your taxes you can download the form from the IRS Web site—that is, if your tax preparation software doesn't have the form, which it almost certainly does. And as for rushing to the post office before midnight—why? Your tax software just filed the forms online.

In the space of half a decade, we've gone from having to conform our lives to the financial world, to having the financial world conform to our lives—an astounding bit of empowerment that's happened so quietly that many of us aren't even aware that it's happened, much less are using it to our advantage. Not every revolution comes bursting through the door. Still, over there in the corner more than six million North Americans are quietly doing their banking online—and an estimated thirty million will join them in the next five years. It's time for everyone to reap the rewards.

Which is where this handy little book comes in. Enclosed in its smallish dimensions is a guide through these revolutionary times. It's for all you folks who want to stop waiting in line at the bank, or trying to get your broker on the phone, but are worried that if you try it on your own, you might screw something up. Well, you won't (really—I'm not just saying that to get you to buy this book). Taking charge of your finances online is easy, and getting easier every day.

This book can't (and won't even pretend to) make you a financial expert. That's your job: You'll have to take the time to become the master of your own financial situation. What it will do is get you started on the way. It will show you how to do it all: Not just how to bank online or trade online, but also how to find and finance houses, cars and credit cards online. It'll tell you where you can learn everything you ever wanted to know about finances without having to budge from in front of your computer. It'll even help with the taxes. Potholes and obstacles? They're there, to be sure. But they're easy to get past, once pointed out. This book will do a lot of waving and pointing and telling you when to swerve.

The bottom line: It's your money and your chance to be at the front of one of the great financial revolutions of all time. It's easier than you think.

Using This Book—and US/Canada

The chapters following cover all the basics of making your money work online—banking, mortgages and loans, credit cards, investments, and taxes. They should be used in conjunction with the **Web site reviews** in the second half of this book, where you'll find US (Part Two) and Canadian (Part Three) business URLs (addresses) to turn knowledge into action.

The information following is written primarily for US users. However, in terms of practicalities, much of it applies equally to **Canada**—setting up banking and brokerage accounts, applying for loans, dealing with credit cards, and using other commercial services online are very similar processes both sides of the border.

2

Online Banking

GETTING STARTED

Take a look at your ATM card. It's a pretty unassuming thing, and yet it represents a sea change in the way banks do business. Before ATMs and the cards that go with them, people had to get money during bank hours. Any banking activity, in fact, required you to actually go into the bank office during business hours. Now, of course, you can do just about all your banking any time of the day through an ATM machine, and many people do—and everyone today assumes that their bank has these ATM functions. A bank without ATM capabilities is a bank that doesn't have many customers.

The way we feel about ATMs today is how we will feel about online banking tomorrow. We won't wonder that our banks have online banking; we'll assume it. And for exactly the same reason as ATMs: Online banking makes managing our money so much simpler. Ask anyone who already banks online. They can't imagine ever going back.

What's the Big Deal?

The advantage that ATMs have brought to customers is pretty clear: ready access to your money, wherever you are. But what does a regular customer get out of online banking?

The short answer is, again, access. With online banking, you can work with your accounts from anywhere, any time of day or night, without having to wait in line. Your money keeps the same hours you do. If you want to transfer funds from checking to savings at 3am in the morning, you can do that. If you want to pay bills wearing a bathrobe, you can do that too. As long as you have a computer connection and the necessary software to access your account, you're golden. Just about the only thing you can't do right now is download money—and with the next generation of "smart cards" coming along, even that will be possible soon enough.

Meantime, here are the pros and cons.

Preparing for Online Banking

So, you've decided you're on for online banking? What do you need to get yourself started?

First and most obviously, you'll need **money**, a **computer**, a **modem**, and **online access**. The money speaks for itself, as does the computer. The modem and online access are likewise self-evident. Not every bank requires an Internet connection in order to bank electronically (some banks have their own internal system). But most do, and every bank that uses a Web-based system requires it. We're assuming for the purposes of this book that you are already online and have some familiarity with the Internet; if you don't, read Angus J. Kennedy's *The Rough to the Internet* to get up to speed.

Assuming you have an Internet connection, you don't really need any software beyond an **email program** and a **Web browser**, typically Microsoft's Internet Explorer or Netscape's

Pros and Cons of Banking Online

Pros:

- **Bank Anytime.** Online banking is open when you are.
- **Know How Much You're Worth.** Banking online gives you the exact status of your accounts, as of the moment you log on.
- **Special Deals.** Many banks offer special rates or introductory offers (such as free bill pay) for customers who bank online.
- **Freedom of Choice.** You can choose to do business with any bank that has online access, wherever it is based.
- **Consolidation of Information.** If you use personal finance software, online banking allows for better integration of your information and the bank's, especially if the bank allows you to access your accounts using that personal finance software.

Cons:

- **Deposits.** If you bank with a bank outside your local area, or a bank that is Internet-only, you'll have to deposit through direct deposits or through the mail. Deposits sent by mail understandably take several days to show up in your accounts.
- **ATM Fees.** If your online bank does not have their own ATMs locally, you may have to pay additional ATM fees each time you access your cash. (Some online banks refund these charges.)
- **Computers (1).** Despite everyone's best efforts, computer systems do go down. If your bank's online service is down, you'll not be able to access it until it's fixed. During particularly heavy usage either of the Net or the bank's servers, your banking session may be slow. And, of course, your own computer can let you down.
- **Computers (2).** Banking online assumes a level of comfort with computers; if you're uncomfortable with computer programs, you'll probably be uncomfortable banking on one.

Continues over

For Small Business

This book is primarily about personal banking. But many banks also offer online services specifically designed for **small business owners**, including online business checking and investments, payroll and retirement plans, credit accounts and other merchant services.

Additionally, both Quicken and Money **Personal Finance Software** are offered in a small business-specific version, which features business-oriented tools such as invoicing, income tracking and business reports.

Navigator. Any online service will provide you with a Web browser when you sign up for their service, and just about every computer shipped in the last few years comes with a Web browser installed.

Web browsers come with **security encryption**—a process that allows the browser to send confidential information (such as your banking account or credit card numbers) across the Internet in a secure fashion. Regular browsers have 40-bit encryption, which is generally safe enough. But many banks require 128-bit security encryption, a level of encryption so high that the US government does not allow it to be sent overseas—only residents of the US and Canada have access to these browsers at this time. Both Netscape and Microsoft feature browsers with 128-bit encryption; if you don't have one on your computer now, you should download the latest version (but not a 'beta' fest) right away.

An optional but handy piece of software is a **personal finance program**. This is a software program that allows you to handle all your finances on your computer. You can use it to track your checking and savings accounts, balance your checkbook, track your investments, keep tabs on what you'll owe the tax man, and more. Many banks allow customers to use personal finance software to access their online accounts. This can be very helpful, especially if you already use the software to deal with your finances—the information can be downloaded into your program instantaneously, saving you from the drudgery of typing it in yourself.

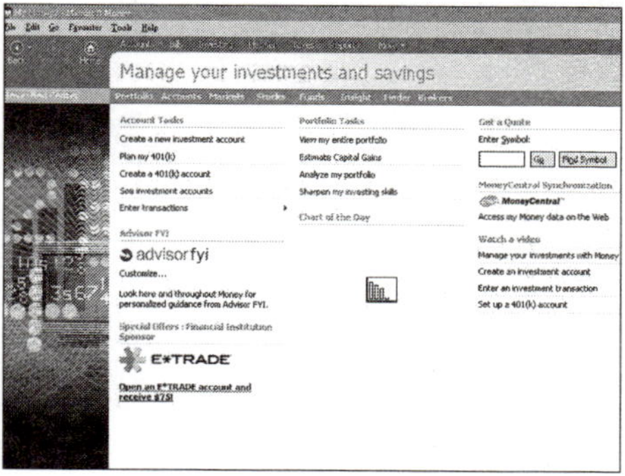

There are two brands of commercial personal finance software which are commonly supported by banks: **Quicken**, by Intuit, and **Money**, by Microsoft. (For the purposes of this book, we'll be concentrating exclusively on Money and Quicken when we discuss personal finance software.) Your bank may support both or just one, or may provide you with their own proprietary brand of software (this is becoming less common). And some banks don't support personal finance software at all, preferring to use Web browsers as the online interface. The sidebar on p.12 (Web-based v. Software-based) outlines the pluses and minuses of the two approaches.

Both Quicken and Money are widely available in stores and online, and if your bank uses one or both, they may even give you a version to use. Can't beat that. The newest versions of Money and Quicken both come with built-in Web capability, allowing you to access your Web-based accounts from the software without having to fire up your Web browser.

Web-based vs Software-based

Which format for online banking—Web-based or software-based—is going to be right for you?

Web-based Banking Might Be Right for You If ...

- You already use the Internet on a frequent and regular basis, know your way around a Web browser, and are comfortable using the Web for online transactions (you've bought something online).
- You don't currently use personal finance software and have no interest in doing so in the future.
- You have a reliable online connection that allows you access to the Web at any time.
- You are confident of the security offered by online browsers and Web-based banking services.
- You want to be able to access your accounts from any online-capable computer, not just the one that has your personal finance software on it.

Software-based Banking Might Be Right for You If ...

- You use (or plan to use) personal finance software for your finances, and want an easy way to reconcile your home accounts with your bank accounts.
- You don't have a regular online connection (banks will provide dial-up access to their servers for software-based banking).
- You have concerns about Web browser security.
- You don't spend a lot of time online, nor have you used the Web for transactions.
- You prefer to have your accounts accessible from only one place (the computer with your personal finance software on it).

Signing Up for Online Banking

Before you apply for your online bank account, here's a checklist of things to do. For this exercise, it's assumed that you already have a bank account and that you are signing up for online banking with your current bank, or that you have a specific bank in mind if you do not already have an account. We'll talk about switching banks and shopping around for the best banking deals later (see Chapter Four).

Step One: Determine Whether Your Bank Has Online Services

Most banks allow their customers at least basic online services, such as balance transfers and bill payments. But how can you know for sure? Easy:

Check Your Bank's Web Page

Nearly every bank has a **Web site**, which you can invariably find just by entering the bank's name as a URL in your Web browser (for example, the Web site for Wells Fargo bank is www.wellsfargo.com).

If that doesn't do the trick, try searching for the bank in a Web directory like Yahoo (http://www.yahoo.com) or Excite (http://www.excite.com), or AOL Search (AOL Keyword: Search). Enter the bank's name in the search area of the main page, and you're likely to get a link. AOL also lists banks that have relationships with its service by state; use AOL Keyword: banking and then the State Banking Centers button.

Not every bank that has a Web site has online banking, but every bank that does have online banking will have information about it on its Web site. Many of these sites also feature online demos (so you can see what the banking process will look like) as well as on-site applications.

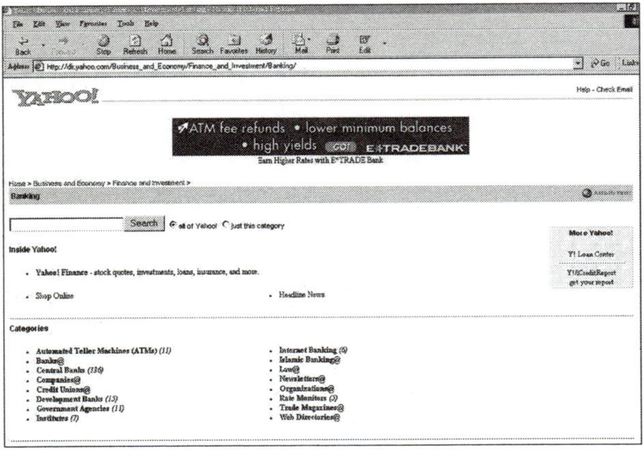

Call Your Bank's Customer Service Number

The bank representative should be able to tell you if the bank offers online banking services, as well as what services are available and what software you'll need to access the services. Depending on the bank, they may also be able to take your application for online services over the phone.

Alternatively, the next time you're in making a deposit or withdrawal, ask your teller about the availability of online services. They can either provide you with information or get you in touch with a bank representative.

Step Two: Find Out What Services Are Available Online

Not every bank gives the same level of online service. Some provide only basic **bill payments** and **transfers**, while others allow a much wider range of services, including **loan and mortgage applications**, **bill presentment**, and **stock and fund trading**. You need to decide for yourself what things you want to accomplish online and make sure your bank can accommodate those needs.

Basic Services

Here are the basic banking services every bank should provide online:

Account Balances: Review the state of your accounts and recent and historic activity.

Fund Transfers: Move funds between your accounts.

Bill Payment: "Write and send a check" online to your creditors, with funds debited against the appropriate account.

Advanced Services

Here are some more advanced services banks can provide:

Bill Presentment: This allows you to see itemized bills online; not only do you know how much you owe, but you also see the breakdown of the charges on the bill.

Account Information Downloads: The ability to take all current information on your accounts and download this as a single file into your computer, either in a format your personal finance software can read or as a spreadsheet or text file.

View Checks or Deposits: See copies of paid checks or deposits, and in some cases download images of them onto your own computer.

Stock and Fund Trading: Invest online.

Loans and Credit Cards: Apply for and manage payment of credit cards and loans online.

Step Three: Learn About the Fees

You thought that all this great technology would come for free? Strange how it comes over that way. In fact, many online banking services come with a fee—albeit quite reasonable ones, due to the intense competition out there in bankland.

Indeed, according to Bankrate.com (http://www.bankrate.com), a Web site that tracks banks and their fees, nearly 65 percent of banks online now offer their services free (up from 38 percent in 1999). Those banks that charge **access fees** average charges of about $5.44 per month.

Although it looks like fees are going down—and many banks offer special deals to lure you into banking online—you should never underestimate the ability of a bank to find new ways to charge you. Anyone who uses an ATM knows that "service charges" have a funny way of cropping up. Common online charges relate to **bill payment** (which is fair enough, as the bank incurs costs here, as they sometimes have to print and send checks by mail). Less scrupulously, if you sign up for an account in which your method of banking is supposed to be online, you can be charged if you step into a bank office and have a teller help you. And if you have a regular account, of course, your normal banking and checking fees will probably still be in effect.

Your bank should have fees described in the online information at its Web site, possibly buried in fine print. Alternatively, check **Bankrate.com**, which has information on online fees as part of its information on overall fees, or **Gomez.com**, which ranks banks by several criteria, including overall cost.

Step Four: Learn About Privacy and Security

If you are sending confidential banking information over the Internet, you want reassurance from your banking institution that the information is being handled safely and securely. Just as important is the knowledge of what information about you (who you are, where you live, how much you have in your accounts) is being bandied about or sold to the highest bidder. To that end, find and read the **privacy and security information** that your bank posts on its Web site.

How Secure Is Online Banking?

One of the chief concerns people have about online banking is that their financial information will somehow be exposed. And this much is true: You should be as careful with financial information that you send electronically as with any other method. However, banking online is safe from prying eyes, thanks to several security methods employed by both your Web browser and your bank. Let's review a few of them.

■ **Web-browser Encryption**: The first and formidable line of defense is the encryption your information undergoes within your Web browser. Encryption means that the information you want to send is scrambled by use of a numerical "key." A random "key" is generated any time you start a secure bank process with your bank; how secure that key is depends on how many bits are used to generate the key. Typically, banks require 128-bit encryption: this is serious encryption, allowing for something on the order of 340,000,000,000,000,000,000,000,000,000,000,000,000 numerical combinations ... and that's a tough one to crack.

■ **Personal Finance Software**: The latest versions of Money or Quicken come with 128-bit Web browsers that you can install, and the software's equally encrypted.

■ **Firewalls**: Suppose the hackers and crackers decide to attack the bank's computers directly. What's to stop them? The answer is a "Firewall"—a computer that acts as a go-between between outside users and the bank's computer system. When you request information from your bank, it goes to the firewall computer, which checks the request, and then, if everything's correct, asks the computers on the other side to forward that information. Strictly speaking, you have never accessed the bank's computers. Hacking a firewall is not easy. And in any case, if you have a regular bank account, its details are still on your bank's computer.

Continues over

■ **The Government**: Let's suppose someone has managed to get past all the defenses to access your accounts online. Well, in the US the same FDIC insurance that protects your money if your local bank branch is robbed protects you if the bank is breached online. Regulation E, which protects credit cards, also applies to online banking. If someone accesses your accounts and manages to sneak off with your money, you can get back all but $50 of it—so long as you report the theft within 48 hours.

The security information should tell you what sort of measures your bank employs to safeguard your confidential information, as well as what **guarantees**, if any, they provide should that information be compromised due to a failure on their part (the information should also tell you what obligations you have to keep your information safe). The privacy information should tell you what personal information they keep, and under what circumstances they provide third parties with personal information about you. It should also tell you how you can opt out of having that information shared in the form of mailing lists and such. If you can't find that information on the site, call or visit a representative. Your security and privacy are important issues (see sidebar above).

Step Five: Learn the Format

As previously mentioned, banks may offer online access through **Web** or **personal finance software**, though happily an increasing number are offering their customers the choice. The one piece of advice to give here is that if you have a choice, stick with it once you've made it; it'll be easier to keep track of your account information that way.

If your bank uses personal finance software, you'll probably have to download some information from your bank to get going. There's also often a delay between the application and when you can start banking online, as the bank processes your application and mails you additional materials. Be patient, and use that interim to become more comfortable with the personal finance software you'll be using.

The Application

You've satisfied your questions about security, privacy, format, fees and services, so the only thing left to do is apply, right?

Nearly every bank that has online banking allows you to make an **application online**. If you do this, you'll be taken into a secure environment on their Web site where you can enter information that includes your name and address, how you can be reached, and the banking options you want. You'll be able to tell you're in a **secure area** because your Web browser will display a lock icon in the bottom left or right of your browser window (if you're not shuttled into a secure online area, don't apply online). You may additionally be asked for employment or salary history, or other information, depending on the bank. If you already have an account with the bank, you'll be asked to provide those account numbers.

You'll also be asked to enter the **name and password** you want to use to access the account. The easiest name to use, of course, is your own, although you may need some variation if someone else with the same name is already a bank customer. Your password should be something that only you know, and something that someone else can't easily figure out (don't use your birthday or middle name). Some banks require you to use both letters and numbers in your password, or may provide you with a random password, which you may then change.

Some banks will process your entire application online, in which case you'll be required to create an "**electronic signature card**"; others will take the process offline at the end, mailing you confirmation materials for you to sign and return before setting up the account. If you are uncomfortable applying online, or have questions about the application process, remember that you can usually apply over the phone or in person at your bank.

If you are a **new customer** to the bank, you will probably be required to make an **initial deposit** (usually at least $100). The initial deposit can either be handled on the site with a credit card transfer, or by mailing a check or money order to an address that the bank provides during the process. If you are a **current bank customer**, the application will allow the bank to make your existing accounts accessible online (unless, of course, you are applying for a new, separate account).

Accessing Your Account

Once you've applied and received confirmation that your account is ready to go, the first thing you should do is **access your account**. If you've chosen to do your banking through the Web, this will be an easy thing to do—just go to your **bank's home page**. The home page commonly has a special button or area where customers can log in.

Once you find the area that allows you to **log in**, enter your name and your password (the password field will show asterisks rather than the password you type in, so type carefully and pay attention to upper and lower case). Once you enter this, your account information page should appear, and you'll be ready to go. Make sure that you've been taken to a **secure area** on the system—check for the locked icons. If you don't see the locked icons, check with your bank. It could be that the bank is using "frames" on their Web site and secure areas of the bank's site don't appear as the main frames on your screen.

Accessing with Personal Finance Software

If you are using **Quicken**, **Money**, or your bank's **personal finance software**, you'll need to configure your software to access the bank's system. This will take more time than accessing the bank's system through the Web. (Personal finance software programs are capable of handling more than one bank account at a time. This is unlike the Web connection, which is directly interfacing one particular bank.) You'll need to enter detailed information about yourself and your account to help your personal finance software figure out which bank it is talking to and which accounts you are accessing.

Fortunately, Quicken and Money come equipped with **wizards** (mini-programs) designed to help you set up your accounts. Just make sure that the information you enter into your personal finance software is exactly the same as the information you've provided your bank. If the information isn't exactly the same, you're probably not going to get very far.

Once you've entered the information in your personal finance software, go to your software's toolbar and **connect with your bank**. You'll then be asked to enter your account name and password. Press "enter," and your software will log on and get the most recent information for your account.

Congratulations, you're now ready to bank online!

3

Basic Banking

BALANCES, TRANSFERS, DEPOSITS, AND PAYING BILLS

Well, here you are with a new online banking account. Whatever shall you do with it? First off, make sure that your paycheck gets paid into your bank account by **direct deposit** (see overpage). Done that? Then it's time for basic banking. This chapter takes you through checking your **account balances**, **transferring funds**, and **paying bills**. Throughout, we have provided options for doing this through your bank's Web site, and using Money or Quicken personal finance software (PFS).

Reviewing Your Account Balance

One of the most useful things about banking online is that you can check how much you're worth—any time of day and as of that moment. **Account information** is usually one of the very first things you'll see when you log on to your banking Web site, and it's just a couple of clicks away on your personal finance software. Here's how it works:

Account Balances—Web

Finding account information on the Web could hardly be more simple. Once you have signed in to your bank's Web site you will either—depending on the bank—be provided instantly with your account balance information, or have the option to click on a link to check your balances. Click and your account balances will appear. There's your money.

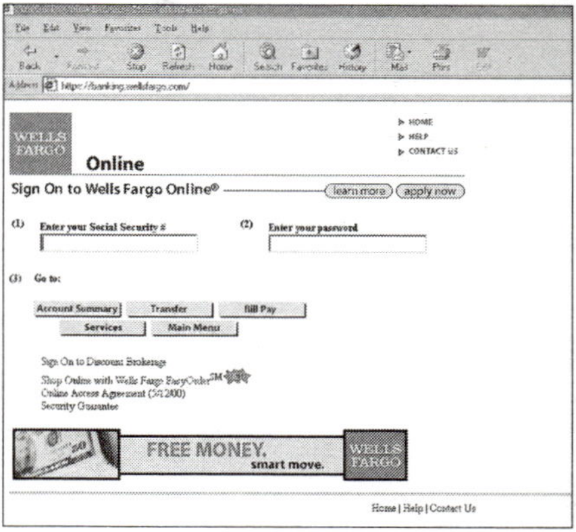

Account Balances—PFS

Getting **account information** using **personal finance software** takes a couple more steps. With both Money and Quicken, you need to go online, select your bank, and then specify information you want to receive (account balances) or send (like transactions you may have started offline). You'll also have to enter your password and PIN. Once you've entered these, click "Connect" or "Send," and you're there.

If you have more than one bank account to keep track of, Quicken allows you to cut this down to one step with a **PIN**

Vault that allows you to access all your PIN numbers with one password. Money will remember your PIN numbers for you if you like—but it's not a recommended option, certainly if your computer is accessible by others, for example at work.

Direct Deposits

With direct deposit, your paycheck (or any other regular income) goes directly from your company's bank accounts to your bank (and instead of a paycheck on payday, you'll get a receipt of the transaction). It's pretty easy to do, saves you mailing or taking the check to your bank, and gets the money into your account faster, earning or paying off interest.

Most companies and government agencies of any size support (or even require) direct deposit. If your employers don't support it, ask them to consider doing so—it's simpler for them, too. Assuming they do, all you have to do is to provide the number of the account you wish the paycheck to go to (usually your checking account), and your bank's routing and transit number (you can get these from your bank).

Ledger and Available Balances

Now you've gotten your account information, you may find yourself looking at two balances for each of your accounts: one labeled either "**Ledger Balance**" or simply "**Balance**," and one labeled "**Available Balance**." The reason for the two balances is rooted in the nature of banks. Banks tend to deal with all account transactions at one time, rather than as they happen during the day. Until those transactions are processed, any transfer of funds that day, such as ATM withdrawals, bill payments or deposits, are noted as "memo posts." These are your bank's way of saying "We know this transaction happened, we just haven't gotten around to making it official." When your bank makes a memo post, it holds back that amount of money pending the processing of the transaction.

So a Ledger Balance is the amount of money that is actually present in any account at that moment; an Available Balance is the amount of money that's available for you to use.

Bear in mind that both ledger and available balances reflect only the activity your bank knows about: ATM, debit card charges and money transfers which are handled in real time (your bank makes a memo post as soon as the request is sent electronically), and regular check payments when your creditor deposits the check in his or her bank. If someone neglects to deposit your check for a couple of weeks, that amount of money will still be listed in your available balance, so you still have to **balance your checkbook**. Sorry about that.

Reviewing Statements

Forgotten checks included, you can find out what's cleared on your account by **reviewing your statement(s) online**. Any transaction your account experiences will be detailed: ATM withdrawals, direct deposits, check deposits and debits, money transfers, automatic payments, the lot.

Statements—Web

Once again, this process is simple. Once you're in your bank's site and viewing your account balances, you will usually see a "**view transactions**" button, which will display all transactions on that account during the last billing cycle. Some banks, like Wells Fargo, allow you to click on the available balance to pull up the transaction list. Decent banking Web sites will allow you to further customize the transactions you can review, so you can see transactions with a certain range of days, or view previous statements.

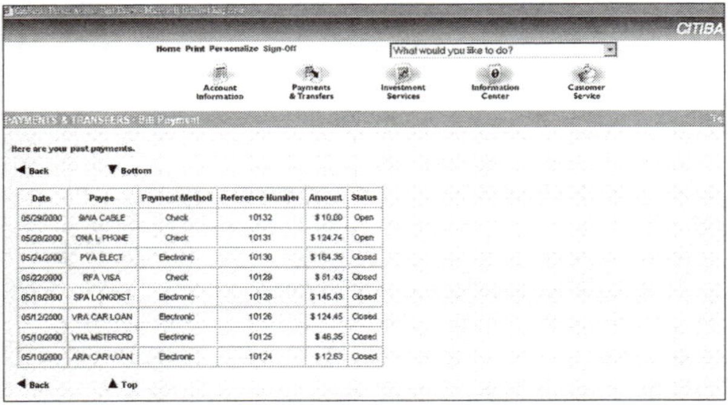

Date	Payee	Payment Method	Reference Number	Amount	Status
05/29/2000	SWA CABLE	Check	10132	$ 10.00	Open
05/28/2000	ONA L PHONE	Check	10131	$ 124.74	Open
05/24/2000	PVA ELECT	Electronic	10130	$ 184.35	Closed
05/22/2000	RFA VISA	Check	10129	$ 81.43	Closed
05/18/2000	SPA LONGDIST	Electronic	10128	$ 145.43	Closed
05/12/2000	VRA CAR LOAN	Electronic	10126	$ 124.45	Closed
05/10/2000	YHA MSTERCRD	Electronic	10125	$ 46.35	Closed
05/10/2000	ARA CAR LOAN	Electronic	10124	$ 12.63	Closed

Statements—PFS

If you're using personal finance software to bank online, chances are you're also using it to do other things, such as handling your offline finances and balancing your bank account. This means that in addition to **downloading the most recent statements** from your bank account, you can **reconcile that information** with information you already have in your software—so you can make sure deposits and withdrawals are for the correct amount. You can also add any additional information you need to keep track of your money.

With **Quicken**, the information you download from your bank is kept from dropping into your account register until you choose the "**Compare to Register**" function. When you do that, you're presented with a list of the downloaded transactions. Click on one, and the software compares the information it has received from your bank with the information that you had previously entered in during money management sessions with the software. You can make any changes or add any information you need to at that point. Then click "Accept" and the information is officially added. Keep doing this with all the downloaded transactions, and your register will be totally up-to-date. Click "Done" and you're done. If you don't want to bother with reviewing every single statement, click the "Accept All" button and then "Done."

Money is similar. After downloading the data when you sign on, access your account information through the Money Home Page by clicking on the account whose statements you wish to read, and then clicking on "**Read Downloaded Statement**." You can choose to simply read the statement, or you can cross-check it with your own register by using the "Reconcile cash activity" page.

All this cross-referencing and double-checking may lead you to ask: Do I have to use my personal software for anything but online banking? The answer is no. However, using personal finance software to handle day-to-day expenses as well as your online banking will help you keep a tight grasp on how much money you really have to spend and where it's going every day.

Transferring Funds Between Your Accounts

You probably already have both a **savings** and **checking account** with your bank: If not, then the move online is a good time to add the option. At times, you'll want to put money into savings from checking or vice versa, and doing this online is just about the easiest thing you can do.

Transfers—Web

Sign on to your bank's Web site and enter your account information. When you are taken to your main page or account information page, select the "**Transfer Funds**" option. You'll be taken to a page on which there are three fields: One for the account from which you are transferring funds, one for the account to which the funds are going, and one for the amount you wish to transfer. Enter the account numbers in their respective fields (some banks will list your available accounts, in which case simply select the account you want in that field). Then enter the transfer amount in that field. Press the "**Send**" or "**Request Transfer**" button (however your bank labels it). You're done. For peace of mind, make a note of the confirmation number or other confirmation information your bank provides. Electronic banking is pretty reliable but you can't assume that there is never an error.

If you regularly transfer money from one account to another (say, tucking away $100 from each paycheck into a money market account), some banks will allow you to **automatically set up** that transfer, usually on a monthly basis. For that, you'll once again have fields to enter the numbers of the accounts you are transferring to and from, as well as the amount being transferred. You'll additionally enter the day of the month you want the transfer to occur (when that day falls on a weekend or holiday, the transaction will be set for the next business day). Send the information and your bank will set up the transfer. Again, note your confirmation information.

Transfers—PFS

It's almost as easy to transfer funds through your personal finance software as it is through the Web.

Using **Quicken**, select Banking from the toolbar, then select Online Banking, and finally the Transfers tab. Select your bank. Select the appropriate accounts in the "Transfer Money From" and "To" fields, enter the amount in the "Amount" field, and then click "Enter." The transaction then waits for you to update your financial information with your bank—when you click "Update/Send," the information is on its way.

Using **Money**, go to the "Accounts" button on the navigation bar; once you're in the Accounts area, select the bank that has the accounts you want to use. A window will pop up asking you what you'd like to do. Click "Create Instructions For" and a new window will pop up. Click on "Transfer" down there on the bottom, and a new box appears. From there, just select the accounts in the appropriate drop-down menu, enter the amount of the transfer and the date it is to take place, and then click "OK." You'll go to the "Connect" window, where you can complete the transaction.

Remember that you can only use your personal finance software to transfer funds between **accounts approved for online banking**. If your personal finance software doesn't know about an account, it can't transfer funds to it.

Transferring Funds Externally

Okay, so you can transfer funds from one account to another at your own bank. But what about if you need to transfer funds out of your bank into an outside account, or into it from an account you hold at another bank? Some but not all banks will allow you to do these transactions online—and whether you can do it all online will be determined by how you make the transfer.

Wire Transfers

If you are making a **wire transfer into your account** from an account you hold at another bank, you may be required to go in person to that other bank with a **transfer form**. This form will require, for both accounts, the account numbers, the name(s) of the person(s) who opened the accounts, and the bank names, routing and transit numbers, plus, of course, the amount being transferred and the date. Your bank may provide a form that can be downloaded or printed to make this easier.

Automated Clearing House

Another way to transfer funds from one bank to another is through the **Automated Clearing House**, which will allow you to perform the transfer process without going anywhere. To **send funds out of your account**, you can enter the information online, or contact a bank representative by phone to initiate the process. You'll need the number, name, and routing and transit numbers for the account you're transferring funds to. Be aware that there may be a delay of one or two business days in completing the transfer, and that there may also be a limit both on the number of transfers per day and the amount you can transfer.

Transferring funds into your account from an account that you have at another bank will probably have to be handled over the phone. Have ready the following information: the number for the account the funds are coming from, the name attached to that fund, the bank the account is in, routing and transit numbers, and the amount of the transfer. Be aware that there may be a delay of a couple of business days in completing the transfer, and that there may also be a limit both on the number of transfers per day and the amount you can transfer. Check with your bank for all the details.

Paying Bills Online

Online bill payment is remarkably similar to a process you presumably already know: writing a check. You fill out the same information: to whom the "check" is to be paid, for how much, and to where it is being mailed. It's not difficult—and the advantage is, of course, no stamps, no envelope, and instant guaranteed delivery.

Unfortunately, Bill Pay doesn't often come free; banks may charge a flat fee for the service, or may charge per transaction, or both. Some banks provide free Bill Pay services if you have a minimum amount in your checking account, or may offer a few months of free Bill Pay as an inducement for you try it out. A select few offer Bill Pay without charge—but not many. So **check the fees**.

Independent Bill Pay Services

One interesting thing about the **Bill Pay services** that banks provide is that they aren't specifically tied to accounts. Your bank may set you up for Bill Pay when you set up an online account (usually by giving you a box you can check off), but it's equally likely that you'll be required to make another, separate application for Bill Pay services. This is in part because a bank needs to show it has authorization to make withdrawals from your checking account without your signature.

The separate nature of Bill Pay services means that you can pay bills online even if your bank account is not set up for online access. Some banks, like the Internet-only Wingspan Bank, will allow you access to their **Bill Pay service** even if you don't have a checking account with them (there's a fee involved, of course). Other financial entities, like American Express, also offer Bill Pay services. This is helpful if, for example, your online bank doesn't offer online bill payment.

Signing Up

As previously mentioned, many banks will allow you to **sign up for Bill Pay services** at the same time you're applying to access your banking accounts online. If they did not, or you decided not to take the option at that time, you'll need to go to your bank's Web site and find the information on Bill Pay. An **application** for Bill Pay services is probably not far off; fill out the application and submit it. Depending on the bank, confirmation may be instantaneous or take up to several days.

If **your bank does not do Bill Pay online**, complain—they need to get with the times. Then get a list of banks and other financial institutions that do allow online Bill Pay.

One place to find such a list is at the home page of **CheckFree** (www.checkfree.com), the online entity that handles the Bill Pay back end for a number of banks and institutions (it also offers a limited range of services itself). Some of these banks and institutions will allow you to pay bills without being banking customers; find one you like and sign up.

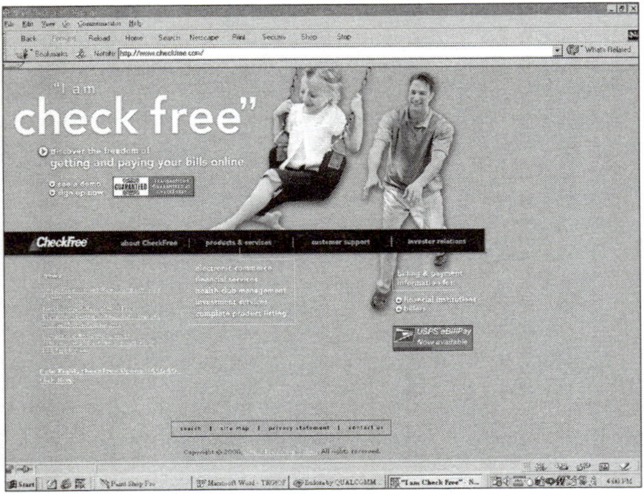

Be aware that many online banks require Web browsers with **128-bit encryption** for Bill Pay services, even if they don't require it for other services. These banks will usually provide you with a link to download those browsers, or you can simply go to the home pages of Netscape (http://www.netscape.com or AOL Keyword: Netscape) or Internet Explorer (http://www.microsoft.com/windows/ie/).

It's Not Instant

Be aware that online bill payment is **not instantaneous**: The amount deducted from your account does not instantly show up in your creditor's account. The process can take anywhere from a day—assuming both your bank and your creditor have the ability to transfer funds electronically—to a week—if your creditor needs an actual paper check (yep—it's possible this online process may end with your bank writing and sending a check in the mail). So when you're scheduling your payments, factor in time for the payment to reach your creditor. Don't have it sent the day it's due; send it up to a week (or more, if you can afford it) in advance.

Bill Pay Through the Web

Once you've signed up for Bill Pay, you can access that area on your bank's (or other chosen Bill Payer's) Web site. In order to pay your creditors, you have to let the bank know who they are and where the money should be sent. To do that, you'll need to set up a "Payee Record" for each of them. Setting up these is a separate process from paying that payee, so initially, paying your creditors is a two-step operation.

Creating Payee Records

In the Bill Pay area, you should see a link or button that says "**Add Payee**" or some variation thereof. Click on it, and you will be taken to an area to enter the payee information. Here's the information you'll need to have ready:

Payee Name: The name of your creditor.

Payee Account Number: This is *not* the payee's account, but *your account with the payee* (your gas company account, phone account number, etc). This number is extremely important for such accounts—without it, a large corporation will have no idea why money is being sent. Obviously it is optional when your payee is a friend or a small business that doesn't use account numbers.

Your Bank Account Number: The bank needs to know from which account you'll be paying this bill. You may have to enter this number manually, or the bank may provide a drop-down list of your bank accounts to select. (Your bank may skip this step and have you enter this information later.)

Payee's Address: The address to which you would otherwise mail your check to your creditor. Some banks will also ask for a phone number.

Amount of Payment: Ah, the painful part—enter the amount you want to send. Some banks leave this out, preferring instead to let you enter the information at a later time, or, if the payment is to be a recurring payment, to set this amount when you fill out that information.

One-Time and Recurring Payments

Once you've entered the payee information, you have the option of paying them. You can opt to do so once only (if it's a one-time payment, or a recurring bill with a different amount each month, like a gas bill), or on a regular basis (this is good for set-amount recurring bills, such as mortgage payments or newspaper subscriptions).

For **one-time payments**, click on the link or button labeled "Schedule Payments" or "Make Payments." Once there, you'll find a list of your payees. Pick the one you want to pay. If you haven't already entered the bank account number you want to pay from, you'll do it now. Likewise the amount you want to send. Enter the date on which you want the payment to be sent—it doesn't have be immediately—and then send the request. Your bank will then send the amount on the date you have specified.

For **recurring payments**, click on the link or button labeled "Repeating Payments" and you'll be taken to an area to set up regular payments. You select the payee from your list and specify the amount of the payment, date of the first payment, and frequency and duration of the payments (some banks combine this area with their "Schedule Payments" area, and list "Pay Once" as an option in a drop-down menu). Most banks can handle conventional time amounts such as weekly, bi-weekly, monthly, quarterly, semi-annually and annually. When you're done filling in the information, send the request for the payment to be sent, and your bank will start automatically paying that bill for the duration of the time specified.

Changes and Tracking Bill Payment

If you need to **change Bill Pay information**, you can do so at any time prior to the send date. This is usually done through the Schedule Payment area or an area labeled "Payment Activity" or "Payment History" that specifically **tracks payment activity**.

This area will also allow you to **track a payment's progress** through the system, so you can see if a scheduled payment was made on time or if there was any trouble with the payment (for example, if you didn't have sufficient funds in your account). Additionally, this area should also allow you to **stop payments** if you so choose, and may also provide a customer service number if you have any additional questions about a payment.

Put some thought into whether you want to pay bills automatically; while it's a timesaver, it may not be the best option for everyone. See the sidebar overpage.

Paying Bills Through Your PFS

Personal finance software was designed from the get-go to pay bills, so extending that ability into the online world is a natural thing for these programs. And in many ways, paying bills online through personal finance software is easier than through the Web; for example, you have the ability to create payee

Should I Set up Automatic Payment of Recurring Charges?

On the surface, setting up an **automatic payment to deal with recurring and fixed charges**—such as your mortgage or car loan payments—sounds like a great idea. It's one less thing you'll have to remember to do each month (or whatever period of time the payment is set up for). However, automatic payment is not a good idea if you are vulnerable to money shortages, or blips in the amount of cash you have available, as they will automatically deduct cash out of your account, whether you can "afford" it or not. Here are some people who might want to think about whether automatic payments are right for them.

- **Freelancers** or people who work on **commission**: These folks often have incomes that vary wildly from month to month—one month they might make thousands of dollars, while in another month they might come away with zip.
- People with a **high number of variable bills**: If your bills don't seem to conform to a regular budget, or you find that bills for phone service, electricity or groceries take up a fluctuating but inevitably high amount of your income, automatic payments might keep you from having the cash on hand to deal with these needs.
- **People prone to "emergencies"**: Your car always seems to need a couple of hundred dollars' worth of work; you are the bank of first resort for cash-strapped friends and family. You're obviously going to need to be ready when emergencies strike.

In short, think carefully about whether your real-world expenses can afford to have money automatically disbursed. If they can, automatic payments are a great timesaver, just so long as you stay aware of the amount of money that goes in and out of your accounts, and factor it in to your budgeting.

records and pay bills at the same time (or separately, if you prefer). And both Quicken and Money have the ability for online Bill Pay independent of your bank account (and yes, both of them charge for it).

Once again, you'll want to check with your bank to make sure they allow Bill Pay through the financial software of your choice. If they allow other banking services through your software, chances are pretty good they will. But be aware that some banks will require you to have the most recent version of the software, which in itself presumes you have a not-too-ancient computer as well.

Quicken Bill Pay

In Quicken, create an **online payee** by choosing the Banking Menu and then selecting the "Online Payees List" option. Click "New" in the online payee list page, and you receive a window in which you can add the appropriate information, including payee name address and phone number, and your payee account number.

From there, **paying bills online** is remarkably like writing checks with the program. In the Menu bar, select "Features," then "Bills" and then "Write Checks." Write the check like you normally would, choosing the online payee in the "Pay to the Order Of" drop-down menu. Check off the Online Payment check box, click on "Record Check," and you're done. The next time you open your Online Center, click "Update/Send," and the payment request goes through.

If you **don't want to create an online payee account**, fire up Quicken's Online Center, select your bank in the Financial Institutions box, and click on the "Payment" tab. Type in the name of the person or entity you want to pay, the amount, and then select the account from which the money will be taken. If the payee doesn't already exist to be selected, you'll enter the pertinent information at that time. Enter the delivery date, click "Enter," and it's taken care of the next time you use the "Update/Send" function.

To create a **recurring payment** in Quicken, go to the Online Center toolbar and click on "Repeating." You'll be taken to the "Scheduled Transactions List," which will be open to the "Repeating Online" tab. The "Create Repeating Online Payment" window will pop up automatically if this is your first time, otherwise click on "New." Pick your first payment date, choose the account you want to make payments from, and then enter the usual information for Payee, Category, and Amount. Schedule how often and how long you want the payments to go on, and then click "Authorize." The next time you click "Update/Send" in the Online Banking Center, the payment will be set up.

Money Bill Pay

For Money, click on the "Accounts" button in the navigation bar, and once you're in the Accounts area, select the bank that has the account from which you'll be paying your bills. A window will present itself, asking you what you would like to do. Select the "Payment" option down at the bottom of the window. The "Edit Transaction" box will pop up. Here you select the account from which you will pay, and enter the rest of the information: Who you are paying, for what services, for how much, and when the payment should be sent. Press "OK" when you've filled out all the information. If you are sending a payment to someone who is not already in your **payee list**, Money will present you with a window at this point, where you can enter payee information. Once you've entered that information, it's stored.

Want to schedule a **recurring payment** online? Okay: Select "Bills" in the navigation bar, and then select "Set up bill and deposits" in the task bar to the left of the main window. In the main window, click the "New" button and a box will appear giving you a choice of what sort of transaction you'd like to set up. Choose "Bill" and click "Next." Another box will appear asking you how often the payment will occur. Pick the "More than once, at regular intervals" option and then use the drop-down box to provide the frequency of the payment. Click "Next" again. A third box asks you to choose your payment method: Select "Automatic Payment." Click "Next" again, and you'll be taken to a final window, where you'll enter the information about which account the payment will be drawn from, who to send it to, the amount, and so on, just like writing up a one-time bill.

4

More Banking Services

GETTING THE MOST FROM, OR CHANGING, YOUR BANK

Okay—you've mastered the basics of what you can do with online banking. But viewing accounts, transferring funds, and paying bills is just the beginning. Beyond checking and savings and their various day-to-day functions, you can explore and sign up online to a host of other types of accounts and banking services. If you're looking for a little more oomph from your savings and are willing to put up with a few restrictions, you can shift around your savings into money markets or CDs (Certificates of Deposit), for example. Plus you can register online for bank credit cards, loans, and insurance.

Or at least you should be able to. If, reading through this chapter, you discover that your bank isn't giving you the service you want online, then you may want to look at alternatives—other banks or credit unions, or online-only financial institutions. These, too, are reviewed in this chapter.

Money Markets, CDs, and More

However well they put it across, interest from a conventional bank savings account is not a lot: Typically less than 2%, according to Bankrate.com. So if you have savings to which you don't need immediate access it pays to check out some of the alternatives—and online they are just a click away.

Some of these savings vehicles are actually better online: A number of banks offer special deals to people who set up accounts online, usually in the form of higher interest rates or lower minimum deposits. It's worth your while to shop around (remembering to read the fine print, of course). Bankrate.com tracks some of these Internet-only deals on their site at http://www.bankrate.com/brm/publ/ratedeal.asp.

Money Market Accounts

Money market accounts are an intermediary between savings and accounts that lock up money for set terms. They usually pay out higher interest than traditional savings, and are insured by the Federal Deposit Insurance Corporation (FDIC) But there are restrictions. Most banks require a minimum balance in a money market account, and by law, you are restricted how many times you can draw from the account—six times per month for most activities (although ATM withdrawals and deposits are often unlimited). The number of monthly checks against the account is also limited, usually to three: After that, you pay for each check, and if you write too many, your account maybe closed.

A step apart are **money market funds**. These are actually mutual funds, where the interest is a dividend on a share of the fund. These function in the same way as money market accounts and generally offer higher rates. They are regarded as extremely safe investments (particularly the ones that invest entirely in US government securities) but they are not insured by the FDIC, so it is possible, if unlikely, that you lose money investing in them. You should read your bank's prospectus on their money market fund prior to investing.

Many banks offer either money market accounts or money market funds and allow you to access information on them online or download that information into your personal finance software. You can usually also set up automatic transfers of money from a savings or checking account into a money market fund or account, by using the Transfer Funds function outlined in the last chapter (see p.27).

Certificates of Deposit

Certificates of deposit—CDs—generally offer higher interest returns than traditional savings or money market accounts or funds, and they are FDIC insured. The catch: Your money is locked up for the term of the CD, which can be as short as three months or as long as seven years, and CDs require a minimum, fairly hefty deposit. If you need to take your money out before the term is up, you pay fees—which might be all the interest your CD has accrued. Again, you'll want to read up on the details before you put your money down.

Many banks allow you to apply for and transfer funds into CDs online and allow you to access information about them online and through your personal finance software.

Interest Checking

If you don't want to bother with more than one bank account, consider at least moving to **interest checking**. The title is self-explanatory: It's an interest-bearing account from which you have full checking privileges. The interest isn't anything to write home about (it's usually the same as or less than a savings account), and you're often required to have a minimum balance in the account. But you have no worries about liquidity. Many banks offer interest checking online, and you can access these accounts just as regular checking and savings accounts.

Other Services: Loans, Credit Cards, Investment, and Insurance

Banks would like you, the customer, to feel that you don't need to go anywhere else for financial services. That's maybe not the case—as a read through the chapters following will hopefully make clear—but bank offers on such things as loans, mortgages, credit cards, and insurance—which you would traditionally obtain elsewhere—are at least worth a look. And, of course, they are offered online.

Loans and Mortgages

Planning to get that new car? Or a new house? Or just build onto the home you have? Many banks offer a range of loan options, from **short-term loans** to **mortgages** and **auto loans**, which you can apply for online. Some banks will even tell you online, within a matter of minutes, whether your loan application has been accepted.

Most banks that offer these services online also provide access to your loan balance and information online, and of course will also allow you to set up automatic online payment of the loan. For more on online loans and mortgages, from banks and others, see the next chapter.

Credit Cards

Credit cards are the lifeblood of the Internet, enabling the whole e-commerce phenomenon, so it's only natural that banks would offer credit cards online as well. Once again, many banks allow for credit card applications and near-instant approval (or not) online, as well as access to card balances and payment online. Additionally, banks and other credit card providers are now offering rebates and other incentives to card holders who shop online. More on all this in Chapter Seven.

Investment Services

Banks want you to keep your money within their reach, so more and more are offering **investment services** that were traditionally handled by brokerage houses and other financial institutions. Many banks will help you set up an investment portfolio, make trades, chart your stocks, and access real-time financial information from their Web sites. They'll also set up retirement accounts, trusts and, if you have the balance for it, help with more exotic maneuvers like margin investing. Again, you'll have the ability to track it all online.

Investing online takes up several chapters later in this book.

Insurance

In November 1999, President Clinton signed into law a bill that swept away Depression-era restrictions on financial institutions that kept them from offering particular services. In this brave new world, financial companies can now offer banking, loans, investments, and insurance services all under one roof. Within a few weeks Wingspan Bank was offering third-party insurance information and quotes on its Web site, and other banks have followed. Once again, you can access information online, while Money and Quicken allow you to track insurance policies, payouts, and more.

Choosing a Bank—Or Alternative

So far in this book, it's been assumed that a) you already have a bank and b) you're happy with the services that your bank offers. But what if a) you don't or b) you aren't? Well, now you get to experience another great advantage to banking online: a truly insane amount of choice. And not just between banks. Credit unions have gone online, and there are growing numbers of Internet-only banks, some associated with traditional banks, others brand-new start-ups.

Bank Options

Gone are the days in which you had to pick between a few banks that had branches close to where you live and work. Now, if a bank has online services, your choices can be based on the services offered, benefits provided, and even the philosophy of the bank itself. Or maybe not? Read on ...

Local vs Non-Local

Despite the choice provided by the online banking world, there are some good reasons to keep your money local. For example, if you decide to bank with an institution whose locations are across the country from you, you probably won't have access to that bank's "local" ATMs—and thus you'll get stung by service charges each time you use a competitor's machine. You'll also lose the convenience of being able to pop into a bank branch and conduct business with a real live human being; and you'll have to send in your deposits by mail—not the optimum situation when you need access to that money sooner rather than later.

On the other hand, non-local banks may provide better banking options or higher interest rates than your local banks—average interest rates on many banking services (both savings and loans) can vary from state to state. This may well outweigh the ATM charges (some banks rebate charges up to a certain amount) and surrender of human contact.

Big Bank vs Small Bank

Locally and nationally, banks come in all sizes, from monoliths like Bank of America and Citibank, who have a multi-state presence as well as lavishly designed Web sites, to small, locally owned and operated banks, like, say, Middleburg Bank of Virginia, which operates only in a couple of Virginia counties and whose Web site reflects that "down home" feel.

Large banks can offer the security of ubiquity—no matter where you go, there they are—which can mean fewer ATM fees and more service (including online service) options. Small banks can offer more personal service and knowledge of the local landscape—which can be important when it comes to loans or business services.

A Bank's Philosophy

Believe it or not, there are banks that maintain a philosophy beyond "make as much money as is legally possible." G&L Internet Bank (http://www.glbank.com), for example, based out of Florida, have a mission statement to "invest and reinvest in the gay & lesbian community." With a little research, you may be able to find an online bank that shares a commitment to your ideals or personal identification. Beyond this, a number of banks, from national banks on down, publicly trumpet their commitment to the communities that they serve.

Of course, you'll want to ask the same finance and service questions of a bank regardless of its ethical commitments.

Credit Unions

Credit unions are an alternative to banks for many people. Unlike banks, which operate as for-profit businesses, credit unions are set up and owned by the people who use their services—by employees of a particular corporation or union, for example, or members of a church. Credit unions offer many of the same services as banks, online and offline, and deposits are also federally insured. However, you have to be eligible to participate by being a member of the credit union's "field of membership," or being related to someone who is. Credit unions also tend to have a smaller number of ATMs in their networks, so you may pay higher service fees.

Is a credit union better for you than a bank? Check out the sidebar below.

Credit Unions vs Banks

Can't decide which is better for you, a credit union or a bank? Here's a quick run-down of the pros and cons.

What Credit Unions Have Over Banks:

- They're not taxed by the government (as they're not-for-profit).
- They generally offer better rates on car loans and credit cards, and on money markets and certificates of deposit.
- They can be more flexible with loan repayments.

What Banks Have Over Credit Unions:

- Anyone can get a bank account (credit unions require certain membership criteria).
- Banks generally offer lower rates on mortgages.
- Banks generally offer a wider ranges of brokerage services and investment products.
- Banks generally offer better ATM services and lower ATM fees.

Online-Only Banks

A growing number of banks are setting up shop entirely on the Internet, with only a token brick-and-mortar "branch" (as required by law). Some of these banks are very well funded—for example, Wingspan Bank, which is an offshoot of First National Financial Services. Others are smaller concerns, whose credentials you'll probably want to confirm on the FDIC Web site (this is easily done—see p.51).

Online-only banks offer a number of advantages to the savvy online bank customer, including a wide range of financial products and services and some excellent financial deals on money markets and CDs. Their low overhead (no real estate or tellers to speak of) also allows them to offer lower fees. The disadvantages? As with non-local banks, there's the risk of additional ATM charges, the delay in making deposits by mail, and the inability to walk into a branch and see a real live human being. Again, review your current banking habits to see whether being with an online-only bank is something that's going to work for you.

How To Choose

Choosing a bank is a serious business: Life is too short to keep moving banks, and most people don't bother. So take the time to figure out what you really want in a bank—the services you need and the accessibility you require, as well as returns you're hoping to get from your money. And use the Web to further your research. There are several sites that provide information on bank rates and services and rank banks according to customer satisfaction. Using these, you can find your future bank, or narrow down the field of candidates.

If you already had your eye on a particular bank, it'll make the process easier. Check out their Web site, which should feature an index of all their services, rates, and special deals, and see if it fits your bill. But don't choose straight away! Even if you have a bank in mind and the information you find on the site appears to suit your needs, you should still look around—there may be other banks that fit your criteria even better. And you still may want to read the reviews of the bank, to learn if it delivers on the service it promises. Think of the information you find on the bank's site as the bar that other banks must leap over.

Researching the Numbers

When it comes to banking, the first priority for many people is the bottom line: Getting the best rates for savings, money market account, CDs, and so on. A good place to collect that information is at **Bankrate.com** (http://www.bankrate.com; AOL Keyword: BRM). This is an independent entity that tracks the rates of bank services such as savings, CDs, mortgages and auto loans, and money market accounts. (It makes money by charging for links to individual bank Web pages—useful for you and uncompromising editorially.) The most useful features of the Bankrate.com site are its rates charts—it gives the national averages for each and allows you to access information on rates in your state; its "High Five" page, which offers the five highest rates in the country in several categories of financial product; and its details of how much banks charge for ATM fees, an important factor if you plan to bank online exclusively.

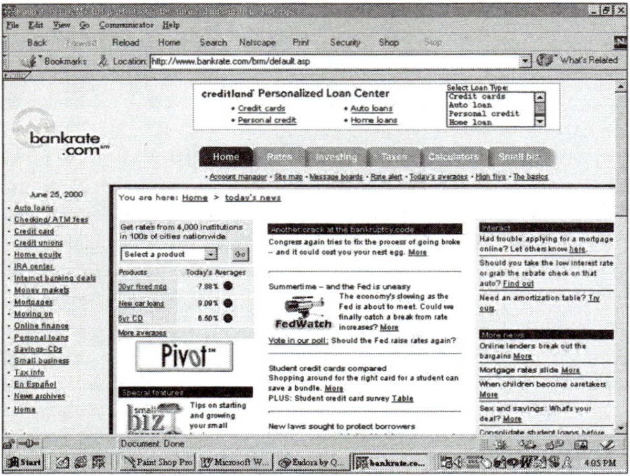

Another source of rate information online is **Rate.net** (http://www.rate.net), which tracks savings, mortgage, and auto loan rates at 11,000 financial institutions in the US. The information is provided on a state-to-state basis, and also though a top ten for the various financial services. Rate.net also provides rankings of the institutions based on financial stability, for those who wish to know more about those to whom they are entrusting their money.

Beyond the Numbers

There's more to online banking, of course, than simply getting the best rates. You want your bank to have the range of services you require, to be accessible when you want to use it, and for their services to be as easy as possible to manage.

To check on these factors, a good place to start is **Gomez.com** (http://www.gomez.com; AOL Keyword: Gomez). This site rates and ranks several different types of e-commerce sites, including online banking institutions. It rates the online banks for ease of use, variety of services, "Relationship services" (personalization through online and offline promotions and services), and even access times to bank servers. Gomez also rates banks based on customer profiles such as "Internet Transactor" (someone who wants to do all his or her banking online) and "Borrower" (someone who is mostly interested in access to capital). These can help you focus on a bank that serves your particular needs.

The drawback to the Gomez.com site is that currently it only covers banks that are either Internet-only, or have more than $2 billion in deposits; small, local banks are not listed and evaluated, so if you're interested in one of those, you have some more homework to do. However, Gomez.com can give you an idea of the yardstick you should apply to any bank in terms of services and performance, so you know what to ask your bank about its services and online performance.

FDIC: Are They Legitimate?

If you're interested in mining raw data about an online bank, its holdings and whether, in fact, the government is aware that this online bank even exists (hey, it happens), there's no better place to go than the source—the **Federal Deposit Insurance Corporation** (FDIC).

The FDIC Individual Banks page (http://www.fdic.gov/bank/individual/index.html) has links to an **Institution Directory** that provides detailed demographic information on every FDIC-insured bank in the country as well as recent and comprehensive information on the bank's deposits, holdings, and other financial particulars. If you can't find the bank you're interested in listed in this particular directory, here's a tip: Think about banking somewhere else.

The FDIC site also includes links to private companies that rank banks (FDIC also ranks banks but does not share those rankings with the rest of us). This page also features the ability for you to rat out any Web site you believe is misrepresenting itself as an online bank.

Switching Your Bank

Once you've found the perfect online bank, all that is left to do is put your money in. If you do not currently have an account at another bank, this is quickly and easily done: Just open up a new online account as covered in Chapter Two (see p.19), deposit money by way of money order or check, and you're ready to go. But if you currently have accounts in another bank or banks, keep a couple of things in mind before you transfer your funds.

First, if you have money in **certificates of deposit** or other investment vehicles that lock up funds for a set amount of time, you probably won't be able to access that money right away (unless you're willing to subject yourself to financial penalties—and there's usually no good reason to do that). You'll have to wait until the term expires before you transfer those particular funds.

Second, if you have a bank account that waives fees in exchange for a minimum deposit, you might actually incur those fees if you simply write a check to your new bank in the amount of your current account, and then close your current account when the check clears. You'll have dropped below your minimum: A lame excuse, sure, but true. So check to see if you might not be better off **closing out your current account first**, and receiving your money at that point.

5

Mortgages and Equity Loans

OBTAINING OR EXCHANGING PROPERTY LOANS ONLINE

For most of us, buying an apartment or house is the single largest purchase we ever make. So it is no surprise that there is a flood of companies online just itching to be the one to get us that money. No surprise, either, that consumers are going for the option of researching and obtaining mortgages online: Deutsche Bank Securities believes that by 2003, nearly a quarter of all mortgages will be initiated on the Net. That's a cool $250 billion for anyone who doubts e-commerce.

The amazing ease with which you can find mortgage and home equity loan lenders online accentuates just how much choice is out there—and how it is very much up to you to get the best deal going. You can find everything you need for every step of the loan and mortgage process, and with a little work, you really can come away with a considerably better deal than you'd find offline.

Step One: Pre-Mortgage Planning

Ready to get that mortgage? Well, hold up for a second. Before we even get to mortgage applications, let's talk briefly about what you should know before you start asking for cash. Here's three things you should have clear in your mind:

1. Whether you are financially ready to own a home—and how much home you can actually afford.
2. The differences between various sorts of mortgage loans—it pays to tell your fixed-rates from your ARMs.
3. The status of your credit.

How Much Can You Afford?

Just as there are numerous sites out there devoted to finding you the mortgage money you want, there is also a passel of sites ready to help you figure out whether you're ready for home-ownership and how much you can swing. In fact (and not too surprisingly), the sites that offer mortgages also offer to help would-be buyers figure out how much they can afford. This is a better idea for them than for you. It pays to separate your information gathering from your mortgage application—give yourself some time to review your findings and decide what you want out of a mortgage before you apply. Borrowing a couple of hundred thousand dollars shouldn't necessarily be a "quick" process.

The best place to start for pre-mortgage planning may be sites that have no immediate interest in getting you to buy a mortgage. One such is **HomePath** (http://www.homepath.com).

This is run by Fannie Mae, the government-chartered corporation that makes its business by purchasing mortgages from lenders (ie, they don't lend money to home buyers directly). Since Fannie Mae's business model blows up if people can't afford their houses, their interest is in making sure people have a clear idea of what they can actually afford and what sort of mortgage is going to be best for their situation.

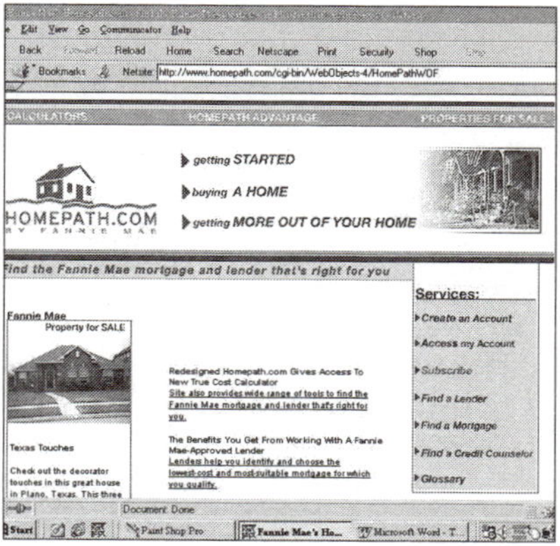

HomePath has three sections. "Getting Started" features information on the pros and cons of home ownership, a test to see if you're ready, mortgage loan basics (including info on the various types of loans), and an online calculator that can help you figure out how much home you can afford. They'll even help you figure out what kind of house you need, if you haven't nailed that one down already. The other sections— "Buying a Home" and "Getting More Out of Your Home"—are intended for people already in the process of buying a house or looking to refinance a mortgage.

Bankrate.com (http://www.bankrate.com/brm/mstep1.asp), which does not sell mortgages, offers an informative mortgage primer that includes calculators on how much house you can afford, as well as information on special programs available for first-time home buyers. **Nolo.com**, an online self-help legal site, also offers a wide range of information for would-be homeowners on mortgages and qualifying for home loans (http://www.nolo.com/encyclopedia/re_ency.html).

What's This About My Credit?

If you have **bad credit**, you're going to have a much harder time getting a house (or a car, or a credit card...). And bad credit pops up where you least expect it. All those gas bills that you put off until the final notice are waving on your credit report. So are all those late credit card payments, accidentally delayed rent payments, ignored college loans, and other financial flubs you may have had. And sometimes bad credit isn't your fault—it's not unheard of for errors to crop on credit reports. If you don't want nasty surprises in the loan process, it pays to get a copy of your **credit report** before you apply for a mortgage or other loan.

You can, of course, do this online. All three major credit bureaus—**Equifax** (http://www.equifax.com), **Experian** (http://www.experian.com), and **Trans Union** (http://www.transunion.com)—will send you a copy of your credit report. The cost at time of writing is typically $8, although it's less in some states and territories. For folks who prefer to keep closer tabs on their credit, Equifax has a subscription service that updates you quarterly concerning your credit report, as does another company called **PrivacyGuard** (www.privacyguard.com; AOL Keyword: Credit Report), which merges information from all three credit report companies into one report. These subscriptions are about $60 annually.

If you've come by bad credit through your own fault, it will stay on your report for seven years (ten years in the case of a bankruptcy). However, if your credit report includes **errors**, you have a right to dispute them—and, if the charge is indeed erroneous, that fact has to be noted to any lending organization that has requested your report in the past. Of course, those erroneous black marks will sit there unless you spot them and dispute them—so get your credit report and go through it with a fine-toothed comb.

Meet the Mortgage Cast

So who is going to sell you that mortgage, and how can you find them online?

Banks and Credit Unions

Online **banks** and **credit unions**—covered in the previous chapter—have been the traditional lender for mortgages and they're still in the business, online and off. Those that allow for online banking generally include mortgage information, promoting their rates and usually allowing you to at least begin the mortgage approval process online.

Mortgage Lenders

Mortgage lenders are companies whose only business is mortgages. They range from small, locally owned and operated businesses, to huge, national corporations that lend to hundreds of thousands of consumers. There are hundreds of them online, and again, many of them will allow you to at least begin the mortgage approval process on their site. Their national organization is the Mortgage Bankers Association of America (http://www.mbaa.org/).

Mortgage Brokers

Mortgage brokers aren't lenders themselves; what they do is work on your behalf to find a mortgage that best suits your needs. While banks and mortgage lenders only show you their own products, a mortgage broker typically works with several dozen lenders at one time, and can thus provide an array of different loan options from banks and mortgage lenders. There are about 20,000 mortgage brokers in the US, according to the National Association of Mortgage Brokers (http://www.namb.org). Many individual brokers have their own Web sites, and the NAMB Web site offers a directory of brokers around the country.

Online Mortgage Sites

Online mortgage sites—companies that work exclusively online to help consumers get mortgages—come in two flavors: referral sites and processor sites. **Referral sites** are basically matchmakers: They work by taking basic financial and personal information about you and matching it to a loan offered by a separate lending institution (you'll typically be given a number of loan options), which then takes your application. Microsoft's HomeAdvisor (http://www.homeadvisor.com) and Quickenmortgage.com (http://www.quickenmortgage.com, AOL Keyword: Quicken Mortgage) are examples of referral sites.

Processor sites represent lenders or mortgage brokers. They collect in-depth personal and financial information, verify credit information, and do scheduling appraisals. They're more of a full-service site and you can complete most of the mortgage process through them. Sites of this type include Mortgage.com (http://www.mortgage.com) and E-Loan (http://www.eloan.com).

Pre-Approvals and Pre-Qualifications

When you visit online mortgage sites, either free-standing or associated with lenders or brokers, chances are you'll see an offer to get yourself pre-approved or pre-qualified for a mortgage. These two terms mean very different things, and are likewise helpful (or unhelpful) for varying reasons.

A **mortgage pre-qualification**, in concrete terms, doesn't mean much—you aren't approved for a loan, and you're not obligated to take a loan from a lender for whose products you are "pre-qualified." Pre-qualification is simply a process in which a broker, lender, or site takes basic personal and financial information and tells you which of their mortgages you could probably get, based on the information you've provided. Pre-qualifications are useful for one thing: Giving you a rough estimate of what sort of mortgages you can get. (What sort of information will you provide in a "pre-qualification" process? See the sidebar overpage.) Many mortgage sites offer pre-qualification quizzes; you can run through one in about 15 minutes.

A **pre-approval** is a whole different bird. Typically, you search for a mortgage after you have found a house to buy. However, if you knows you are looking for a house in a certain price range and a certain place, but haven't found the particular house, you can get "pre-approved" for a mortgage. This means that a lender has given your credit history a once-over and, on that basis, cleared you for a mortgage for a certain amount at a certain rate. Now all you have to do is find a house to go with the mortgage—and you are at an advantage when you make an offer to a seller. You still, however, need to go through the usual mortgage process once it's accepted. You may be cleared but the property hasn't been.

Online sites that pre-qualify buyers for loans offer to get the buyers immediately into the pre-approval process. Be aware that while pre-qualifications are free and quick, pre-approvals take time and money. Much of the pre-approval process can take place online, but you'll still need to mail or fax financial information to your lender. The mortgage process isn't completely wired just yet.

Pre-Qualification Questions

You should have answers to the following questions ready before you begin filling in the forms for pre-qualification or pre-approval:

- Is the loan for a new mortgage or for refinancing?
- What kind of home are you looking for (detached single family, condominium, etc)?
- What is the estimated price of the home (ballpark figure), and also its location (city and state)?
- How long do you plan to own the home? (This will help to suggest types of loans.)
- What is your income and the income of your spouse or other co-signer?
- What is your current indebtedness (credit cards, loans, etc) and also those of any co-signer?
- Are you credit worthy? Have you missed loan or rent payments, or been in bankruptcy, in the last ten years?

Refinancing Your Mortgage

You're not interested in moving—you just want to get a better mortgage interest rate on the home you already own. No problem: Almost every online institution that offers mortgages is also in the business to **refinance your current loan**. If you are in an expensive mortgage, you have the chance to save thousands of dollars over the life of your mortgage by refinancing. You just need to do the sums. Read on ...

Online Info and Calculators

To find out just how much you can save by refinancing, and whether now is a good time for you to take the re-fi plunge, a good first stop is Fannie Mae's **HomePath.com**. This offers a specific section on refinancing your mortgage (http://www.homepath.com/hrp1.html) as does **America Online** (AOL Keyword: Refinance).

There are also a number of **online calculators** that can help you figure it out. Bankrate.com features one in their mortgage section, as does Homepath.com. Mortgage sites such as Quickenmortgage.com and Mortgage.com feature them as well, as do most bank sites that offer refinancing.

It's Not Free

Refinancing doesn't come for free—even online. **Fees** for refinancing will likely include the following:

- application fee
- title search and title insurance fees
- cost of an appraisal
- loan origination fee

as well as any legal service fees relating to your loan. And if your original mortgage has a **pre-payment penalty**, you'll be stuck for that as well. These can add up anywhere from $1000 to $3000, and sometimes more.

When you're using the online refinance calculator, you should remember to include these fees in your estimation (some calculators allow you to break up the fees, while others ask you to provide them as a single lump sum). These fees can erase any saving you might get from refinancing, so be sure not to omit any of them. If you don't know what your fees will be, check out CalcBuilders's "How Much Will My Closing Costs Be?" calculator (http://www.calcbuilder.com/cgi-bin/calcs/HOM9.cgi/). It comes with costs already in place (which can be modified, of course).

Some lenders offer **"no-cost" refinancing**, which means you won't have to provide money up front for the refinancing. However, these "no-cost" mortgages usually come with a higher interest rate. One way or another you will pay to refinance your mortgage.

Home Equity Loans and Lines of Credit (HELOC)

If you're looking for cash for high-end projects, like remodeling the house, buying a boat, or sending junior off to college, you can use the equity in your home to get a **home equity loan** or a **home equity line of credit** (a HELOC). This is ueful credit (derived from years of mortgage payments, don't you know) but serious borrowing: if you default on payment, as with a mortgage, the bank can come after your home.

A home equity loan is for a specific amount of money, given as a lump sum, and it is paid off at a fixed rate. A HELOC is a line of credit that you can access at any time for the length of the agreement, and it has a variable rate (usually the prime rate plus a couple of percentage points). Since both home equity loans and HELOCs are tied to your home, the interest you pay on them is tax deductible up to $100,000.

Most **banks** and **mortgage lenders** online provide home equity loans and lines of credit, and allow you to apply online. Before you do so, you can **compare current rates** for equity loans and HELOCs all over the country on Bankrate.com's home equity channel (http://www.bankrate.com/brm/rate/loan_home.asp)—there's also a calculator that will show you how much you can expect to pay for your loan per month. HSH Associates also lists current rates for major cities at (http://www.hsh.com/heqsample.html). If you're wondering whether a loan or a line of credit will be better for you, Finance.com has a calculator that can help you decide by showing you how much a loan will cost you compared to the line of credit (http://finance.com/cgi-bin/calcs/HEL4.cgi/finance).

Some banks and mortgage lenders will cut you a deal on your equity loan or HELOC if you have a banking account with them or pay for your loan electronically—check with your intended lender and see what sort of deal you can cut. A little cut up front can save you serious cash down the road.

125% Second Mortgages

If you watch any amount of cable television, you've probably seen the ads for mortgage lenders who will provide homeowners with second mortgages worth 125% of the value of their house (and the further exhortation to use that money on whatever you want—like a vacation or a wedding, both good ways of building up your debts). These sorts of loans are called **"high-loan-to-value" loans** and they have big drawbacks.

For one, the amount of the loan that exceeds the value of the home (the 25% in the "125% loan") is not tax-deductible. Second, if you should need to move before that part of the loan is paid off, you'll have to come up with the extra money. Third, though consolidating debt with a 125% second mortgage can make for smaller monthly payments, you can end up paying more in the long run if one of the debts rolled into the second mortgage was a loan at lower interest rate.

Most larger banks and mortgage lenders tend to steer clear of offering high-loan-to-value loans, preferring to stick to loans that offer up to the value of the home. The whole high-loan-to-value lender industry underwent a shake-up in the late 1990s, with some of the highest-profile lenders filing for bankruptcy. Be that as it may, **high-value-to-loan lenders** are online, if you want to find them. One lender with a national presence is ditech.com (http://www.ditech.com). Another well-known name is Kemper Financial

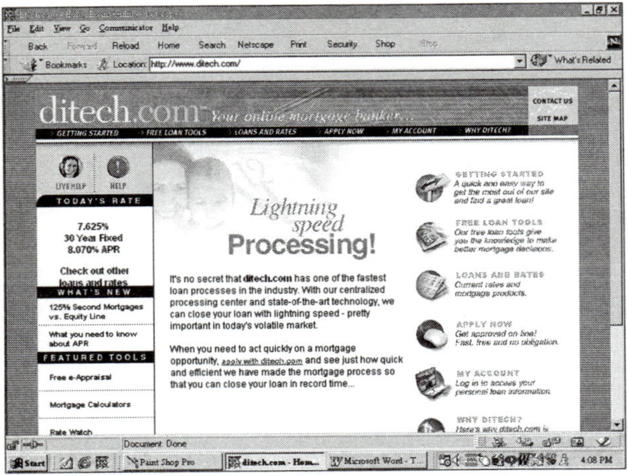

(**http://www.kempermortgage.com/**). One mortgage site that explicitly advertises connecting consumers to 125% loan lenders is Home Loan-USA (**http://www.homeloan-usa.com/**).

Reverse Mortgages

If you're aged 62 or older, you can use the equity in your home for a **reverse mortgage**, in which a bank or lender provides you with a lump sum, a line of credit, or monthly payments that augment your other income. You keep title of your property, and the loan comes due only if you move or in the event of your death (in which case the lender sells the house and recoups the investment, or your heirs pay off the mortgage if they want to keep the house). So while you can't take it with you, you can use it right up until the end.

At this time, there's little information about reverse mortgages on bank and mortgage lender sites. But the National

Reverse Mortgage Lenders Association Web site (http://www.reversemortgage.org/) contains detailed information about the reverse mortgage programs currently available, links to reverse mortgage lenders in US states and Canadian provinces, and a walk-through of the reverse mortgage application process. These programs can be confusing, but they're for real—Fannie Mae (see p.55), for one, buys reverse mortgages in the secondary mortgage market.

6

Car Loans and Personal Loans

BORROWING AND BUYING

After home mortgages, the two most popular loans online are **car loans** and **personal loans**. If you're itching to get that new car or boat, or money for that vacation, fine—the Net has a myriad of options for you to consider.

Buying Autos—Without Driving!

Here's a nice irony: You can do every part of the car-buying process—from researching a car to getting a loan to actually buying a car—without having to drive anywhere. You just need to remember to drive your motor once you get it.

Arm Yourself! Know the Values

If there's any stereotype deeply ingrained in the psyche, it's the auto salesman: the fast-talking, glad-handlin', always-grinning fella who crams you into one of his cars (preferably one of the more expensive models) and has you driving it off the lot before you know what's hit you. It's a harder trick to achieve online, where there's less in the way of haggling, but it pays to know what the salespeople know.

The first thing the salespeople know is: How much that car you want really costs—which is to say, what the dealer had to pay the manufacturer for it, or what the "blue book" value is, if the car is used. For these values, it's smart to go right to the source: **Kelley Blue Book** (http://kbb.com/), the "bible" of new and used car values. For new cars, you enter your zip code, then select a category of car, and then make and model. You'll get both the dealer invoice (the price of the car and destination charge) and suggested retail price. You'll also find the dealer and suggested retail price for all the option packages and accessories for the model.

For used cars, input zip code, make, model, and year, and the extras you'd want, and out comes the "retail value" for that car—the price a car dealership in your area would typically pay for that car. Kelleys also offers an option that allows you to see what your "trade-in" value would be for this car—good both for trading in a car and knowing what dealers actually pay for the cars they sell to you.

Don't stop there—get a second (or third) opinion. **Edmunds.com** (http://www.edmunds.com/) also provides dealer and suggested retail prices on most new and used makes and models, and their various options as well (although not broken down by zip code). **Cars.com** (http://www.cars.com/) also provides the inside scoop on dealer and retail prices, broken down by zip codes. Kelly Blue Book and Edmunds.com do not sell cars directly, but Cars.com does (through CarsDirect.com).

If you check more than one of these sites for the value of your intended car, you'll likely find differences in the costs. On the day I checked, for example, for the retail price of a used 1990 Ford Escort (Pony, two-door hatchback), Kelly listed $1895, Cars.com $2175, and Edmonds just $1530. Of course, you'll want to quote the lowest price when it comes time to talk money with the salesperson.

You might also want to check out the **list of rebates, incentives, and holdbacks** on Edmunds.com (http://www.edmunds.com/edweb/holdback.html). Dealers have to move inventory, and every so often most makes and models of cars have rebates or deals on financing, or dealer incentives ("holdbacks") to move the product. The Edmunds list also features information on **leases**, if you'd prefer to rent rather than buy. Cars.com also lists rebates in a special Deals & Coupons area (go to their main page and click on the "Deals & Coupons" link in the E-Store heading).

What's the Best Car for Me?

You need to get a car but haven't settled on make and model? The Internet can help you make that decision. Knowing exactly what you want makes you less vulnerable to high-pressure sales tactics. If a dealer doesn't have what you want (at the price you want it), you know that you can go somewhere else and get it—there are a lot of cars online.

Beat the Dealers!

You buy a car once every few years at most, while auto salespeople sell cars every single working day of their lives. They have the advantage, unless you do the research to control the negotiation process. This is where the Net really shines: It's full of sites itching to tell you how to beat car salespeople—indeed, the entire dealership—at their own game.

One of the best of these comes from a great finance site you'll be hearing a lot about in these pages, **The Motley Fool** (http://www.fool.com, AOL Keyword: Fool). The Fool's "Buying a Car" area (http://www.fool.com/car/buyingacar.htm) is a comprehensive compendium of selling tricks and tactics. It tells you the "why" behind everything, from why they take your set of keys when you go for a test drive to why salespeople hand you off to the "manager" to close the deal. More than that, you'll learn what you need to do to get the upper hand in the process.

A rougher but no less informative site can be found at **CarBuyingTips.com** (http://www.carbuyingtips.com/). Site proprietor Jeff Ostroff needs some design tips himself, but the information on scams and strategies salespeople use is right on the mark. Another good site—and a quicker read—is **SmartSense's Car Buying Guide** (http://www.smartsense.com/).

There's also a Web site you might just want to check once you've found a (used) dream car. **Carfax** (http://www.carfax.com, AOL Keyword: Carfax) is a service that tracks the **history of a car**. A full report, which will let you know who owned your car, when they owned it, and what damage or mileage they put on it, costs $14.95 (there's also a $19.95 deal for unlimited reports for 60 days). Alternatively, a brief "Lemon Check" is free, and will let you know if any red flags are raised.

Continues over

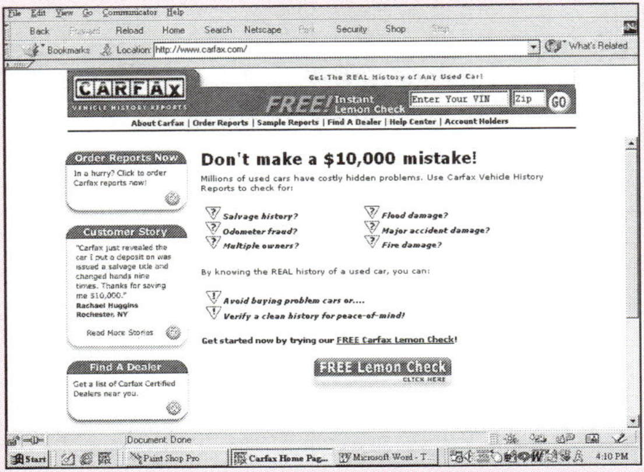

Cars.com (http://www.cars.com) has a **criteria search** where you select the things you need (four doors, say, or an automatic transmission, or a sunroof), and what you want to pay, and it rolls out a list of **new cars** for you to consider. On AOL, go to Keyword: Auto and click on Decision Guide, and you'll get a very detailed quiz on what you want in seeking out the car of your dreams. A Web version of the same guide is available at Personal Logic (http://www.personallogic.com), under the heading "Car Match."

Both of these guides are for new cars only; if you're looking for a **used car**, try AutoTrader's **decision guide** (http://www.autotrader.com/decision/), which is as detailed as the Personal Logic quiz (on AOL, enter Keyword: Used Cars and click on Determine the Right Car For You). With both the new and used car searches, don't count on the price quoted as being the best out there—run the car through Kelly Blue Book or Edmund's first.

But should you buy new or used? This is a book about money and not buying cars—and it's a personal decision at the end of the day. Finance-wise, a few factors to throw in along with the price are **warranties** (automatic on new cars, usually extra—if they're available at all—for a used model), **insurance rates** (more expensive for a new model), and **interest rates** (more expensive for a used car).

Warranties

One of the ways auto dealers make their money is to load customers up on things like options and **extended warranties**, which are not included in the initial price of the car. It's up to you to hold the line on these things at the time you're buying the car. And it's worth noting that if you're interested in getting an extended warranty for your car, you may be able to do better online than in the dealership, both in cost and in where the car service can be performed.

There are several sites that offer extended warranties: **Warranty Direct** (http://www.warrantydirect.com/) claims to be the largest—you can see the services they offer and can send information to get a quote, but they won't show you the quote without getting contact information first. **Warrantygold.com** (http://www.warrantygold.com/) allows you to see the quote before asking for contact information. There are also a number of warranties tailor-made for **specific brands** such as GM, Ford, Chrysler, or Toyota, offered by dealers rather than the auto companies. See the guide section of this book (p.231) for site addresses.

Getting Auto Financing

You've researched your car's price, steeled yourself for the negotiations, and squared away all the various ways you can have the price of your car jacked up on you. Now, there's one more thing to do before you step into a showroom or go car hunting online: Get your financing. Yes, the dealership will no doubt have financing available. But remember: When it comes to selling that car, the dealer is not your friend. By walking in with your financing in place, you walk in with the advantage.

Before setting out on your quest for car money, you should know pretty much what car you want and what you want to pay, be sure you don't have bad credit (see p.56), and, most important, be clear that you can afford the car you want.

A good rule of thumb is that the monthly cost of your car (that's car payment, insurance, gas, and maintenance) should not exceed more than ten percent of your total gross income. You can push this up a bit if your total debt is low, but ten percent is generally a good ballpark figure. An alternate calculation is twenty percent of what you have left after you've paid everything else that month, including mortgage/rent, credit card payment, utilities, and so on. If you're having a hard time figuring out what you can afford, this calculator from Giggo.com can help: **What Car Can I Afford?** (http://www.giggocar.com/yourloan/howmuchspend.asp). On AOL, enter Keyword: Auto Loan, and the same calculator will pop up.

If you want to exceed these figures, that's your choice, but you'll have a hard time finding financing, and when or if you do, it'll likely be at terms that are not to your advantage.

Finally, before you begin applying for loans online, have all the information you'll need ready. Beyond your credit report, this will include **documentation** of your current income, employment history, financial obligations (mortgage/rent, credit cards, college loans, etc), and other personal information such as your Social Security number and personal references. If you have a co-applicant for the loan joining you, make sure you have their information as well. Not every lender will want all this information online—some will get basic information and then opt to call you. But you're better off having it on hand anyway.

Remember if you apply for a loan online to make sure you're using a secure Web site before you enter in your information. If you're not sure or have questions—don't use the

Web forms. Most Web sites will also give you a 1-800 number option to apply. Use it.

Who Wants to Finance My Car?

The answer: Everybody wants to finance your car. Your bank or credit union wants to. The car dealership wants to. Finance companies want to. Even the manufacturers want to—with or without the dealerships in the way. And they're all online and ready to work with you. So the question is which car financing option is going to get you the best deal.

Banks

Once again, banks are the first place most people think of for their lending needs. If you get your financing with the bank at which you already save your money, you may be able to winch down your interest rate by allowing automatic deductions from your checking or savings account. Some banks, like First Union (http://www.firstunion.com, AOL Keyword: First Union) also offer additional car-buying services for a fee, doing the work of shopping around for the best price, ordering and inspecting the car, and offering purchaser protection if the car is not to your liking.

Credit Unions

Car loans are a place where credit unions have a traditional advantage over regular banks and other lending institutions, offering better interest rates to their members. There are also other perks available online: CUCarClub.com (http://www.cucarclub.com/), for example, helps credit union members get a no-hassle deal on cars from local franchises. Carfax, the service that provides car histories, also has a special deal for credit union members (http://www.carfax4cu.com/).

Online Financial Institutions

General lenders like E-Loan (http://www.eloan.com) and LendingTree (http://www.lendingtree.com) provide loans (or connect consumers to loan makers) as part of their range of loan products. And a number of companies specialize in making car loans only, such as Giggo.com (http://giggo.com), 1-800-Car Loan (http://www.carloan.com), and Auto Loan Online (http://www.auto-loan.com).

Many of the Internet financial institutions that deal only in car loans are targeted specifically at consumers who have had **credit problems in the past** and might therefore be wary of approaching traditional lenders. If you fit into this category, you'll probably want to do a little more legwork to make sure whatever you're offered at these sites can't be bettered somewhere else.

Automobile Sites Online

If you're looking to buy a car online, the **auto sites** figure they might as well try to get you your loan online, too. This is often done through partnerships with online lending sites: Auto-by-tel (http://www.autobytel.com) farms their loan process out to LendingTree.com, while Microsoft's CarPoint (http://www.carpoint.com) offers loans through People First Finance (http://www.peoplefirst.com) and E-Loan.

Dealers' Online Sites

Real-world dealers are putting up full-service Web sites to entice online shoppers back into the showroom, and part of that process includes putting up financing information. However, this financing information is usually pretty rudimentary—often just a form the dealership can use to contact you (remember that their ultimate goal is to get you come on down and let them work their wiles on you).

Car Manufacturers

If you know what sort of car you're going to want to buy, you can check out the **manufacturers' financing arm** to see what sort of deals and options you can get out of them. General Motors' financial arm, GMAC Financial Services (http://www.gmacfs.com/), offers traditional loans and loans for consumers with "less than perfect" credit, and gives information about incentives like their "College Grad" program. Ford Finance (http://www.fordcredit.com) will inform you about special deals available locally, when you enter your zip code. Chrysler Finance (http://www.chryslerfinancial.com/) allows you to pick a car model, trick it out online, and then help you figure out how to pay for the just-designed dream car.

Almost all major manufacturers, both import and domestic, have financing arms available through their company Web sites. In addition to lending information, these finance sites also feature information on leasing options available to you. (Should you lease instead of purchase your next car? Check out our sidebar overpage for more information.) Be aware that when it comes time to apply online, many car manufacturer financial sites will shunt you back to a local dealership, which will process the loan application. So rather than sidestepping the dealers, you may merely be delaying the inevitable.

Check Your Rates!

The fabulous thing about applying for loans online is that you can know within a matter of minutes whether you have a loan or not. But (recurring theme here) just because something can be done fast doesn't mean that you're getting the best deal. Before you go through the loan application, **check rates** at Bankrate.com's Auto Loans area (http://www.bankrate.com/

Lease or Buy?

It's nice to have a new car. But is it so nice that you'll want to do it every two or three years? That's essentially the question you'll need to ask yourself if you're considering leasing a car instead of buying. But there are also some finance points to consider:

- Lease payments are typically lower than car loan payments. But you're also usually required to put at least a couple of thousand dollars down at the time of the lease.
- At the end of two or three years, you walk away from the car—and if you don't have another car to replace the leased car, that "walking away" part will be literal.
- At the end of the lease, you walk away from your car with no additional cost...as long as you didn't exceed the agreed mileage (mileage in excess can be an additional 24 cents a mile) and your car isn't dinged or shows "unusual wear and tear." In fact, you could end up paying thousands more at the end of your lease if you're not careful, both when you sign a lease and as you drive the car.
- You can use your current car as a "trade-in" to help finance your lease—but dealers don't always give you trade-in value and some are not beyond ignoring its value altogether in the lease.

There are a lot of hidden costs involved in a lease, and it's up to you to know them all. Start with the overview of leases from Bankrate.com at (http://www.bankrate.com/brm/green/auto auto3a.asp), and follow it up with the lease overview from theWhiz.com (http://thewhiz.snap.com/1999/06/990628c.asp).

brm/rate/auto_home.asp). You can find out what rates are both nationally and where you live, for new and used cars, and who is offering the lowest rates, under which terms. It also has finance calculators to figure out how much you can really afford.

Now you're ready to buy a car. Should you do it in a dealership, or online? The sidebar below weighs the pros and cons.

Buying Cars: Online vs Dealers

When it comes to deciding where to buy your car, online or in a dealership, new or used, what it really comes down to is what sort of person you are and what your tolerance is for haggling.

If you're the type of person who does poorly in negotiations or doesn't mind paying more for the convenience of shopping from home, shopping online is a good bet. Most car buying online these days is "no-haggle"—which means that the seller lists a price for a particular car (or for the particular options which you use to customize the car) and then you either take it or leave it. In exchange for the low-pressure car buying experience, you may not get the very best price—but you're in control of the process. A more serious drawback in buying a car over the Net is that, unless the car is actually physically nearby, you won't be able to test-drive it until it arrives at your door, paid and purchased.

If you're the sort of person who takes pride in making car salespeople cry as you strip away all their hidden profit centers, use the Net for research only—and then head over to the dealership. If you use the online resources effectively, you should be able to back the dealer into the corner—and have the satisfaction of delivering the coup de grace in person.

Personal Loans

Suppose you want a large chunk of cash for something other than a house or a car: For example, you've found yourself in a temporary financial bind, and need to pay for car repairs and the kid's tuition. Or maybe you just want to buy yourself and the spouse a pair of matching jet skis. There's a loan type for this: **personal loans**. These are loans provided by banks and other lending institutions which have no stated purpose. You can use them on anything you want. They come in two different flavors—**secured** (usually tied to your checking or savings accounts or some other collateral) and **unsecured**—and are available in lump sums (which generally have a fixed interest rate) and as lines of credit (which usually have fluctuating interest rates).

Personal loans can provide you with quick and ready cash but they come at a price—interest rates that are just this side of usurious. Small unsecured personal loans can have interest rates upwards of twenty percent. That's just plain nuts. Secured personal loans and larger unsecured loans come down from those dizzying heights, but rates for these types of loans are still typically six or eight percentage points higher than mortgage rates or new car loan rates. In fact, in many cases, you might be able to find a better rate from a credit card than you could from an unsecured personal loan.

Such is the nature of personal loans that many banks and lenders, who allow other loan applications online, prefer to do their personal loan applications the "old-fashioned" way: by phone or through the mail. One can always, of course, go into a neighborhood bank branch as well. This is one loan option, in fact, where it may actually be better to do the loan face-to-face. Your banker or lender might be able to provide you with some loan options you might not have considered, which will cost you less in interest. Also, frankly, in the case of small, unsecured personal loans, a little bit of face time with a real human being can make a difference.

Be that as it may, personal loans are readily available online, largely through banks and credit unions, some of which will take your application online, while others will simply send you additional information. LendingTree.com (http://www.lendingtree.com) will take your information and present it to a number of lenders who will then bid on your application, presumably allowing you to get a better rate. Some banks will

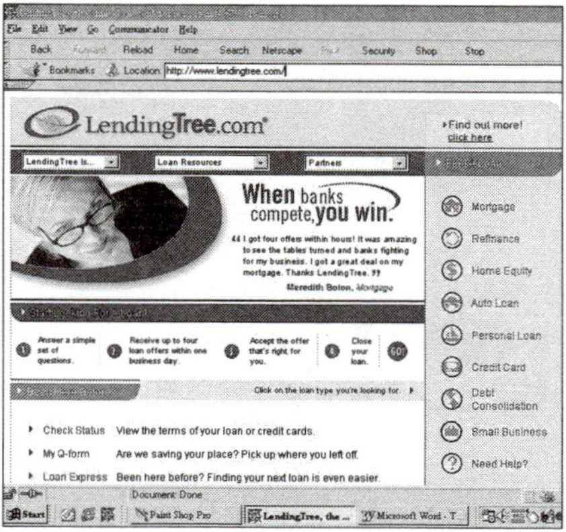

trim your interest a quarter point or so if you allow for automatic electronic deductions from a checking or savings account. Finally, as with auto loans, **credit unions** generally offer lower rates for personal loans than banks; if you belong to a credit union, make that your first stop, online or off.

Institutions who do take applications for personal loans online usually ask for very detailed information about your current income, debt load, and the like. So be ready to have all the pertinent information at hand, including the names of all the institutions to whom you owe money (and how much).

If you're still hot for a personal loan, there's one stop to make before you apply: Once again, Bankrate.com publishes **information on the current rates** for personal loans nationally and in each state in its "Personal Loan" area (http://www.bankrate.com/brm/rate/personal_home.asp). The site also features a beginner's guide to personal loans, the tone of which implies that you're better off looking for some other way to finance whatever it is you're financing. No argument here.

7

Credit Cards

USING THEM, CHOOSING THEM, GETTING THEM

Credit cards have made the Internet what it is today—of the billions of dollars in Internet commerce, almost all of it is handled by way of credit card transactions. And the Net is returning the favor, helping connect consumers to credit cards. Everyone from platinum card holders to people just emerging from bankruptcy can head online and find a card that suits their needs. And more than that: Not only can you find your cards online, you can service and make payments on the cards as well. Plus credit card companies are sweetening the deal by offering consumers special offers (and protections) when they use their cards online.

It's a big area. This chapter runs though how you can make sure your transactions are safe, your rights and protections online, and what credit card companies and others are doing to encourage you to shop on the Net. Then it moves on to finding the right card online, what happens when you apply, and what to do if you find you've gotten in over your head with credit card debt. Yes, the Net can get you deep into credit card debt, so it's only right that it can help get you out of it.

Are Cards Really Safe Online?

Let's assume you already have a credit card—not a bad bet since there are over a billion cards in circulation in the United States (four per person on average). Then you can use it to go online and buy stuff. What sort of stuff? Anything. Books, CDs, movies, clothes, sports equipment, cars, pet supplies, even groceries and gasoline. If you can buy it in a store, you can buy it online—any time of day. And as with all things Internet, choices are vast: Looking for that rare edition of a favorite childhood book? You'll find it on the Net.

Be that as it may, many folks are still hesitant to punch their credit card number into a Web site form and press "send." Hackers break into Web sites all the time, after all—what's to keep some crafty teenager from jotting down your credit card information while it's whizzing across the Net? And once he's got it, what's to keep him from charging thousands of dollars while you go about your life, totally unawares (that is, until your bill arrives)? Well, the answer is pretty much the same as with banking. When you go online, a wall of security exists around your card, protecting it from prying eyes, and you from financial harm. Let's outline your protections, which occur on three levels: technological, governmental, and retail.

Technological Protections

The first line of security in online transactions is one discussed in Chapter Two of this book: **Secure browsing**. Both major browser brands, Netscape Communicator and Microsoft Internet Explorer, come equipped with an encoding feature known as Secure Socket Layer (SSL), which is activated when you browse online and enter a **"secure" area** of a Web site. So long as you're sending information in a secure area, your information is almost ridiculously safe. You'll know if you're in a secure online area when you see a locked padlock icon on your browser: For Netscape, the padlock is on the toolbar and in the lower left-hand corner of the browser. For Microsoft, the padlock icon is visible in the lower right corner (America Online users use a version of Internet Explorer, which also shows the padlock in the lower right-hand corner).

All major online commerce sites feature secure purchasing and ordering, but some smaller commerce sites ("Ma and Pa" Web sites, as it were) do not. So be alert: You should see the locked padlock icon before you enter any credit card or personal information into Web browser forms. If you don't see a locked padlock, do not enter your credit card or any other personal information, and find some other way to make the payment instead. If you're not sure if the form is secure, assume it is not (better safe than sorry).

Governmental Protections

In the event of someone stealing your credit card or credit card information, online or offline, the US government offers some measure of protection. Simply put, you are not liable for any charges made to your **credit card** once you report it (or the credit card information) as stolen to your credit card company. Also, even if it takes you several days (or weeks) to notice your card or information has been stolen, the maximum amount for which you can be held **liable is $50**. These protections are in force whether the fraud is online or offline, so using your credit card online is as safe as using it in the "real world." And to be honest, theft is less likely online.

That must certainly be the view of Visa, which has introduced a **Zero Liability policy** for fraudulent purchases, meaning that consumers who have their Visa cards stolen and used will not be responsible for any charges incurred, online or offline. This reassuring warranty covers all Visas, whoever they have been issued by.

However, if you're using a **debit card** rather than a credit card, you may not have the same level of fraud protection. Strictly speaking, debit cards (which use money that you already have in your checking account) aren't credit cards. So check with your issuing bank to make sure you know exactly what protections you have in place—or, simpler, make sure you use a credit card rather than a debit card when you shop online—maybe even a credit card you reserve for this purpose.

If you are the victim of credit card fraud, it's up to you to clean up any messes that fraud makes on your **credit reports**. It'll be a hassle, but it'd be more of a hassle later, say, when you're trying to buy a house or a car and you have to explain those charges.

Retail Protections

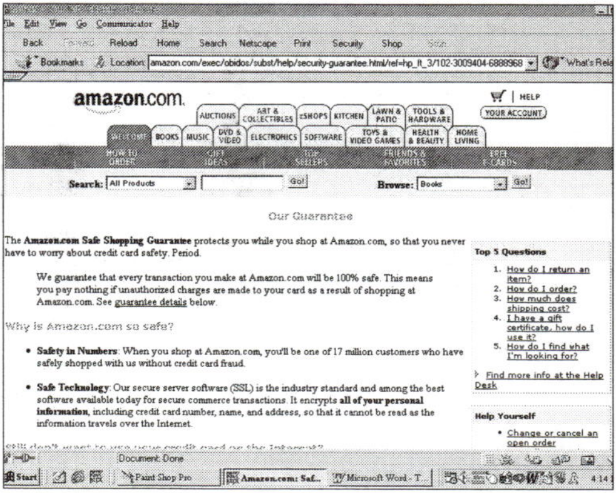

Commerce sites know that many consumers still feel edgy about using their credit cards online, and some of them go the extra mile to ensure customer security and privacy. Amazon, for example, offers to refund any amount of fraudulent purchase up to $50 (ie, the limit of your legal liability in credit card fraud), a lead followed by many other online shops. If you're on **AOL** and shop through the Shopping Channel (**Keyword: Shopping**), any purchase you make from any of their certified merchants is likewise covered for the first $50.

If you are concerned about security, you can usually find the guarantees retail sites offer just one click from their homepage, following a link labeled Security Information (or some variation) or in the site's Help section.

Electronic Wallets

Retailers aren't the only ones attempting to convince you of the safety and convenience of buying online. Credit card companies themselves are offering advanced technology and special deals to entice you to punch in your credit card number online. Why? Well, beyond the money they'll get from you, they also a collect a tidy transaction fee from the retailers. Call it enlightened self-interest.

Leading the charge is **American Express** (http://www.americanexpress.com) and its "Internet friendly" charge card known as **Blue**. Card members are provided 100 percent protection against fraudulent online purchases made with their card. The card also lets members use American Express' **Online Wallet**—a service that stores members' shipping information so they don't have to enter it every time they make an online purchase. And it has an option for something called a **smart card reader**. This is a piece of hardware that plugs into your computer and requires a

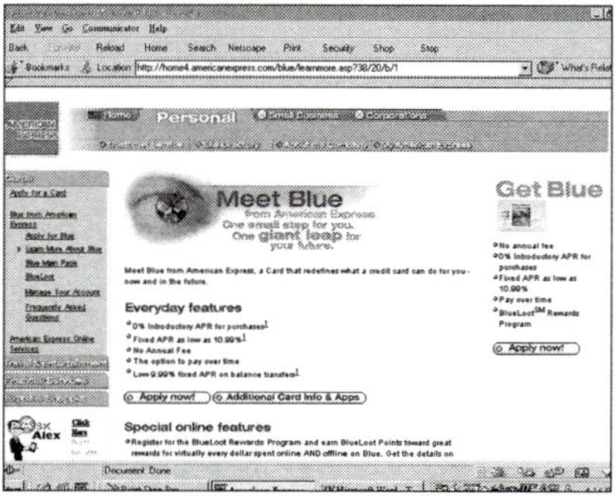

Getting a Card Is Not Very Hard

The ease with which it is possible to get a credit card, particularly on the Net (which can offer card approval in minutes), highlights one important point. Which is: folks these days have too much credit. The average American credit card holder has thousands of dollars in consumer debt on his or her cards, cards which typically carry interest rates of 16, 17 or 18 percent—and sometimes even higher. The average credit card holder will spend nearly a thousand dollars in interest each year, money that buys nothing except time to rack up more interest. It's not even tax-deductible, like your mortgage interest.

Before you go card shopping, ask yourself if you actually need a new credit card, and what you plan to use it for. Looking for a card with a lower interest rate than your current card(s), to help lower your interest load and to consolidate your debts, is one excellent reason. Having a credit card with consumer protection to use for shopping online, in preference to using a bank debit card, is another. Looking for a new card so that you'll simply have more credit available to you is not a great idea. After a certain point, even credit card issuers start looking at how much credit you have available versus your income and refuse to issue any more cards—and by that time you would be swimming in debt.

PIN number in order to authorize an online purchase. So, if a card is stolen it can't be used to make online purchases without the PIN.

While Amex Blue is currently the only card with a smart card reader, other credit card providers are offering electronic wallet services. Providian offers a wallet service for their **Aria** line of Visa cards (http://www.aria.com), which keeps track of shipping and credit card information, offers 100 percent fraud protection, and offers access to hundreds of merchants. **Discover Card** (http://www.discovercard.com) also offers an electronic wallet (Desk$hop Virtual Card) from their site.

Finding the Right Card Online

Credit cards are not created equal. Some have low credit limits while others have no credit limit at all. Some have an annual fee; others don't. Some offer a low, fixed interest rate, while others (frankly, most) have a high interest rate that fluctuates well above the prime lending rate. Some are unsecured, meaning there's no collateral needed to back them up, while others are secured by the cash you have in your bank. And some credit cards aren't credit cards at all. There are also **charge cards**, such as American Express and Diner's Club, which must be paid off at the end of each billing period, and **debit cards**, which are tied directly to your checking account.

In reality, there are really just two types of credit cards: The kind you want, and the kind you can actually get. The kind you want has a low fixed interest rate, no annual fee, a high credit limit, and a whole raft of free consumer perks, like airline miles and a concierge service. The kind of card you get is based on your credit history, your income, and the research you do to find a good deal. We can help with the latter. The online world is packed with sites designed to connect you with credit cards, and everyone out there is offering **deals** right now to pull in and maintain your custom as you shop online.

Banks and Credit Unions

Banks have been the primary outlet for credit cards for decades and the two largest credit card brands—Visa and MasterCard—originated as banking consortiums. Nearly every bank you can name offers a credit card, and most offer several, with rates and fees varying according to the consumer's income and credit history. Many larger banks like Wells Fargo or Bank of America will take credit card applications online and can offer an instant acceptance or rejection, and almost all banks with Web sites offer information on their credit card products online. Banks will also allow you to set up payments online as well, drawing directly from your bank accounts.

Many **credit unions** offer credit cards to their members, at interest rates that can be lower than usual. Most credit union Web sites carry information about their credit card products, and some will also allow members to apply for the cards online, although few give instant approval online.

Net-Only Card Providers

Want a card that's untainted by the offline world? You can get one either through **online-only banks** like Wingspan (http://www.wingspanbank.com, AOL Keyword: Wingspan), or through an Internet-only card issuer like **NextCard** (http://www.nextcard.com). These cards come Internet friendly, with online shopping protections, online access to account information, and discounts with online merchants, plus some other interesting goodies—NextCard, for example, can personalize your card with a photo you supply.

Online brokerages are also getting into the act; for example, E*Trade (http://www.etrade.com, AOL Keyword: Etrade) offers a Visa, which, like its other online-only compatriots, comes with online shopping protections, and also offers cash back on online purchases.

Or perhaps you fancy a credit card with a big "AOL" symbol? Or a "Yahoo!" emblazoned on the front? These are two of numerous online sites which offer cards to their members or visitors. And they often come with special deals. AOL Visa (AOL Keyword: AOL Visa) offers reward points, online shopping protections, and a month of free AOL service. Yahoo Visa offers membership points and online shopping protections. Other sites offering cards include Lycos (http://www.lycos.com) and iVillage (http://www.ivillage.com).

Online Stores

How about a Sears card? Or Target? Or Nordstrom? You can get all of these and more online: Sears (http://www.sears.com), Target (http://www.target.com), and Nordstrom (http://www.nordstrom.com, AOL Keyword: Nordstrom) are just three of the many retailers who offer their **in-house cards** online, and will (of course) accept these cards when you shop online at their stores. One warning: In-house credit cards typically have **sky-high interest rates**, even compared to other credit cards: 21 percent APR is not unusual. If you get one of these, check the rate, and pay it off every month.

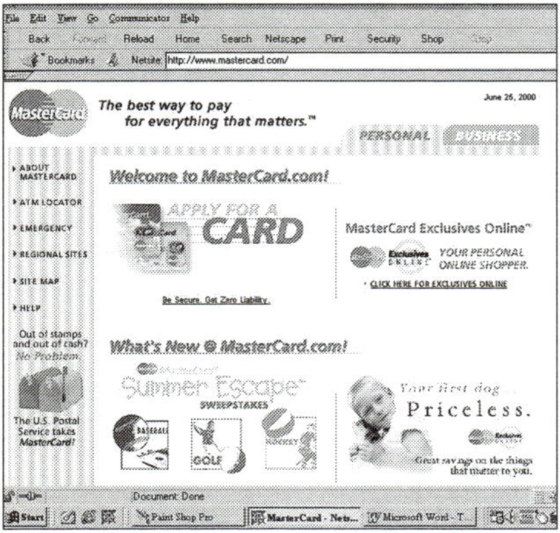

If you prefer to have a card that is not restricted to one store, some retailers offer **branded Visa or MasterCard credit cards** with special deals in their stores. For example, outdoors outfitters REI (http://www.rei.com, AOL Keyword: REI) offers a Visa card that offers REI members their "patronage refund," 100 percent online fraud protection, and travel insurance up to $100,000. Computer maker Dell (http://www.dell.com, AOL Keyword: Dell) provides a Visa that provides 0 percent interest and no payments for six months on the initial Dell purchase.

Credit Card Issuers

Eliminate the middleman. **Visa**, **MasterCard**, **Discover**, and **American Express** all have Web sites on which you can apply for their cards. Visa and MasterCard will point you in the direction of one of their member banks' Web sites, while Discover and American Express will take your application directly on site. And let's not forget **Diner's Club** (http://www.dinersclub.com), the first true credit card when it debuted in 1950. It accepts applications online.

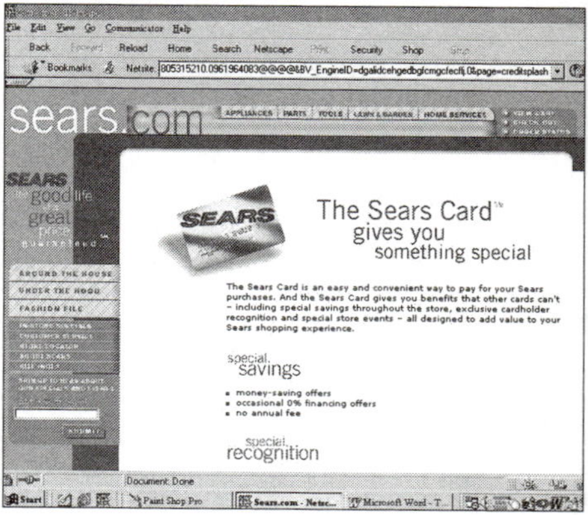

The big issuers are also getting keen on deals. For example, the **MasterCard** Web site (http://www.mastercard.com) offers MasterCard Exclusives Online, while **Visa** (http://www.visa.com) offers its own collection of retail, travel, and business bargains. **American Express** and **Discover Card** offer similar member deals on their sites.

Not to Mention Kiss...

Additional to all of these options, there are credit cards issued by thousands of universities, fraternal organizations, airlines, special interest groups, magazines, sports teams, and rock groups (yes, metal masters KISS offer a Visa) whose credit cards can be applied for online.

Narrowing the Search

You could spend weeks going from site to site, jotting down the specifics of each card, trying to decide which card is right for you. You don't want that—you want a direct connection

Credit Card Factors

APR: This is the interest you pay on any balance you leave on your card. The average is between 15 and 18 percent. A good APR is 12 percent or below. A truly excellent APR is 10 percent or below. You'll often see cards advertised with APRs in the 4 to 8 percent range, but beware: Those are introductory fees, and they'll go up, usually in three to six months.

Charge cards, like American Express, do not charge interest. However, they must be paid in full at the end of the billing period.

Annual Fee: This is the amount you pay for the privilege of using the credit card, and can range from nothing to $300 (for the American Express Platinum card).

Benefits: The goodies that you can get by using the card: Air miles is one of the most popular. Discover Card offers cash back. Many premium cards offer travel services and shopping deals. But these things don't come free: Cards with benefits usually come with annual fees.

Charity Deductions: This is painless giving but be aware that if you use a credit card that contributes a percentage of each sale to a specific charity or organization, that contribution is not tax deductible for you. You would do better to give direct.

Secured Cards: Folks with bad credit or no credit at all may find themselves in the position of having to get a "secured" credit card—one that's tied to the money they have in a savings account (either directly or as a ratio). These credit cards can help to rebuild credit, but they naturally tend to have low credit limits and higher-than-average APRs. Don't get this sort of card if you can avoid it.

Ease of Use: Will you be able to use this particular card in your favorite stores? In the restaurants you like to go to? At the Web sites you buy stuff from? Not every place will take every card, so make sure you get the card that's right for your lifestyle.

to the right card for you. As long as you know what you want, that can be arranged.

What are some of the things you should be looking for in your credit card? Our sidebar opposite fills you in.

Several Web sites maintain listings of cards and providers, based on users' criteria. As with other financial services, a first stop should be **Bankrate.com**, whose Credit Card area (http://www.bankrate.com/brm/rate/cc_home.asp) keeps regularly updated lists of credit cards based on overall rates, best deals for people who pay off their cards monthly or carry a balance, best card rebates, best secured cards, and the best cards in standard, gold, and platinum flavors. Another useful site in this vein is **CardTrak** (http://www.cardtrak.com). It provides extensive lists on the best standard, gold, and platinum cards, as well as information on the best rates offered by reward and "affinity" cards (cards associated with a non-banking entity, like an orchestra, football team, or charity).

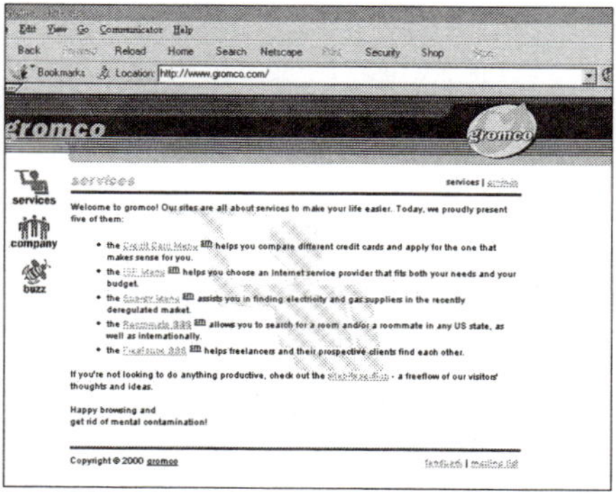

Alternatively, there are sites that will provide you with a list of suitable cards, culled from information you provide. **Gromco**'s Credit Card Advisor (http://www.gromco.com/cca/) will generate a list of suitable cards from its database, based on your need in terms of interest rate and annual fee, and on your income and credit history. The list also provides links for terms and conditions of the cards, as well as a link to apply online. The main site for

MasterCard provides the same service, connecting consumers to their cards based on features and rewards. **American Express** offers the same service to help you determine the best card out of the ones they offer.

If you like the idea of the card companies coming to you instead of the other way around, **LendingTree** (http://www.lendingtree.com) will take your application and present it to a number of banks. They will then bid on your business, offering the credit cards which they think will suit the needs you've specified. Then you choose (or not). Another site, **Priceline** (http://www.priceline.com), is teaming up with NextCard to allow consumers to specify the exact terms they want on their credit cards. The catch here is that if NextCard accepts your terms, you're obligated to get the card.

However you choose, take some time to research, and remember not to jump at the first offer that looks good to you. If you find a card that works for you, do a little more work and see if you can't find one that's a little bit better. The difference of a percentage point may not seem like much at the front end, but it can save you hundreds if not thousands of dollars over the life of your credit card.

Applying For Your Card Online

You've settled on the card you want; now it's time to apply online. This part is almost too easy.

Here's what you'll need for your typical **online application**: information on your current salary and employment history, your current housing situation (whether you rent or own, and how much you pay for either), any additional income you might have, your banking situation (if you have a checking or savings account, and whether those accounts are with the bank you wish to give you a card) and your Social Security number. This information is pretty uniform across all applications, though some will require more information, especially ones that will give you an "instant" thumbs up or thumbs down.

It's important to remember that when you apply for a credit card online, you really are applying for a **card right then**. With most applications, once you've been approved online, your credit line is opened and your card in the mail, and any fees you owe for the card will be billed. You should also be aware that the fine print of these online applications allows the bank or credit card company to run a **credit report** on you.

Another reminder: When you apply for a card, make sure your **application is secure** by checking the padlock icon on your browser (see p.82). If your padlock icon is not "locked," do not apply online. Apply either by phone or through the mail. Or apply for a similar card online that features a secure application. Most credit card companies suggest using a browser capable of 128-bit encryption, and some actually require it.

There's also one other point to consider: The card you think you are applying for may not be the card you get. Many cards, particularly ones with variable rates, will assign you an interest rate based on your credit history and your income. If your credit history does not meet their criteria for the lowest rate, you'll be **given a card with a higher rate**; they won't ask you first if you want it (you agreed to take the higher rate—it's in the fine print of the Terms & Conditions). If this happens, your course of action is clear: Cancel the account, cut up the cards when they arrive, send them back to the issuer registered mail, and then let the credit bureaus know that the account was closed at your request (this last part is important). Don't take anything less than what you expected to get.

When Credit Cards Go Bad

One of the consequences of easy credit online is that it's all too easy to find yourself swimming against the tide in high-

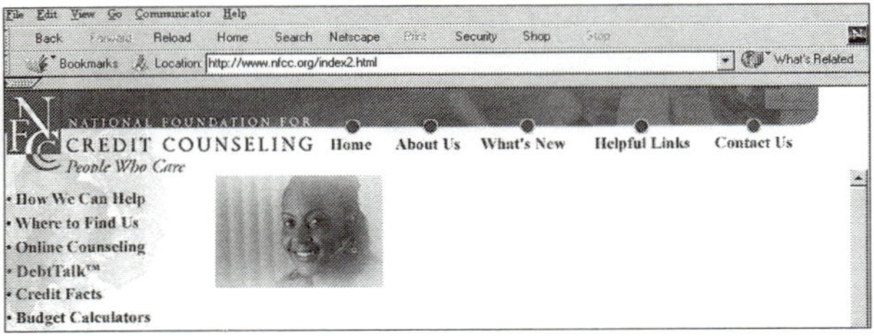

interest debt. If you find yourself edging toward this position, there are sites online than can help you get out. You could start by checking into the **Motley Fool** site. Their Getting Out of Debt feature (http://www.fool.com/credit/credit.htm) offers practical steps to keep your debt in check, and tips and tricks from readers. The well-known financial magazine **Money** (http://www.money.com/money/101/lessons/9/intro.html) also offers a useful online tutorial on keeping debt at bay.

If it's too late for that, and you're in serious debt trouble, it may be time to start thinking about **debt consolidation** and other tactics to bring your finances under control before your barrel into bankruptcy. The National Foundation for Credit Counseling (http://www.nfcc.org) can put you in touch with credit counselors where you live, or can help you start your credit rescue process online. Two other non-profit companies online devoted to helping consumers are Myvesta (http://www.myvesta.org), the online site of the Debt Counselors of America, and Metropolitan Financial Management (http://www.debt-help.com).

8

Financial Intelligence

GETTING INFORMED ONLINE

Never in the history of money has it been so easy to take control of your individual financial destiny—banking, investing, and borrowing with minimal human intervention. So easy, in fact, that you need to remind yourself that personal finance requires planning—and homework. You don't have to be scared of being in charge of your money, but you should be prepared. Fortunately, there's a lot of help out there on the Internet, and this chapter is essentially about where to find it: where to go online to get a grounding in basic financial planning, and where to go next, for a dive deep into the world of financial intelligence, particularly as it relates to investing.

Just the Basics

Most people think of financial advice and intelligence in terms of investment advice. But you do more with your money than simply invest it. You use it to buy things. You use it to pay your mortgage. You use it to send your kids to college. For every way there is to use money, there's a way to use it smarter and better, so you have more of it after you're done.

If you're just beginning to get your feet wet in financial planning, pick your site, take your time, and read as much as you can on the subjects you want to know about—and then when you're done, pick another site and read through that. Not every site will give you the same advice and information, so the more you read, the more you'll know what the range of opinions is concerning money in your everyday life.

TheWhiz.com

There are a number of sites that cater to such needs and that are written for people who have never browsed *The Wall Street Journal* and would hope never to. **TheWhiz.com** (http://www.thewhiz.com, AOL Keyword: TheWhiz) is one of the best examples of this sort of site. This has financial advice broken up into the most common aspects of everyday life: cars, insurance, banking, school, spending, and even a category for "play" (where the articles examine things like the cost of getting hitched in Vegas or theme park vacations).

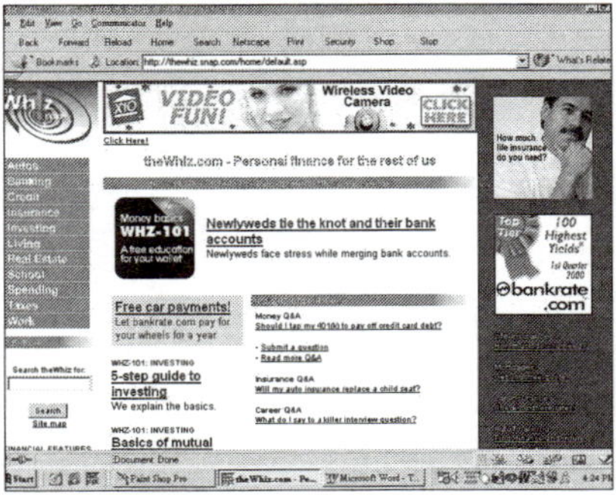

In addition to current articles, each subject also features an archive of selected stories, designed to address most questions the average person is going to have in that category. TheWhiz.com also features guides under the "WHZ-101" rubric, which covers the basics of things like buying cars and homes, using online banking, and (of course) investing online. The writing style angles toward the smirky, but the underlying financial advice is solid and easy to understand.

RicEdelman.com

Attitude is something that many of the "novice" financial planning sites have, but none more so than **RicEdelman.com** (http://www.ricedelman.com, AOL Keyword: Edelman). Ric Edelman is well known for his series of popular financial planning books, and while his site features wall-to-wall advertising for these books (and audio tapes, and radio shows, and television appearances...), it also features extremely useful step-by-step planning departments, covering specific financial events like weddings and estate planning as well as more general topics. The site even provides a "top ten" list of articles for people who don't have a whole lot of time (although this is entirely the wrong attitude to have when it comes to your money).

Edelman's financial advice is unconventional at times (for example, he suggests that instead of trying to work down a mortgage, you should instead get a big mortgage and never quite pay the thing off), and he occasionally comes across as a know-it-all blowhard. On the other hand, he backs up his strategies with actual numbers (his rationale for never paying off the mortgage is that it's the cheapest loan you're likely to find), and his style is clear and confident. The site is designed to give you the information you want in an efficient way.

The Motley Fool

The Motley Fool site will be explored later in this chapter, for its investment advice. For starters, however, the Fool's "Personal

Finance" area (http://www.fool.com/pf.htm) should be your next pit stop. Like the Edelman site, the Fool's personal finance area is designed to walk you through specific life events, with a series of articles that constitute a step-by-step approach. Its disadvantage is that its financial planning information is not nearly as complete as at the other sites mentioned above (it covers buying a home, a car, and a college education, and also includes three features on bringing down personal debt). What is there, however, has the right mix of information and relaxed style.

SmartMoney.com/AOL Money Basics

Covering the same ground but slightly more buttoned-up, you have **SmartMoney.com**'s "Planning" area (http://www.smartmoney.com/intro/answers/). Like theWhiz, SmartMoney provides articles and planning guides for most of life's major events and purchases, from cars to colleges, with a tone that leans more toward the professional than the chummy. Perfect if you want a site to give you the facts, not be your best pal.

SmartMoney.com also provides the content for **America Online's Money Basics** area (Keyword: Money Basics), which concentrates primarily on the 1-2-3s of investing. For more general financial planning tips on AOL, you'll want to go to the Advice & Planning area (Keyword: Advice & Planning). This area is actually one of the better ones out there for comprehensive information, thanks to AOL's ability to aggregate content from other sources, including all the sites mentioned above. The area may in fact have more information than you want (unless you've been burning to figure out your "Pet Finances," which is an actual subsection), but in cases like this, better too much information than too little.

Financial Planning by Demographics

The sites above are designed to be "one size fits all"—which is to say that the advice provided will likely fit whether you are male or female, black or white, young or old. It's not unreasonable, then, to look for financial planning information with your specific demographic in mind. You'll find it, no matter who you are or what group you identify with.

Women

The largest range of "niche" financial planning sites is for women: There are several specifically aimed at women's planning and investing needs. Begin at **Women's Financial Network** (http://www.wfn.com/), which features a "milestones" section, covering starting out, marriage, children, and retirement, in addition to a full slate of investing and finance articles and areas.

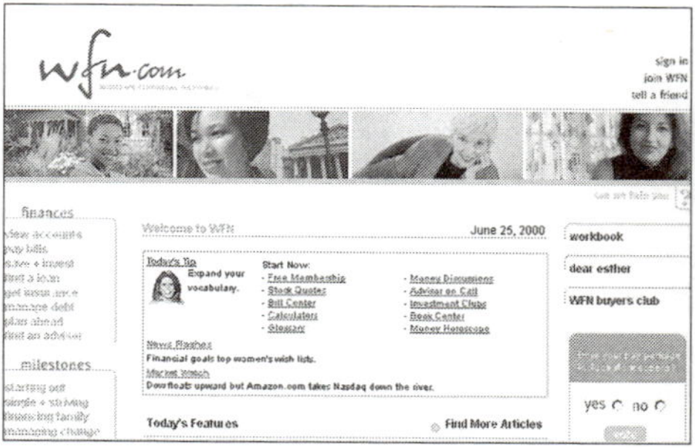

General women's sites also have detailed money and financial planning areas: **iVillage** has MoneyLife (http://www.ivillagemoneylife.com/), whose financial planning series is called "Life Stages." **Women's Wire**'s Money section (http://www.womenswire.com/money/) features news from Bloomberg, a financial news wire; the navigation isn't very good, but the information is. **Oxygen** features the women's financial site **Ka-Ching.com** (http://www.ka-ching.com). **AOL's Women's Money** area (Keyword: Women's Money) features content from iVillage, Women's Wire, and Oxygen.

Gays and Lesbians

There are also a number of sites catering to particular gay and lesbian financial issues. One of the most comprehensive is the **Gay Financial Network** (http://www.gfn.com), which features breaking financial news to accompany gay men and women's particular money conundrums. Gay community site **Planet Out** also offers financial planning advice (http://www.planetout.com/pno/money/planning/), as does **Gay.com**'s Financial Channel (http://content.gay.com/channels/finance/).

Age-Specific

Feeling your age, whatever it is? Fear not. You've got sites ready. For **20-somethings** and Gen-Xers, there's **Greenmagazine.com** (http://www.greenmagazine. com), which dispenses useful investing and financial lifestyle advice with a characteristically detached voice.

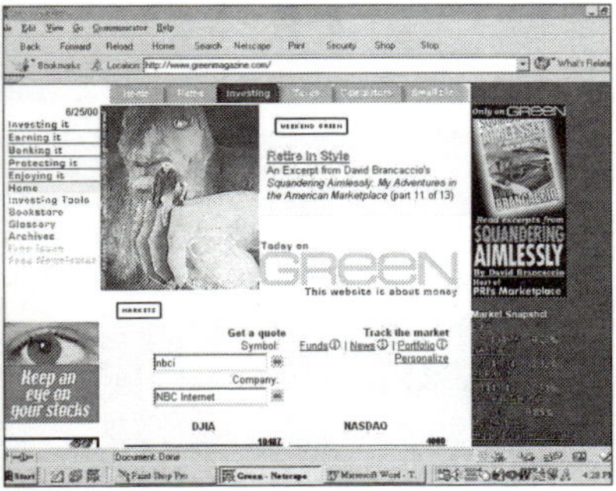

Boomers and above can head to **ThirdAge.com**'s money area (http://www.thirdage.com/money/), whose emphasis is on retirement and job- related financial issues. **Seniors** can rely on the American Association of Retired People (**AARP**) for a suite of financial planning features (http://www.aarp.org/indexes/money.html).

African-Americans and Latinos

African-Americans looking for financial planning advice might begin at **BET.com**, whose money area (http://www.bet.com/MONEY/) features the latest news, as well as investment and planning articles written specifically for the site. **Blackstocks.com** (http://www.blackstocks.com/) also features a detailed financial planning area under its "University" heading, though the content is taken directly from **Money.com** and is more general in nature.

Spanish-speaking Latinos and others can turn to **Consejero.com** (http://www.consejero.com/), which offers financial planning articles aimed at the United States and other Spanish-speaking countries.

Stocks, Funds, and Investing Financial Information

Now that you've gotten solid on the basics of money and financial planning, let's slide into the fast lane: Time for **stocks, funds, and investing** financial information. When it comes to such advice in the online world, there's a distinct shift—from finding information to deciding whether you can trust the information you find. Would-be investors are always looking for the next hot tip on a stock and that eternal hope blossoms online in unhealthy ways. As a result, you can get bilked, or just plain lose your shirt, if you're not careful. So this section starts with who and what not to trust, when it comes to financial information online, before covering the more reliable and indeed invaluable intelligence sources.

Financial Advice You Should Not Trust

Trust me. Here are some locales for tips that are definitely to avoid. And if you don't think investing scams could happen to you online, you are invited to peruse the Security Exchange Commission's Internet Enforcement Program Web site (http://www.sec.gov/enforce/intrela.htm), which features a current list of Net-related litigation involving investment fraud. It'll give you a new perspective.

#1: Investing Tips from Online Message Boards

Many online financial sites, including some of the most trustworthy, feature **message boards** and **discussion groups**

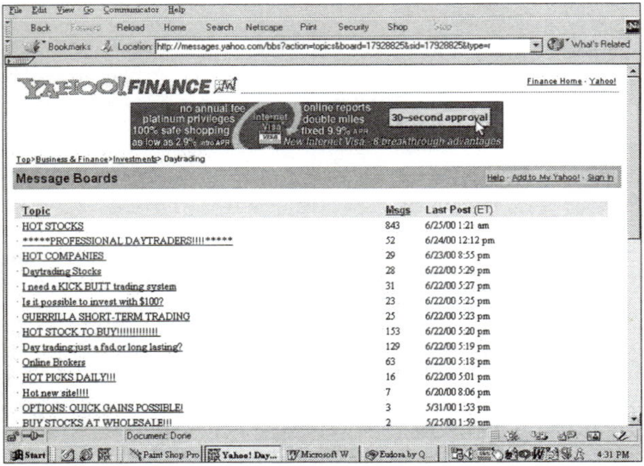

where site readers and members can trade opinions on current financial events, recount investing experiences, or just trade posts socially. These message boards can be great for interaction with other investors, but thanks to their essentially anonymous nature, you know nothing about any of the other people on the board. They could be just other investors talking about their experiences, or they could be con artists pushing a fraudulent stock. Or they could be idiots.

America Online, which has extensive personal finance message boards on its service, actually has a Message Board Disclaimer: "People using the Investing Forums should exercise the same degree of common sense that they would in any situation in which they interact with strangers whose personal and financial motivations are unknown. Recommendations to buy or sell stock, and similar 'tips' contained in Investing Forum postings, should not be used as a basis for making any investment decision." That's right on the nose.

#2: Investing Tips from Usenet Newsgroups

"Newsgroups" are message boards that are not associated with any particular Web site or Internet service provider—they're more of a community resource, fashioned in the old days of the Net as a pioneer outpost. Anyone with a basic Internet connection can access them and post comments, opinions, or (as is often the case) unwanted ads for a stock or financial product. Ads on newsgroups are a breach of newsgroup etiquette and invariably concern a worthless investment product (it's the Usenet equivalent of "spam" that you get in your electronic mailbox). In regards to other tips and advice you'll find on newsgroups, the same advice applies as with message boards—you don't know the source, and you don't know their motivations. Read, participate, but be smart.

#3: Investing Tips from Online Chat Rooms

There's an ad for an online broker which features a guy in a chat room asking for hot stock tips. Someone replies "VBNM" over and over again. The guy gets very excited, and then the ad cuts to an office party and a woman's butt jiggling on a keyboard as she laughs, hitting "VBNM" on the keyboard over and over again. Keep this image in mind whenever you're in a financial chat room. It'll help.

#4: Investing Tips from Spam Email

You don't pay attention to spam mail any other time, so why start when it comes to your money? Anyone with a truly hot stock tip wouldn't be spending his or her time mailing people they don't know about it.

#5: Investing Tips from (Most) Online Newsletters

Why not? Again: You often don't know who is writing these newsletters and what their motivations might be when they tout one stock or another. The SEC requires people who write newsletters to disclose if they are accepting payment for stock recommendations, who is paying them, and how much. But just because the SEC requires it doesn't mean they're doing it (especially if they're trying to pull a scam).

Now, the flip side of this is that many legitimate stock analysts, financial journalists, and financial magazines and Web sites will send out newsletters to interested investors; it's cheap advertising for them. Not every online financial newsletter is a con. It's up to you to research the author of the newsletter and the stocks they spotlight.

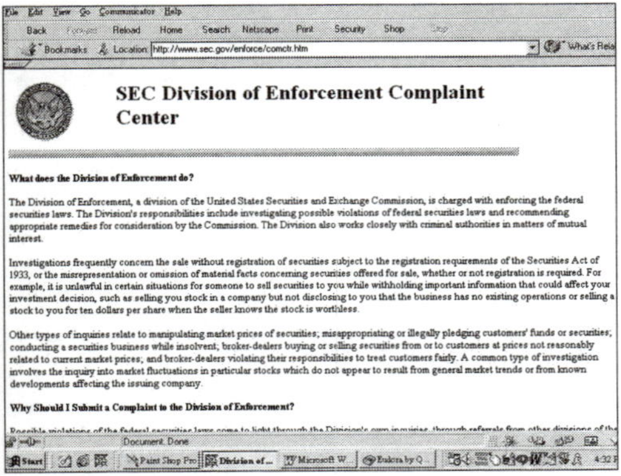

Financial Newspapers Online

For all the advances of upstart Web sites, **print newspapers and magazines** remain the "gold standard" when it comes to informational integrity. Most major newspapers and magazines pre-date the Internet and adhere to standards of journalistic integrity seemingly untainted by the trillions of dollars they report on every month, week, and day. These days, almost every serious newspaper and magazine has a Web version. Some of these sites repost the articles printed in the print version for that day or week, but more and more of them are offering "online only" features, which can include portfolio tracking, stock tickers, stock symbol research, frequent story updates, and more.

All the Pretty Doodads

Here are the multimedia elements that you'll find on every self-respecting financial site on the Web:

Market Snapshots: The current position of the major financial markets in the US: the Dow Jones Industrial Index, the NASDAQ, and the S&P 500. Many sites will then allow you to click on a specific index title to bring up more detailed information on that day's trading.

Stock Quotes: Enter the stock symbol in the text field, press "Enter," and the current position of that particular stock is called up ("current" being a relative term: stock prices on free sites are often delayed by 15–20 minutes). Many sites will then allow you to do more intensive research on the stock you've called up, including historical charts (see how the stock has done over a month, a year, or ten years), a company snapshot (who the company is and what it does), analyst ratings (whether professionals feel the stock should be bought or sold at the moment), and so on.

Portfolio Services: As part of their customization process, many sites will allow you to construct a "portfolio" folder, which will allow you to track the progress of the stocks you have invested in or are otherwise interested in. These portfolios typically allow you to enter the amount of stock you have in each company, so you can see your net worth fluctuate all the live-long day. This can become very distracting.

Market Games: Online competitions in which players are given a sum of fake money (typically $100,000 or so), which they then "invest" in particular companies. The player with the most "money" at the end of the game period wins, though the prize is not usually as grand as the theoretical money that's been earned (in the case of AOL's Market Game, for example, you get a T-shirt). Still, it's a risk-free way to invest like an idiot.

Our sidebar on p.105 defines some of the most useful financial site elements.)

The papers recommended below are among key sources—useful for beginners and experienced investors alike. Bear in mind that this is the tip of the iceberg: There are thousands of newspaper sites on the Web, likely including your local paper, and almost all of them have some business news online.

Wall Street Journal

The king of all finance media is, of course, the **Wall Street Journal**. Its Web site (www.wsj.com) features the full text of the daily newspaper as well as a host of Web-only features, including a thirty-day article archive, detailed stock information including links to analyst reports and SEC filings, and a "Personal Journal"—a page which you can set up to show you the information that's important to you.

The site also features message boards where the conversation is (shall we say) slightly more refined than you might get elsewhere. This latter observation is at least partially due to the fact that you have to pay to access the *Journal* site: About $60 a year, slightly more if you use the monthly billing option. The subscription also covers the subscription to **Barron's Online** (http://www.barrons.com), which features the text of the printed *Journal* plus detailed coverage on online investment sites.

If you prefer not to have to pay for the *Wall Street Journal* content, point your browser at **DowJones.com** (http://www.dowjones.com), which offers a slimmer selection of WSJ information, along with stock quotes and a business search engine.

The New York Times

The New York Times (http://www.nytimes.com, AOL Keyword: NYT) offers its entire business section for free, although you will have to register to access the site (not necessary if you access the *Times* from AOL). In addition to the full daily helping of business news, the *Times* offers capsule company research of 10,000 companies through **Hoover's Online**, the ability to construct and track a portfolio, and the usual assortment of charts, indices, and bank rates.

The Washington Post

The Washington Post Online also features a well-stocked business and tech section (**http://www.washingtonpost.com/business/**) which has a very well put-together business research area. Enter the ticker symbol, and the site pulls up the most recent articles on the company from the *Post* and the newswires, as well as press releases and a capsule from Hoover's.

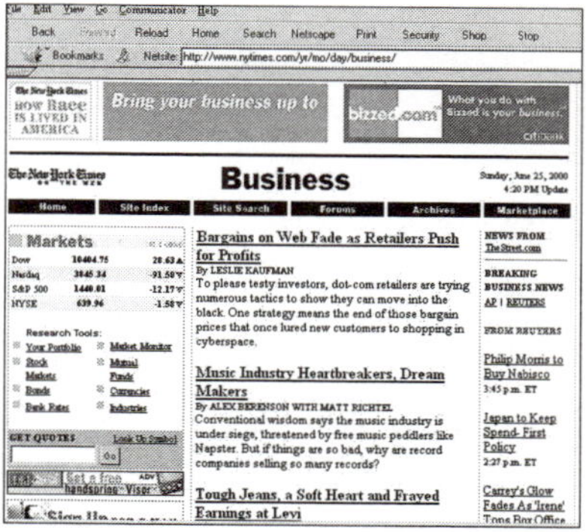

The Los Angeles Times

On the West Coast, **The Los Angeles Times** business site (**http://www.latimes.com/business/**) features news, stock and mutual fund research, and a nifty feature that allows you to download annual reports in Adobe Acrobat format.

The Financial Times

For a view of the financial world that actually deigns to consider the rest of the world, head to **The Financial Times** (**http://www.ft.com**). It has financial and business news from all over the world as well as industry spotlights, premium market reports, and market indices from the Nikkei in Japan to the DAX in Germany.

Financial Magazines Online

The most popular business and finance magazines have also made the leap into the online world, offering much if not all of their weekly magazines online and then sweetening the offerings with market research and other online goodies.

Money

Money.com (http://www.money.com, AOL Keyword: Money) presents *Money* magazine articles, columnists like Michael Sivy and Jason Zweig, daily news updates from the magazine staff and from CNNfn.com, and an interesting set of Web-only treats, like financial planning walk-throughs, a virtual investing game, and an array of investing tools and finance calculators.

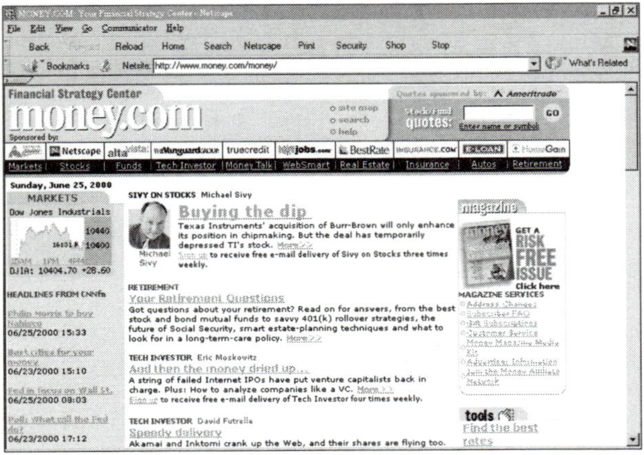

Business Week

Business Week (http://www.businessweek.com, AOL Keyword: BW) elects to charge an access fee for the majority of its weekly magazine columns and articles online (unless you access through America Online, in which case you can see it for no additional charge). However, the site also features extensive and valuable free content, including a daily briefing area and areas on investing, global business, and technology—even if you're not paying for the core content, it's worth the visit.

Smart Money

Smart Money is the *Wall Street Journal*'s glossy magazine for investors, and its online counterpart, SmartMoney.com (http://www.smartmoney.com, AOL Keyword: SmartMoney) offers links to free annual reports and mutual fund prospectuses in addition to a well-stocked larder of investing and personal finance stories and analysis.

Forbes

Forbes magazine's online site (http://www.forbes.com/) also features a range of stock and mutual fund research tools, but its best features center on the magazine's infamous lists of the richest people in the country and world. Among the financial tools at the site are several that track the companies that have contributed most to these accretions of wealth.

Fortune

Speaking of famous lists, **Fortune**'s "Fortune 500" is the most famous of all. The magazine's Web site (http://www.fortune.com, AOL Keyword: Fortune) features it prominently all year round, and gives visitors the stock research tools to learn more about those companies, along with content from the weekly magazine.

Lights, Camera, Web site: TV Sites

Print is not the only "old line" media to make inroads online: Each of the major financial cable networks and television news operations hang their shingles online as well, most with a fairly impressive array of content and multimedia doodads.

CNN ...

CNNfn (http://cnnfn.com, AOL Keyword: CNNFN), for example, provides text versions of the biggest financial news stories of the day, as well as written commentary, but also provides streaming media versions of its television shows from the Web site (to accommodate bandwidth issues, the visual portion is about the size of a postage stamp). It also features a very robust investor research area that makes it very easy to see which stocks have been upgraded or downgraded by analysts, which companies are expecting stocks split or earnings warnings, and what events are coming on the economic calendar.

... And the Rest

Other TV sites provide other interesting features. **CNBC** (http://www.cnbc. com/) offers a scrolling stock sticker that users can program to show only the stocks they are interested in (this requires free registration), while **Fox Market Wire** (http://www. foxmarketwire. com/) offers stock alerts and full reports to its registered users. **CBS MarketWatch** (http://cbs.marketwatch.com, AOL Keyword: MarketWatch) provides online clips of its analysts offering advice and commentary, and **ABC News'** Business site (http://www. abcnews.go.com/sections/business/) serves up stock "picks and pans" from analysts Standard & Poor.

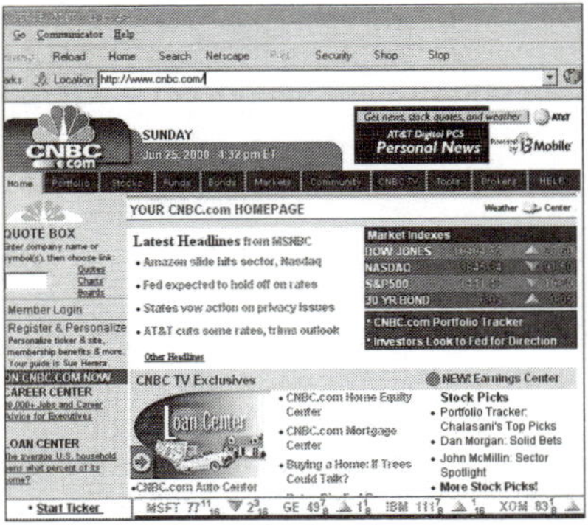

Online Financial Sites

The old financial media has successfully populated the online world with their sites. But what of the financial sites that were born and bred online? Are they worth paying attention to? The answer to this is a qualified yes: A few of them have become both immensely popular and deeply influential in terms of popular investing. This is not least because these sites dove into market analysis in a typically online sort of way—with a sense of adventure and irreverence concerning the subject at hand.

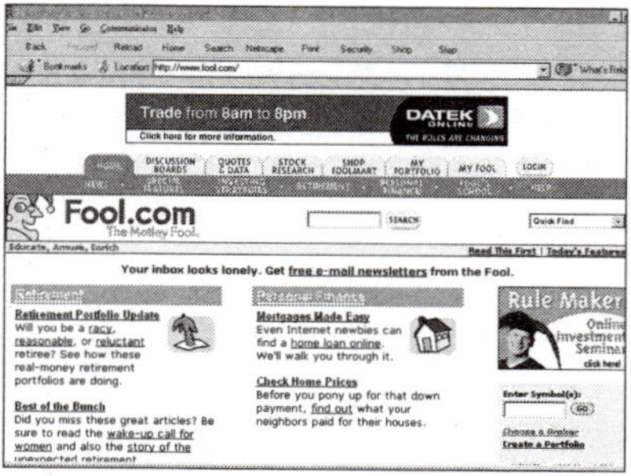

The Motley Fool

Easily (and justifiably) the most famous of these online-origin sites is **The Motley Fool** (http://www.fool.com, AOL Keyword: Fool). The Fool motto is "Educate, Amuse, and Enrich," and the Fool writers do all three, primarily by approaching investing as something any fool could do, as long as he or she keeps to a few simple rules.

The Fool site features extensive educational investing articles and programs (located in its "Fool's School" and "Investing Strategies" areas) and lots of thoughtful but thoroughly smart-ass analysis of stocks and current market events, both from its writers and in its member-driven message boards. The Fool has since expanded into books, radio, and television, but the heart of their operation is the Web site, and it is highly recommended both for novice investors and for those who want a fresh perspective on the investing game.

TheStreet.com

Another online site with a reputation for challenging journalistic expectations is **TheStreet.com** (http://www.thestreet.com, AOL Keyword: TSC), a reputation earned thanks to its co-founder and chief columnist James Cramer. In addition to writing about events in the market, Cramer is a hedge fund manager, which means that he works in the world he writes and opines about. This has led to some minor scandals—check out the sidebar below on the James Cramer affair. However, Cramer's point of view is that to write knowledgeably about the field you have to work in it (and in any event, if he writes about a stock he trades, he has to disclose that fact). However

What James Did

James Cramer said mean things about a stock, and the stock's price fell, and someone cried foul.

More precisely, Cramer, a hedge fund manager, asked one of his associates to research a specific stock (Wavephore), to see if he could borrow some of their stock to sell it short (he believed the price of the stock was being artificially inflated). He made mention of this fact while he was a guest on CNBC's Squawk Box, additionally labeling the company as a potential "Fraud-U-Net" company. After Cramer's appearance, the stock rocked, Wavephore complained to the SEC, and CNBC dropped Cramer as a guest.

Cramer did nothing wrong (he didn't actually buy any stock to sell it short, he just inquired about it), but the fact that he runs a hedge fund and acts as a commentator caused people to question both his objectivity when it comes to commenting on stocks and the appropriateness of his doing so at all. It also points to just how volatile stocks (particularly Internet stocks) can be, and why investors need to take time to research the fundamentals of the companies they invest in.

you feel about this, TheStreet.com makes for exciting and sometimes confrontational reading. Technically the site is a premium service (membership is about $100 a year), but it also features a generous helping of free content, including message boards and an investment basics area.

The Online Investor

If you'd prefer less attitude when it comes to learning the ropes in the investing arena and in researching your stocks, you can check out **The Online Investor** (http://www.theonlineinvestor.com, AOL Keyword: OLI). OLI's chief writer Ted Allrich presents his information in a calm, reassuring, no-nonsense style—perfect if you just want the facts. The site itself is disarmingly low-tech, but the information is very good.

Sage

Prefer to learn about and research mutual funds? You'll want **Sage** (http://www.sagefinancial.com, AOL Keyword: Sage), which is to the world of mutual fund investing what Motley Fool has been to stock investing—even more so, as Sage co-founders Alan and Stephen Cohn have been ranked as two of the ten most influential people in fund investing by the *Wall Street Journal*. Sage features an extensive educational area on funds and investing in them, along with interviews and chats with fund managers, analysis of market events and how they affect fund investors, and (of course) lots of member message boards.

Online Aggregate Sites

Think clicking around the online world for financial information is too much of a bother? Save your clicking finger some exercise by visiting these sites that aggregate financial information and financial information providers into one convenient, easily navigable online experience.

America Online's Personal Finance Channel

This fact may upset "Web-only" purists—and I should declare an interest given that I'm a contributing writer—but probably the single best collection of personal finance information online, especially for new investors, is **America Online's Personal Finance channel** (AOL Keyword: PF). It features all of the online-only sites mentioned above, as well as many of the print/television financial sites, including Money, Fortune, CNNfn.com (all owned by Time Warner, which is now owned by AOL) as well as CBS MarketWatch, Smart Money, and the Whiz. Most of this may be available elsewhere online, but AOL's "keep it simple" philosophy makes the information easy to find and use.

AOL's finance channel also features most every multimedia, stock research, and financial planning option available online, including chats and message boards, either through its own resources or through its partners. And it's also where AOL members can begin their online banking and trading sessions.

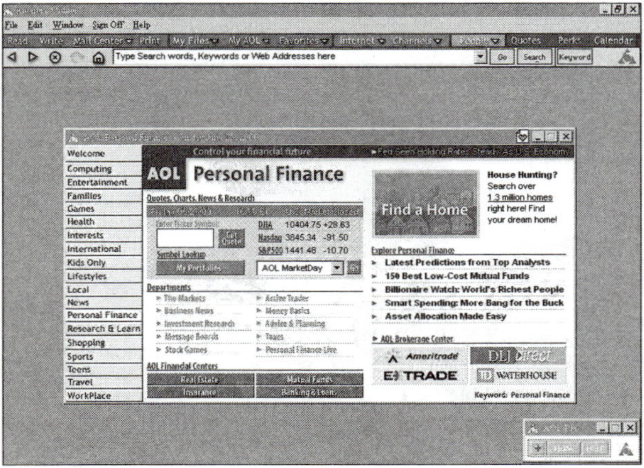

Microsoft's MoneyCentral

In direct competition to AOL's Personal Finance channel is **Microsoft's MoneyCentral** site (http://moneycentral.msn.com/home.asp). MoneyCentral offers online banking and trading access, personal finance planning, financial news and information (from MSNBC and CNBC), and a host of market and stock researching tools.

Quicken.com

Quicken.com (http://www.quicken.com/) also offers a broad range of financial planning and investing news and services, including banking, trading, and insurance services. The Quicken.com site integrates with recent versions of Quicken software, so if you use the program to keep track of your finances, you'll get quite a bit of exposure to this particular aggregate site.

9

Online Investing

CHOOSING AN ONLINE BROKER AND MAKING THE FIRST TRADE

Go ahead, admit it: this is why you bought this book in the first place. And that's okay—more than okay, it's great. Online investing is the single greatest financial innovation of the Internet era, helping to bring millions into the market arena by allowing them to control their investments at a low cost, and with simple-to-understand tools. As Prometheus stole fire from the gods and gave it to humans, so does the Internet demystify investing and make it available to anyone with a computer.

But (there's always a catch) with power comes responsibility. Fire is a swell tool to have, but it can burn down your house; by the same token, playing fast and loose with online investing is a great way to lose a large chunk of your retirement nest egg. Despite the TV commercials about truck drivers owning their own island states or the self-affirmations of being "modern capitalist mavericks," investing online is like all other money matters—you need to look well before you leap.

This chapter runs through the set-up exercises of learning what sort of investor you are, which online broker is likely to be right for you, and what you'll need to do to sign up for your online brokerage account. Then we'll walk you through a trade, using your new brokerage to buy stock with a market order. These are the basics of what you'll need to get going.

In Chapter 10, we'll talk about the different types of investments you can buy as well as some of the other types of orders you can place for stocks. We'll even talk about the phenomenon known as "day trading." But first things first. Let's get you set up to trade online.

What You Need to Start Investing

If you've decided to go forward with online investing, you'll need a couple of things before you begin.

Money

The first and most obvious component is a reasonable sum of money. Most online brokerages expect you to deposit some amount of money into your trading account when you apply and to keep a **minimum account balance**. This amount is typically in the $2000 range, but can be as low as $500 or as high as $5000. If a minimum balance is required, you could be charged fees if you drop below it, and if you trade frequently, you could drop below your balance just from your brokerage fees (even low-priced fees add up). So make sure your investment egg is large enough to clear the hurdle.

128-Bit Encryption

Second, if you haven't yet gotten a Web browser with **128-bit encryption** for your online banking or other online financial transactions (see pp.17–18), you'll probably need to get one now. Almost all online brokerages strongly recommend you use a 128-bit browser to trade, and several require it. Many of the online brokers that require secure browsers include download links on their sites.

What to do if you're somewhere **outside the United States and Canada**, and don't have access to 128-bit browsers? Well, in one sense the point is moot, since you would not be allowed to trade on most US-based trading sites to begin with. However, many of the leading US online brokers also sport sites specifically designed for **non-US investors**; for example, E*Trade features an international branch (http://www.etrade.com/cgi-bin/gx.cgi/AppLogic+Home?gxml=hpa_international.html) that does business in Europe, Asia, Australia, and Canada; DLJ Direct (http://www.dljdirect.com, AOL Keyword: DLJ) has branches in the UK and Japan.

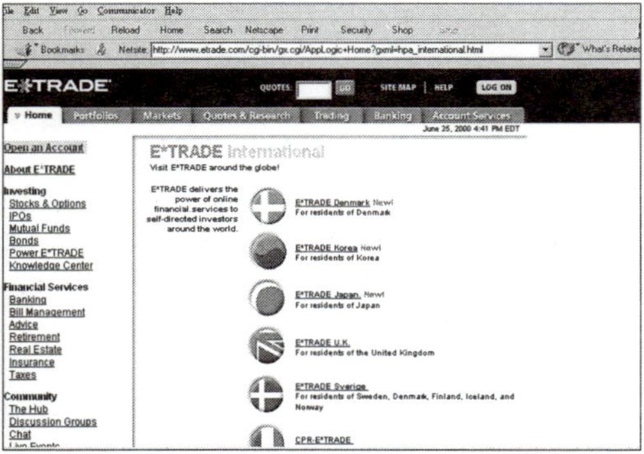

Understanding

Third, and this should probably go without saying, don't invest online if you're not actually clear on how to invest. You need at least a basic understanding of **how stock, mutual funds, and other investment vehicles work**, and **how trades are accomplished**, both online and off.

If you read Chapter Eight, you'll know where to find sites online that can give you a grounding on how to invest and how the financial world works. The site beginning investors are likely to get the most use out of is **Motley Fool** (http://www.fool.com, AOL Keyword: Fool). If you go nowhere else before you begin to invest, at least go there; the site has some excellent teaching tools and is written in a style that makes the fundamentals a snap to understand.

Investor, Know Thyself

From this point forward, let's assume you've done your homework and you feel confident with trading online. Join the crowd! Now let's look at the sort of investor you are, and what you're likely to be looking for in an online brokerage.

Investment goals are like fingerprints: No one has exactly the same set. Be that as it may, most investors can be lumped into a few broad categories, and folks in those categories are likely to have certain needs to be met by their online brokerages. Here are the categories:

Aggressive Investors

These are the people that online brokerages dream about: They're constantly checking their portfolio, trading for short-term gain, and have need of the freshest information on stocks, funds, and financial news. They'll also want access to IPOs and options. "Day traders" (see p.147) are included in this category, although not every aggressive investor is a day trader. These folks want low-cost trades, a minimum of system congestion for fast-order execution and fast-order confirmation, and access to the latest (but not necessarily the deepest) financial information.

Serious Investors

These investors don't trade as often as aggressive traders, but do so on a regular basis, upgrading their portfolios after careful consideration of their stocks and of where the market is going. Serious investors tend to be less concerned about lightning-fast trading ability or very low trade costs; instead they place a premium on the best financial information they can find.

These folks crave comprehensive financial data, access to member-driven content like message boards and chats, and investment tools that can help chart a solid financial course.

Long-Term Investors

These people aren't worried about being millionaires overnight: Their goal is solid but not necessarily pyrotechnic growth in their net worth over a substantial portion of time. Since this type of investor trades infrequently, low-cost trades and up-to-the-nanosecond stock information are not so much an issue; what they want is access to a wide range of investment choices, including mutual funds and bonds, and financial planning tools capable of charting long-term goals.

Convenience Investors

These investors may belong to any of the above categories, but are also looking to have all their financial needs dealt with in one place, including banking, credit cards, bill payment and more. These folks want financial services and lots of them, placing them at a premium above things like low-cost trades or deep investment data and stock information.

Before You Sign: What You Need to Ask Online Brokerages

From AB Watley to Wyse, there are dozens of online brokerages offering a wide array of services. Some cater to the high-speed aggressive investor, while others provide a range of services that are attractive to long-term or convenience investors. As you travel through the sites of the various online brokers, here are some questions for you to keep in mind.

Keep in mind also that a number of sites will also allow you to use an interactive demo to see what trading on their site will be like and which will provide answers to many of the questions here; be sure to take advantage of them.

How Much Does It Cost to Trade?

Prices for online trades range from as low as $4.95 for investors with a high volume of trades at E*Trade (http://www.etrade.com, AOL Keyword: Etrade)) to as high as $29.95 at Charles Schwab (http://www.schwab.com). Most cluster around the $15 price point for market orders (the most common sort of stock trade), with some additional costs for large trades (more than 1000 shares) or other types of orders, such as limit or stop orders. This cost is going to be more of an issue for investors who plan to make a lot of trades; investors who plan on buying and holding their stocks for long periods of time should probably concentrate on other factors. Related to this:

What Other Fees Can I Expect?

Do they charge for transferring funds from other accounts, or for closing accounts? If you have an IRA, what do they charge for the custodian fees? If you drop below your minimum, what are you charged? Are you charged extra for large trades (over a thousand shares)? Are you charged if your account is inactive? Various brokers charge at least one or two of these fees—find out which ones you'll be liable for.

What's the Minimum Account Balance?

Most online brokers require somewhere around $2000 as the minimum balance in a cash account (the most common sort of brokerage account), although several, including Suretrade (http://www.suretrade.com) and DLJ Direct (http://www.dljdirect.com) have no minimum balance. Minimum balances are going to be an issue with folks who have smaller amounts to invest, or with investors who make a high number of trades or otherwise run up fees because of their investing activity.

Who Are These People, Anyway?

Every type of investor (but particularly long-term investors) should be interested in the reputation of the brokerage they potentially may do business with: Whether the company is an offshoot of an older, more established brokerage house (like DLJ Direct or Charles Schwab), or whether they were born and bred on the Net itself. It's also worth knowing if the brokerage has had any sanctions brought against it by the National Association of Securities Dealers (NASD), or if other customers have had problems with the broker and its services.

Check out the broker through the **NASD site** (http://www.nasdr.com/2000.htm), which features a searchable engine on brokerage firms and individual brokers; the information includes any Disclosure Events (ie, bad stuff) that have gone down at the brokerage. You can also find out what disciplinary actions the New York Stock Exchange has handed down to brokers and firms by visiting its Regulations page (http://www.nyse.com/regulation/regulation.html) and clicking on "Disciplinary Actions."

What Sort of Online Security Is on Offer?

Does the broker put up firewalls to protect its servers from hackers? Do they offer 128-bit encryption for their accounts? Will they log out your account if it is idle (thus protecting you if you step away from your computer and someone else sneaks a peak)? The more security protections your broker offers, the better off you'll be. If you can't readily find security information browsing a site, go somewhere else with your business.

How Secure Is Your Money?

Check to see if the broker you are looking at is covered by the Securities Investor Protection Corporation (SIPC) (http://www.sipc.org/), which will cover your securities up to $500,000 (or $100,000 in cash holdings) if your brokerage tanks. If a broker is not covered by the SIPC, you're probably better off not trading with them. Another question: How will they protect your money from online fraud?

How Can I Make a Trade?

Will the brokerage let you trade over the phone as well as online? Will they let you talk to a real live broker? Will using those services cost more? Will you be comfortable with the options you'll have available to make your trades?

What Can I Invest In?

Aggressive investors will want to be able to work with options and IPOs and possibly also "penny stocks" and over-the-counter stocks. Long-term investors will want access to mutual funds and bonds as well as stocks.

What Sort of Information Can I Get?

Aggressive investors should be looking for access to real-time financial data (which is offered for free at some brokerages, while others offer it for a fee), while serious and long-term investors will want a whole sheaf of data available: Charts, news, stock screenings, company analysis, and investment-planning tools and calculators for a start.

What Sort of Customer Service Can I Get?

If something goes wrong with your account, will you be able to get support over the phone or through email? How useful is that help going to be? If you need help navigating the brokerage Web site, will you get it? Customer support is important for everyone, but especially for newer investors.

What Other Sorts of Services Are Available?

Convenience investors will want to know if they can bank with their broker, and if their broker offers credit cards or ATM cards. Aggressive investors will want to keep an eye out for services like "after-hours" trading. Investors who use Quicken or Money to handle their finances will want to know if they can download information in those formats.

Narrowing the Field

You've decided what features and services are most important to you; now comes the "fun" part: narrowing down your potential brokerage list. There's a hard way of doing this, which is visiting the site of every single brokerage you can find and looking for all the details. Then there's the easy way, which is to take advantage of sites that have already done much of the comparison shopping for you, leaving you only to examine the finalists.

Our first stop is **Gomez.com** (http://www.gomez.com, AOL Keyword: Gomez). Gomez.com is an evaluative site that each quarter ranks several dozen online brokers in a number of relevant categories, including ease of use, overall cost, onsite resources, relationship services, and an overall score. They also break the brokers down into investor categories, so you can find the right broker whether you're an aggressive trader or a long-termer. Each ranking comes with a review and a detailed score on the brokerage's various services; you can evaluate the brokerages individually or side by side. Gomez.com also offers some basic tutorials on the process of trading online.

Another excellent resource comes from **Xolia.com** (http://www.xolia.com), which offers a very useful Online Broker Decision Center. Using a starting list of several dozen online brokers, Xolia narrows the field through information provided by the user: what the initial deposit will be, how you wish to conduct trades, what additional offerings you

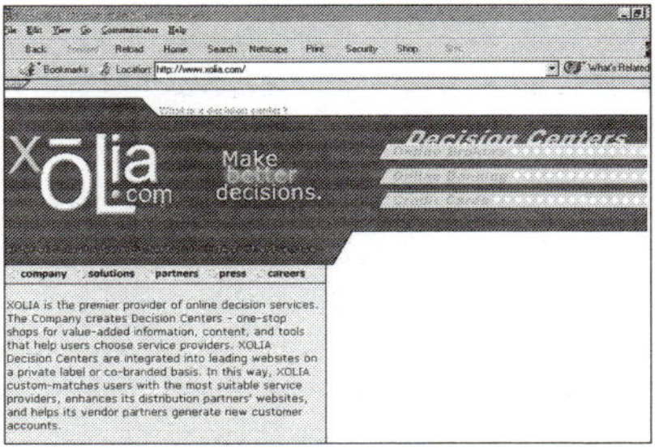

Some Myths of Investing Online

Online investing is a great thing—but it doesn't quite live up to the hype around it. Here are some myths that need dispelling:

■ Trades Made Online Are Instant

Trades done online are no faster than trades made with traditional brokers, and given the nature of market orders (in which your trade request joins a queue of others to be executed), and factors such as trade volume or your broker's system status, your trade could take minutes or even hours to be executed.

■ Trading Online Is Cheaper

Each individual trade is indeed cheaper online than with a traditional broker, but people who trade online also tend to trade more often. The cost savings for each trade can thus be swallowed up. Online brokers also charge other fees (see p.121).

■ Online Trading Yields a Better Rate of Return

Trading online gives you more control over your stocks. But if you're watching the stock ticker and trying to sell every time one of your stocks dips, you'll lose out. First, there's the cost of the trade. Second, If you've held the stock for less than a year, you'll be required to pay a higher tax on your capital gain. Third, if the stock goes back up, you'll lose the gain you could have garnered.

■ I'll Be Able to Get in on IPOs with an Online Broker

Initial Public Offerings (IPOs) are the first public issuance of stock by a company, and during the Internet era, they've taken on legendary proportions, with stock values going up hundreds of percentage points in the first day. But IPOs are initially handled by an underwriting firm (which brings the stock to market and sets the opening price), and unless you're a large institutional investor in that firm, you're unlikely to take part in the initial purchasing. You'll have to place an order and wait for it to be filled. However, some online brokerages do cater specifically to IPO investors.

want, and so on. After the field is narrowed, users can click on the broker to receive a broker profile. The site also features a nicely done side-by-side comparison tool that allows you to compare the features of three online brokers at a time (use the advanced setting for the best, most detailed information).

By using either of these tools, you should be able to narrow down your field of broker candidates to a manageable number. Go visit your finalists and see which one best suits your needs.

Setting Up a Brokerage Account

Once you've found a broker you like, it's time to **apply for an account**. Here's what you have to look forward to. (This section assumes you are starting up a new account and are not transferring an account from some other broker.)

Hold On

First, a little bad news: Usually you won't be able to start trading the moment you apply for an account for the simple reason that you haven't sent along any money yet. Some online brokerages, such as E*Trade, will allow you to begin basic trading immediately if you have funds transferred electronically from an existing bank account or other trading account (there will still be other forms, such as a signature card, you'll need to send along by regular mail). By and large, activation of your account will happen once your application has been approved and your initial deposit makes it to your broker's system—a process that could take a week or more.

Individual or Joint Account?

When you apply, you'll be asked to choose the sort of account you'd like to have. The first issue to consider is ownership. If you're trading for yourself and only yourself, you'll pick an **individual account**—the easiest sort of account to open.

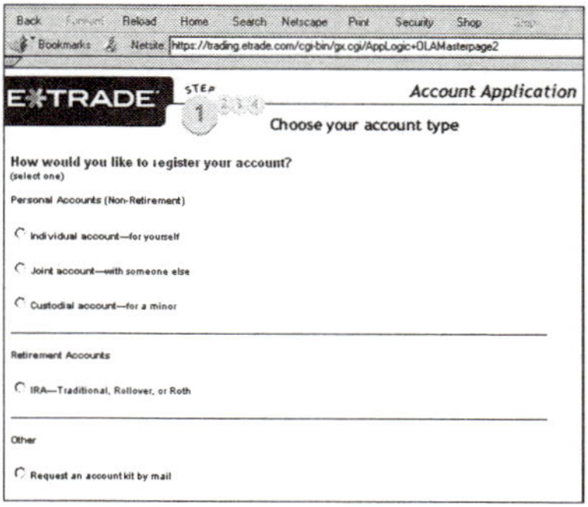

If you are opening an account with a partner or someone else, you'll choose to open a **joint account**. These typically break down into two main types: *Joint tenants* with rights of survivorship (if one of the account holders dies, the surviving account holder takes control of the entire account), and *tenancy in common* (if an account holder dies, his or her portion is controlled by his or her estate). There are also *community property accounts*, for married couples in community property states, and in some states, married couples can also choose *tenancy in entirety*, an option that keeps property from being seized to pay for the debts of one account holder. Be aware that with joint accounts, the party opening the account is the one responsible for paying the taxes on the account.

Other account types include **custodial accounts** (held in trust for a minor's name but managed by an adult), **investment club accounts** (which are managed and controlled by a group of investors), and **trust accounts**, which are registered in the name of a trust or estate. There are also a wide range of **business accounts** available.

Cash, Margin, or IRA?

Your second issue to consider is the sort of account you'd like to open. The most common option is a **cash account**, which simply means that you use cash that you deposit into the account to buy stock, funds, or whatever other investment vehicle you want. Then you have **margin accounts**, in which your cash is collateral for a line of credit that the broker extends to you the line of credit being equal to the amount of your own cash in the account. Finally, there are **option accounts**, which allow you to take options on stocks rather than trade the stocks outright.

Both margin and option accounts usually require a larger initial deposit and are somewhat more complicated than cash accounts. They will also involve a credit check. We'll be dis-

Getting an IRA Online

Many brokers will allow you to set up an **Individual Retirement Account (IRA)** through their service. IRAs have a number of advantages for investors: You can contribute to them tax-deferred in the case of a traditional IRA, or receive disbursements tax-free when you retire (in the case of a Roth IRA). The drawbacks are that you can contribute only $2000 a year into a single IRA account, and that the money in the account will not be available to you until you're 59 and a half (the account also needs to have been open for five years in order for you to access the money).

Many sites feature **education IRAs** (for your kids' college expenses) and **rollover IRAs**, so you can bring over money from other retirement vehicles, such as 401(k)s, into your IRA account. Online brokers typically require less money to open an IRA account than other types of accounts.

What can you do with your IRA with on online broker? Typically, whatever you can do with a regular cash account, which includes trading stocks or investing in mutual funds or bonds. Note, though, that your trading fees will come out of your IRA account, so be careful how often you trade. As with the other accounts you'll have on your online brokerage, you'll be in charge of how the money is invested. So, give it careful consideration; after all, that's your retirement money you'll be working with.

cussing the details of each in Chapter Ten; generally speaking, however, if you're a beginning investor, you're probably best advised to steer well clear of them and stick to a cash account. For the rest of this chapter, in fact, we'll assume you've chosen to open a cash account.

You can typically also choose to open an IRA, which is handled differently than other investment accounts. Check out the sidebar opposite for details.

Personal Info

Once you've decided on the type of account and ownership thereof, it'll be time to enter your **personal information**. You'll need to provide: your legal name, your citizenship and residency status, employment information, and social security number. If you have a joint account, the other applicant will also need to provide the same information. Depending on the broker, you may be asked to include additional information: Income, dependents, home and work phone numbers, and such.

The Customer Agreement

At some late point in the application process, you'll be confronted with a very long and very legal document called the Customer Agreement. While the temptation will be to glaze over this document and get on with your trading, you really need to read the whole thing and make sure you understand it, as it constitutes the ground rules between you and your broker. It includes clauses you'll want to know about, such as the No Investment Advice clause (ie, it's not their job to tell you how to invest your money), and clauses on arbitration (in other words, you may be agreeing to waive your right to sue the brokerage in court). Read it all, and if there's something in there you don't agree with, don't continue.

> 3. No Investment Advice. You acknowledge that E*TRADE will not provide you with any legal, tax or accounting advice or advice regarding the suitability or profitability of a security or investment. You also acknowledge that E*TRADE's employees are not authorized to give any such advice and that you will not solicit or rely upon any such advice from E*TRADE or any of its employees. You assume full responsibility with respect to transactions in or for your Account and your investment decisions. E*TRADE and its officers, directors, employees, agents and affiliates will have no liability with respect to transactions in or for your Account and your investment decisions.

In the Post

After you are finished with your application online, you may be required to print out the application, sign it, and send it to the broker along with the initial **account deposit** (typically in the form of a check or money order, although you can transfer funds from another trading account, or have the money wired from your bank). The broker may also send you some additional forms in the mail to sign and return.

If you choose an "**instant trade**" option, you'll be required to provide your bank account information and routing information, so the broker can transfer the money. Otherwise, you'll receive confirmation of your ability to trade once your money has arrived at the broker. During the application process, you will have received a screen name and will have chosen a password; use these to sign on to the service.

Congratulations, you're on! Once your money has cleared, you'll be ready to trade.

Making That First Trade

Okay—for this exercise, we're assuming you've signed on for a cash account, that you'll be making a market order on a stock, and that you have a specific stock in mind which you wish to purchase. If you don't have a stock already in mind to purchase, don't buy one just for the thrill of making your first trade—take time to research, either with the research tools and information provided by your broker, or on the financial information sites covered in Chapter Eight.

First Step

First: Sign on to your broker by calling up the Web page and entering your account information where it says "**Member Logon**." When you enter that information, you'll be taken to your front page, which will usually contain recent news and links to analysis provided or licensed by the broker. It should also provide links to information concerning your account: your **portfolio balance**, your **transactions**, the **status of recent trades**, and so forth (since this will be your first trade, most of this information won't yet exist).

Last-Minute Check

Your front page should also contain either a link to a **research area** or a field that allows you to enter a stock symbol and have information on that stock pop up. If it's the former, click on the link and enter your stock research area, and then enter the symbol of the stock you want to research; if the latter, enter the stock symbol in that field and press enter.

Before you make your trade, do some final research on the stock. Your research area should include **stock prices**, the latest **news on the stock**, **company and analyst reports**, and **historical graphs and charts**. Check the most recent price of the stock: Is it trading at a price you are comfortable with? Check the stock price over the course of the day and over the past few months: Are you comfortable with its performance? Does the stock have extreme price swings in the course of a single trading session that could affect the price at which you purchase the stock?

Check out recent **analyst coverage** of the stock—do the pros feel confident with the stock and where it's headed? Do they rate the stock as a "**Strong Buy**" or a "**Buy**"? What do they expect the earnings to be? Read the latest news—are there new products or events on the horizon that will make the stock react? By the time you're ready to make your first trade, you should know all of this information, of course—but there's nothing wrong with checking it one more time.

Now Trade

Now you're satisfied that you're ready to buy that particular stock. Click on the "**Trade**" option that your online broker

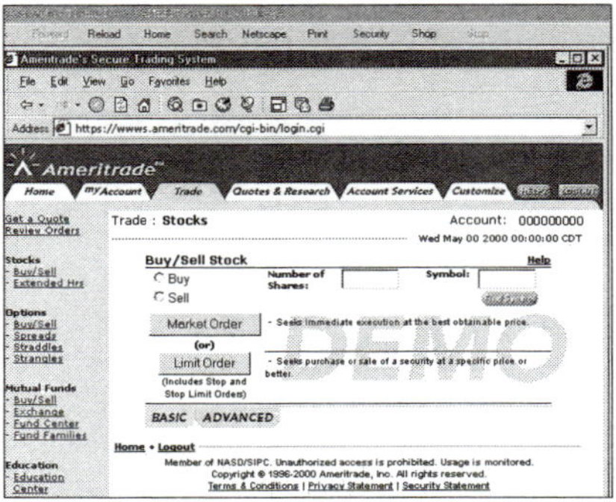

provides (you may need to go back to your home page for this, depending on how intelligently the site is designed).

The page that comes up may have a number of bells and whistles on it, but you should be concentrating on just a few elements. First, the "**Buy/Sell**" area, in which you select whether you are buying a stock or selling it. There may be other options besides buy and sell—we'll go over these variations in the next chapter. For now, you're choosing "buy".

Next, you provide the **symbol of the stock** you want to purchase in the "**Symbol**" or "**Stock**" field; for example, if you want to buy Microsoft stock, you'd enter `MSFT` (if you don't know the symbol, most brokers will offer you a search engine that will provide it to you). Next to this should be a field into which you'll enter the **number of shares** you want to buy. While brokers prefer that you buy and sell in blocks of a hundred (or multiples thereof), as a practical matter you can buy any amount of stock you choose. Finally, the page should give you the option of having the order be a **market order**, or another type of order, like a **limit order** or a **stop order**. A market order puts your purchase request in the queue, where it is taken and fulfilled in the order it is received; the other varieties of order place certain limitations as to how your order can be fulfilled. Again, we'll cover these in the next chapter; for now, choose market order.

Confirm That Order

Once you've made your selections, click on the button at the bottom of your screen which reads "**Preview Order**" or "**Confirm Order**." You'll travel to a page that reads back your order to you, so you can make sure you didn't make an error typing in the order (say 1000 shares instead of 100, or entering stock symbol IBN when you meant IBM). Make sure your order is exactly what you want it to be—once executed, it can't be cancelled.

If your order is correct, click on the button that reads "**Confirm Order**" or "**Place Order**." From there you should be taken to a **Confirmation Page** that will once again restate your order and will provide you with a tracking or confirmation number for that order and also a link to a page on the site where you can **track the status** of that order. Many brokers will also issue an **email** when you make the order, and again when the order is fulfilled.

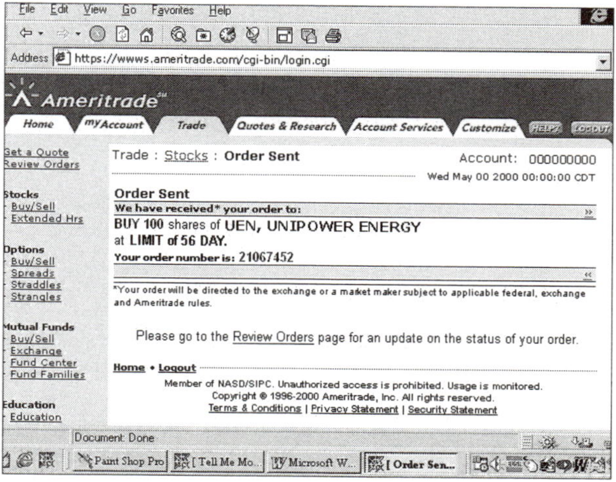

Capital Gains—Investment Tax

Sure, it's fun to buy and sell stock online, but those dreams of high-adrenaline trading come with a wakeup call: **taxes**.

This is actually pretty simple: Here in the US, you're taxed more if you sell an investment within a year of purchase than if you sell after that first year. Any profits you take on an investment that you've held less than a year are a **short-term capital gain** and considered at tax time like any other income you might have. So you'll pay the full tax burden on those gains. However, profits on investments held longer than one year are taxed at the **long-term capital gains** rate: ten percent if you're in the fifteen-percent income tax bracket, and twenty percent for everyone else. So, in essence, a short-term capital gain comes with an additional tax bite of anywhere from five to nearly twenty percent.

The amount of money you save on the long-term capital gains rate vs the short-term rate effectively increases the richer you get (funny how that works), but it's nevertheless a substantial savings for everyone in every bracket. So think before you decide to execute a rapid-fire trade: In the long run, you could make even more money by holding your fire.

Keeping Tabs on the Price You Paid

The cost of your trade will be debited to your account; be sure to keep track of how much you're spending on trades since it reduces the amount of money you have available to trade with. Your broker will provide you with a page that tracks your available funds—your **Account Balance**.

Be aware that **market orders** are not fulfilled the instant you place them. Order fulfillment can take seconds, minutes, or even hours, depending on the state of the markets, the system status of the broker, and how the broker chooses to route the order to the market. As a result, the **price you purchase**

your share for may be more (or less) than you expected, depending on how much the trading numbers have shifted between when you placed your order and when it is executed.

Right—It's Time to Sell!

The good news is that when you wish to **sell your stock with a market order**, the process will be the same, except you enter "sell" instead of "buy". So in essence, you've now mastered the art of basic buying and selling online.

Given how easy it is to do, you may feel like you should do a lot of buying and selling and **fine-tuning your portfolio**. But remember: The idea of investment for most people (and this probably includes you) is to build a solid portfolio for the long term. If you planned carefully in the beginning, you should keep the "fine-tuning" to a minimum. Resist the urge to fiddle, and before you buy or sell, ask yourself: Is this trade absolutely necessary for my long-term goals?

There's also another reason not to fiddle with your stocks too much: taxes. See the sidebar opposite to learn how long-term investing can save you a bundle at tax time.

10

Advanced Trading

FROM MARGIN ACCOUNTS TO DAY TRADING

If you followed the last chapter, you are up-and-running by now with an online brokerage account and you've made your first stock trade—a market order on a cash account. Once you're confident about these basic trades, you may want to start looking at some of the more advanced investment variations available online. These include different variations of trades such as **limit orders** and **stop orders**, investment vehicles such as **mutual funds** and **bonds**, and higher-risk **margin and option accounts**. Also covered in this chapter on advanced trading are a couple of current buzz phrases—

"**after hours**" and "**day trading**"—adrenaline-fueled trading experiences, which may or may not be right for you.

Finally, we'll explore some of the other (less scary) investing options to be found online, such as **mutual funds**, **bonds and treasuries**, **IPOs**, and "**penny stocks**."

Limit Orders, Stop Orders, and More

When you make a **market order** for a stock, what you are doing is asking to have your order for a certain amount of stock filled as soon as possible and at the best price available. This means that whatever price a stock is selling for at the moment your order is executed is the price you pay—and likewise, in reverse, if you are selling.

In many cases, this isn't a problem, especially if you're looking at a long-term investment; most stocks will not swing wildly in price between the moment you place your order and the moment the order is filled. And long term, such variation is likely to be negligible. But what usually happens is not what always happens. Hot stocks—for example, in recent months, new tech or Internet companies—see **wild price swings** in a matter of hours, and any delays in executing a stock order can mean a considerable price difference.

Fortunately, you are not entirely at the whim of the market. You can **specify certain parameters** within which your stock is to be bought or sold, the better to control your trading experience. Typically, these variations of stock orders will cost you a little more to execute than a regular market order, but if price and control are important to you, it's worth the extra few bucks. Here are the variations:

Limit Orders

With **limit orders**, you specify that you wish to buy or sell a stock only when that stock reaches a certain price. When you buy a stock, the limit specifies the upper limit which you would choose to pay; when you sell, it specifies the lower limit at which you would sell. So you're guaranteed a minimum buy or sell price (though you are not guaranteed, of course, that the stock will actually manage to reach your limit price).

This type of order can be useful if you're buying or selling a **volatile stock**, since it limits your exposure. It's also useful if you're selling **fewer than 100 shares** of a stock; such amounts are known as **odd lots** and usually have to be bundled with other orders—which means they may not get the best price when sold or bought through a market order.

Stop Orders

Stop orders are similar to limit orders in that they are activated when a stock reaches a certain price point. Unlike limit orders, however, stop orders are then executed regardless of price—so if the stock is experiencing wild price swings, you could still end up paying more (or less) than you expected, or selling for more or less than you want. You can use these to cut your losses if one of your stocks dips below a price you are comfortable with. But be careful: You may suddenly find yourself selling a stock you actually wanted to keep.

Stop-Limit Orders

As the name implies, **stop-limit orders** are a combination of the two orders above: Your stock goes to market if a particular price point is reached, but will not sell for less than what you specify (or be bought for more than the amount you choose). The drawback to this sort of order is that unless your specific requirements are met, your trade may not be executed.

Time-Sensitive Orders

Additional to stop, limit and stop-limit orders, investors can usually further specify the **timeframe** in which they wish their orders to be executed—which could be as short as a few minutes or as long as it takes. These options are, in order of chronological duration:

Fill or Kill: Means what it says—if the order can't be filled as soon as it hits the floor, it's canceled.

Day Order: The order is valid for that market day. If it is not filled in that time, it's canceled.

Good Until Canceled: The order stands until it is fulfilled. This could be in the next minute or several decades from now. Don't forget to cancel such orders at some point.

All or None: Not specifically a time-dependent order, this order specifies that all of the shares in your offer to buy or sell are indeed bought or sold, or that none of them are. Some brokerages will only allow you to make this sort of order if you have a specified number of shares (for example, E*Trade requires at least 300 shares).

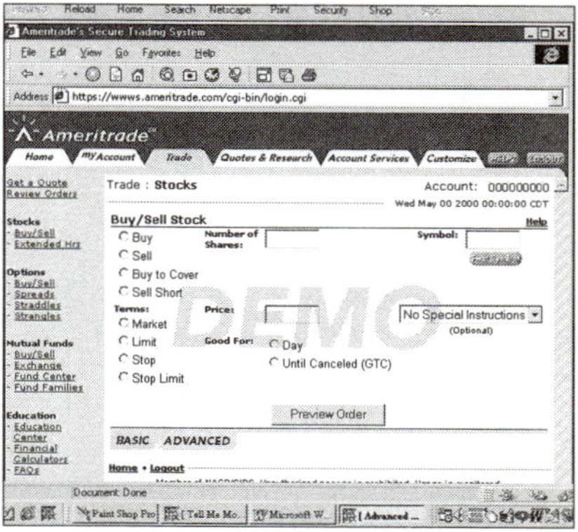

Most online brokerages will either allow you to place limit and stop orders (and the various time-sensitive orders) from the same page you place market orders, although some (such as Ameritrade) choose to feature those options on an "Advanced" page. After you have made the order, you should be allowed to confirm the order again before it is actually placed, same as a market order.

Margin and Option Accounts

For most investors, in for the long term and without a mass of spare cash with which to speculate, a **cash account** is both the smartest and safest way to go with online brokerages. However, there are other options available, notably **margin** and **option accounts**. These are riskier than straightforward cash accounts and require more attention from you—but they have their rewards.

Margin Accounts

Margin accounts are in essence credit lines: By putting up a certain amount of cash, you are allowed by a brokerage to access a credit line equal to that amount. You then use both sums to invest, effectively doubling your access to the market (with a few exceptions). In return for access to credit, you'll be charged interest, usually a few percentage points above the prime rate (the rate drops progressively the more money you have in your account). By law, margin accounts require a **minimum $2000 deposit**, and you can't use an IRA account to buy on margin.

You can buy most stocks and a number of government securities making use of a margin account. Exceptions include stocks worth less than $5 and initial public offerings (IPO stock will not be available for a while afterwards, either). Additionally, certain NASDAQ stocks are not available on margin. If you have a margin account, you can still use it to purchase such stocks but you have to shoulder the financial burden without use of the credit line—and those investments won't count toward your credit with the brokerage.

Since you're asking for credit when you apply for a margin account, your **credit report** will be accessed and assessed.

Selling Short

If you have a margin account, you have another option besides the simple "buy" and "sell" of a cash account: You'll also be

Margin Account Gains and Risks

First the Opportunities . . .

Margin accounts allow you to **buy more stock** using less of your own money, thus possibly increasing your profits. Rather than buying 100 shares of a particular stock using just your own money, you can buy 200 shares. If the stock price moves upwards, your profit on the broker-assisted shares consists of the difference of the value of the stock when it was purchased, and where it has moved to (minus, of course, trading fees, interest on your credit line, and taxes). Also, as the amount of credit you have is tied into the amount of your own money in the account, as your worth goes up, so does the amount you can borrow.

And the Risks . . .

Not every stock goes up in value, alas. When the value of a stock you've purchased with credit goes down, you are on the hook for the difference. And as the value of your stocks decreases, so does the amount of credit you have available to use.

Additionally, if your stocks hit a bad patch and equity value of your portion of the margin account dips below a certain percentage (35 to 50 percent depending on the broker), you'll be subject to a **margin call**. This is a fancy way of saying that you are overdrawn. If you get a margin call, you will either have to deposit additional funds into the account to get your percentage back up to acceptable levels, or sell some assets, generally at a loss. If you don't do anything within three days, your broker will—usually by selling stock. This makes holidays fun.

But wait, there's more. If you attempt to purchase a stock on margin without sufficient equity funds in your account, you'll be on the receiving end of a **Fed call** (so called because they are required by the government). Again, you'll either have to deposit additional funds or liquidate assets—and again, if you don't take action within three days, your broker can.

Continues over

In short, playing with margins can get you burned if you don't have funds on hand. This is particularly the case if you are using a margin account to invest in volatile stocks. During the market correction of April 2000, some Internet stocks lost seventy percent of their value within a couple of weeks. Investors who were trading on margin, assuming that tech stocks would just keep roaring along, got slammed with margin calls and ended up losing their shirts.

So don't trade on margin if you can't afford to lose money.

able to "**sell a stock short**." This is an extremely risky ploy to make a little money, so again, don't try this if you're not willing to take a bath.

The concept works like this. If you believe a certain stock is going to decrease in value, you "borrow" shares of that stock from your broker and sell them at a particular price (say, $100) with a "**sell short order**." Later, when the stock has dropped enough (say, to $75 a share), you place a "**buy to cover order**," which buys back the stock. The "borrowed" stocks are returned to your broker and you keep the profits ($25 for each share of stock, minus fees, interest, and taxes). In effect, you've made money on a stock while most of the stock's investors have seen the value of their holding go down. You can typically execute these orders on the same page you do your other stock orders, or on a special "Advanced" page.

The **problem with selling short** is that there is no limit on the amount of money you can lose. If a stock price goes up instead of down, you are responsible for paying the difference between the price you "borrowed" the stock at and its current value (and it can keep rising forever). That difference eats into your equity position in your margin account—and if it gets too high, you're looking at a margin call.

Other things about selling short you need to know: A sell short order can only be executed after an **uptick** or a **zero-**

plus tick (which is to say, the stock has to hold steady or go up slightly from its previous market value—this is to keep short sellers from totally slaughtering a stock's value), and the stock has to be **marginable** (see p.140). Your brokerage also has to be able to borrow the shares in order to lend them to you—if it can't, you won't be able to sell short the stock.

Option Accounts

Some brokerages that allow margin accounts will additionally allow you to get an **option account**—a margin account that provides you access to options.

Options are not stocks; they are contracts that allow you to buy or sell stocks (or other securities) at a particular time, at a particular price. Because of their inherent risks and complex nature, many brokerages require an extra step in the application process before they allow investors to work with options. E*Trade, for example, mails out a booklet entitled "Characteristics and Risks of Standardized Options" by the Options Clearing Corporation (OCC) to everyone who applies for an option account. Why the extra warning? Because more people (about eighty percent) lose money with options than make money with them. Of course, people wouldn't work with options if there were not an upside. Options can be used as a hedge against a drop in stock price (by placing a "put" on the stock that allows you to sell if prices drop below what you are comfortable with), or they can allow an investor to benefit from a stock's performance without actually owning the stock.

Options work like this: You purchase the right to buy a stock at a certain price at a certain time (a **call option**) from a stockholder, or purchase the right to sell a stock at a certain price at a certain time (a **put option**). The buyer (or holder) pays a premium for the option to the seller (or writer). In both the case of the call and the put, the buyer is not obligated to buy the stock—good news if the stock goes in the opposite of the intended direction. However, no matter what, you have to pay the cost of the premium.

Why do eighty percent of people lose money buying options? Because it requires precision timing: When you buy on option, you're betting that you know where a stock's value is going to be at some point in the future. This is not a bad deal if you are extremely well versed in the minutiae of the stock you have optioned. However, for most of us, it's more like gambling than not. You'll even lose money if you're right about the general path of a stock's price, but not the timing at which it arrives at your strike price (that's the price at which you've said you'd sell or purchase the stock). Also bear in mind that you need to factor in the price of your premium, so you have to do better than your strike price to make a gain.

Before you make any decisions on trading options, make sure you're clear on what they represent, what you need to do to be a successful options trader, and above all, the risks to your money. The Chicago Board Options Exchange has an extensive education area on options (`http://www.cboe.com/education/`). For a less complicated (and less comprehensive) overview, you can also check out the Motley Fool's page on options trading (`http://www.`

fool.com/FoolFAQ/foolfaq0055.htm). The Fool is generally disinclined toward trading options, and its page gives a reasonable explanation why.

After Hours Trading

In the United States, the trading day occurs **between 9:30am and 4:00pm Eastern time**. That's when the vast majority of trades and other investing business are accomplished. However, for years, large, institutional investors have participated in **"after hours" trading**—a secondary market that is open when the market day has ended. And now individual investors can do likewise, through online brokerages.

After-hours access is good in the sense that it allows individual investors the ability to react quickly to things like earnings reports or company warnings (which are typically released after the markets close, in order to give investors a night to think about the implications before they make trades). It also allows investors who might be busy during the trading day (you know, with actual work) to plan and execute trades on their schedule.

Be that as it may, there are significant differences between trading during the market day and trading after hours. The most important is that the after-hours market is smaller in volume than the market during the trading day: This means both less liquidity in the market and a higher potential for volatility in prices. As a result of this, most online brokerages allow **only limit orders** in the after-hours market. This is for your own protection: If an institutional investors' move in the after-hours market causes a stock's price to go way up or down, little investors could get swamped like a dinghy in the wake of an aircraft carrier. Also, be aware that trading halts may be placed on particular stocks by the SEC or by the stock exchanges if news significantly affects a stock's price—in those cases your order will be canceled.

To further increase the chances of your trade going through, most brokerages will only allow you to trade **round lots** (100 shares, or a multiple thereof) on the after-hours market. You may additionally be unable to specify a "fill or kill" or "all or none" order, which means that some of your order may be completed, but some of it may not. If that's the case, depending on your broker, you may not be able to cancel the untraded portion of your order. If you're **left with an odd lot** as a consequence, you'll have to enter the rest of the order as a new order during the regular market day. Orders on the after-hours markets are typically **day orders** (meaning that they will either be fulfilled during that after-hours trading session or canceled).

Additionally, **timing is of the essence** in the after-hours market. When you enter an order in the after-hours market, it waits in line to be fulfilled like it does during the trading day. However, you'll notice the "line" more. For example, a limit order you've placed waits in line with other limit orders at the same price. The ones entered earlier are fulfilled before yours. If the price moves after those orders have been filled, your order may go unexecuted.

One final note: As a practical matter, the regular market and the after-hours market are **two separate markets**. Orders placed in one will not be fulfilled in the other. As an example, if you place a stop order during regular hours, and that price is reached on your stock during after-market trading, your stop order will not be executed. The separate nature of the markets also means that the prices of stocks may be different in after-hours trading than it was during the regular trading day. So don't assume that the last price of a stock during the regular trading day will be the beginning price of that stock in the after-hours market (or vice-versa).

When can you trade after hours? It depends on your broker. E*Trade offers after-hours trading from 4:05pm through 6:30pm; Morgan Stanley Dean Witter (**http://www.msdwonline.com**) offers 4:30pm through 8:00pm; DLJ Direct offers 4:15pm to 7:00pm in the evening and also 8:00am to 9:15am in the morning (all times Eastern). There's no particular standard time, so check out the brokerages and determine which offers the best hours for you.

Online, there are a couple of **compendiums of after-hours trading information**. Online financial commentators TheStreet.com offer up a Guide to Extended Trading Hours (**http://www.thestreet.com/basics/nightowl/777198.html**), while the National Association of Securities Dealers has placed a number of reports and results from working groups on its Web site (**http://www.nasd.com/eh_module_menu.html**). However, be aware that this is an area still in rapid development—things are changing with online after-hours trading, and changing fast.

Day Trading

Here's all almost everybody in the world really needs to know about **day trading**: DON'T.

You want more? Basically, most people can't hack it either financially or mentally. To be a successful day trader, one must be willing to put in a substantial capital investment for equipment, a substantial time investment for research and making trades (successful day traders are glued to their computers from the moment the market opens to the second it closes), and must be willing and readily able to lose thousands of dollars every single day in pursuit of profits. It's not for someone who wants to have a life outside of investing—and especially a beginning investor. Don't feel bad about this fact: Day trading is quite frankly a life not fit for humans.

If you decide to go ahead and day trade, good luck—and with the therapist. Here's what it's about.

What Day Trading Is

Basically, day trading is the art of **buying and selling stock rapidly** (all stock is bought and sold within the trading day), with the goal of making a profit on incremental price changes. Rather than picking a stock and holding onto it for years or decades in the hope the value will grow over time, you pick a stock with the hope the price will tick upwards 25 cents by the end of the day (or, frankly, within the next five minutes). Day trading requires constant scrutiny of stock movement by the trader; this can get so intense that day traders find it difficult to tear themselves away from their screen to eat lunch, even to go to the bathroom (thus giving a new meaning to the term "Buy and hold").

Because success relies on small stock movements, volatility is both the day trader's friend and mortal enemy. It can lift the value of a stock or send it crashing down, all within the space of minutes (almost all day trading occurs on the NASDAQ exchange because it is twice as volatile as the NYSE). All stocks bought in the trading day are sold at the end of it—there are almost no carryovers, which means that day traders eats any losses they have at the end of the day (some traders may hold onto a stock for longer than a day, but few do). A day trader can easily make over 150 trades in a single session.

What Day Trading Requires

Besides nerves of steel, a feel for the market, and an encyclopedic knowledge of the world of finance, here's what you'll need to get started in the big bad world of day trading.

First, you need a large sum of money you can afford to lose; even experienced day traders can lose thousands of dollars at a pop in their quest for capital gains. Day trading professionals suggest **$100,000 as a minimum** level of capital investment in order to day trade successfully; it's enough that you can lose a fair chunk and still keep going for a while. If you can't afford to lose money, don't day trade. If you can afford it, but it makes you sick to think about losing huge sums of money, don't day trade. Everyone who day trades loses money at one time or another, and some days a lot more than others.

Second, as speed of response is critical in day trading, you need to deck yourself out with a **computer workstation** that can accommodate your need for speed. This will include a decently fast and robust computer system (500 MHz or better and 128 MB of high-speed RAM—this will allow you to accommodate trading software and keep your computer from choking on the real-time data you'll be piling into it), as well as dedicated, **high-speed access to the Internet**. This means a cable modem or DSL connection, if they are available in your area, or an ISDN line at the very least. If all you have available is a dial-up connection (ie, a typical modem), you might want to rethink your idea to day trade online at home. Also be aware that even cable and DSL connections fall prey to Web congestion, just like any other sort of Web access.

A decent computer will cost you anywhere from $1200 to $2000; cable modem and DSL access typically starts at around $40 or $50 a month. Many cable and DSL providers offer faster and more reliable service to businesses for a higher fee—you should consider such a service.

Third, if you're serious about day trading, you may want to consider using **specialty software**, designed specifically for day trading and its needs. Tradecast (www.tradecast.com) is an example of this sort of software. It includes access to real-time NASDAQ Level II stock information (which tracks changes as orders are processed and filled, as well as providing information on who wants a stock and for how much—essential for a day trader), a streamlined process for making orders, a subroutine that continually checks for interrupted access to the Internet, interactive and constantly updated analytical tools, and dynamic streaming data. The software also includes access to Tradecast's system, which claims to process orders in seconds (with the usual caveat that busy days and lots of online traffic can make things crawl). Other providers of similar software include the rather dramatically named Executioner (http://www.executioner.com/), eSignal (http://www.esignal.com/) and Speedtrader (http://www.speedtrader.com/).

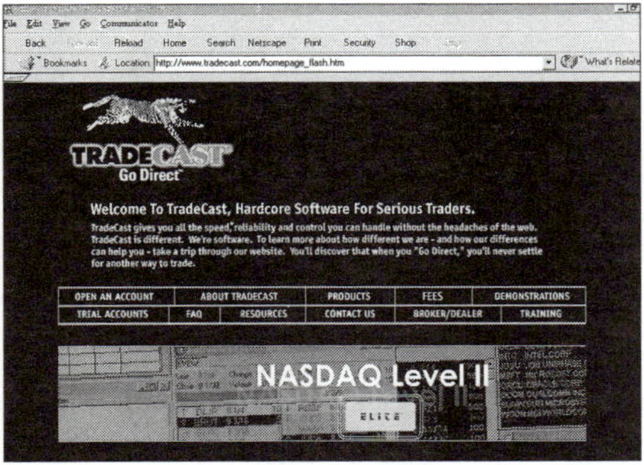

These software packages aren't cheap: Tradecast's "Elite" package runs to $179.95 per month (fee waved if you trade more than fifty times a month), Speedtrader's Level II program is $200 a month (waived for twenty or more trades a month), and the Executioner II software clocks in at $250 a month (waved for fifty or more trades per month). This cost does not include the cost of opening an account on these respective trading systems (which require a deposit of anywhere from $1000 to $5000) or for the cost of making trades (usually around $20 a trade—which is why they'll eventually waive software fees). Other fees include licensing fees for NASDAQ information or for access to ECNs (Electronic Communications Networks—how the brokers connect to the markets and to each other).

Web brokerages can and do offer some day trader-like information. AB Watley (http://www.abwatley.com/) features an "Ultimate Trader" option that allows for free NASDAQ Level II quote access and (not free unless you make a ton of trades) data access, as well as reduced fees for a high volume of trades. This option requires $20,000 in the accounts. E*Trade provides NASDAQ Level II information for its "Platinum" users, defined as those who make more than 75 trades in a quarter. Web Street (http://www.webstreet.com) provides NASDAQ Level II information to its members for an additional $50 per month, or free if they make 25 or more trades a month or have $250,000 or more in their accounts. In short, for most of these accounts, you have to lay out some serious dough, either in account balances or in trade volume.

All these costs will cut into your profits, and your profits will be taxed at the short-term capital gains rate rather than the much less onerous long-term rate. In effect, day traders start off in the hole relative to other investors, and have to dig themselves out before they can make a real profit.

Oh—and by the way, yes, you can day trade using a **margin account**. But that is a monumentally bad idea.

Funds and Bonds

There are plenty of other investment options online beyond the stocks you'll find on the New York Stock Exchange and the NASDAQ, and in the case of **bonds** and **mutual funds** they can be a very good, reduced-risk part of any long-term portfolio. Here's a quick run through.

Mutual Funds

If you're interested in investing but aren't especially interested in personally picking the right stock or portfolio of stocks, you might want to consider a **mutual fund**. In a fund a professional fund manager picks a collection of stocks (and maybe other investment vehicles, like bonds): Your job is to evaluate these choices and the performance of the fund, and decide whether or not you want to buy in. When you own a fund, you don't actually own shares in the companies the fund invests in, but you do benefit from the performance of the stocks it holds.

Mutual funds have several advantages for investors. They are managed by professionals (whose sole job is to make their funds as profitable as possible); they're diversified and thus reduced risk (if one stock in the fund drops badly, it may be balanced out by upswings in other stocks); and they're liquid, which means if you want to sell, you can, and without having to worry about whether you get a decent price for your stock.

The downside? Reward is proportionally reduced (a single hot stock performance in the fund can be counterbalanced by falling stocks or overall lackluster performance), and you have no control over the stocks in the fund. Funds also come with costs—the cost of buying or selling the funds, along with administrative fees, marketing costs, and "loads"—the cost of buying in or out of a fund. The good news is that just as online brokerages have lowered the cost of trading, they've also lowered the cost of buying and selling funds. There are also a wide range of "no-load" funds as well.

Ethical and Index Funds

There are thousands of funds available, aimed at just about every type of investor: funds for those who want aggressive

Spiders, Diamonds, and Triple Qs

Index funds are good for investors who don't want to obsess too much about how their stocks are doing. They more or less mirror the index they are modeled after, so when the market is up, so is the fund—and vice versa. Other investment trusts precisely follow the ups and downs of particular indexes: **"Spiders"** (stock symbol: SPY) follow the **S&P 500**, **"Diamonds"** (DIA) follow the **Dow Jones Industrial**, and the **NASDAQ-100 tracking stock** (QQQ) quite naturally follows the NASDAQ.

While these trusts perform similarly to index mutual funds, there are significant differences: Index funds can only be bought and sold at the end of a trading day, whereas trusts are available to be bought and sold during the regular trading day. Trusts also feature lower expense ratios than most index funds. But there are drawbacks—notably the fact you can't put additional money into a trust without ringing up a commission fee from your broker. This means trusts are better suited for people who plan to make a single (or infrequent) large buy-in rather than sock away a certain amount each month, as many people do with index funds.

You can learn more about Spiders, Diamonds, and Triple Qs by visiting the American Stock Exchange Web site (http://www.amex.com/) and clicking on the "Index Shares" button.

growth and have a high capacity for risk, funds for those who want their money to quietly accrue value, funds that invest in one particular sector, like tech or pharmaceuticals, or in a particular geopolitical area, like international funds. There are "**ethical funds**," too: funds that invest in eco-friendly companies, for example, or avoid investing in companies that sell tobacco and other "questionable" products.

There are also funds that mirror the performance of the markets in general, known as **index funds**. Why would anyone want a fund that simply mirrors the market? Perhaps because the markets outperform managed funds—funds picked and run by a human—roughly nine times out of ten. There's another kind of investment vehicle similar to index funds—"**Spiders**" and "**Diamonds**"—for more on which see the sidebar on p.153.

Index funds are a really useful way to invest while managing risk (although there is still risk involved) and thus an ideal part of any long-term investment portfolio. If you haven't considered them, check the amusing "plain language" disclosure on the Web (http://www.ipsfunds.com/risks.html).

Buying and Exchanging Funds

The great majority of online brokerages allow their members to **research, buy, and sell funds online**. Typically speaking, buying or selling funds with your online broker will be much the same as buying or selling a stock: You'll enter the fund symbol and the amount of the stock you want to purchase (reflected either as a dollar amount or as shares of the fund). You may also be asked how you want to deal with any **dividends or capital gains** the fund may generate—either reinvest or pay out into your account (if you choose to pay out, you'll have to pay taxes). You may also have the option to **exchange your funds**—which means that under certain conditions you can exchange shares of your current fund with shares of another fund run by the same company.

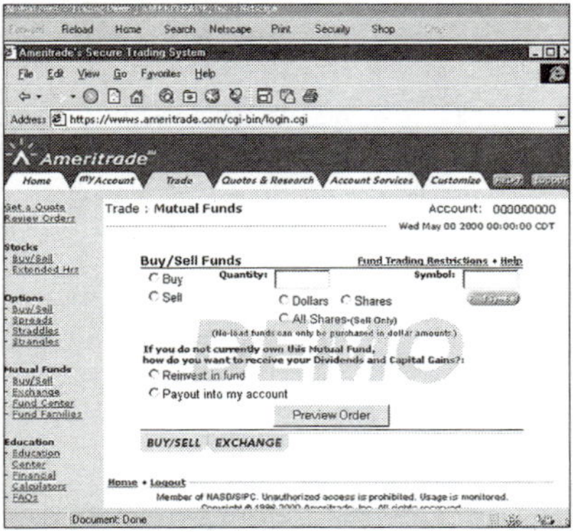

After you've written up your order, it'll be presented to you again so you can confirm the order is correct; if it is, your order will then be processed.

Bonds

Bonds aren't considered a very "sexy" investment, nor do they generally offer the sort of returns that stocks and funds can achieve. What they can offer is security: Short of the collapse of the United States government, for example, US Treasury securities will pay what they're supposed to pay, when they're supposed to pay (and if the government has collapsed, your bonds are probably the least of your problems).

Bonds also benefit from a tax quirk: Certain types of them are partly or totally tax free—effectively raising their rate of return. How this works is that bonds issued by one type of government in the US cannot be taxed by another. States and cities can't tax US bonds, the US can't tax state and municipal bonds. Additionally, bonds from your own state aren't taxed locally, either. So if you buy Ohio state bonds and you live in Ohio, you'll have no tax obligation on that bond. Not a bad thing if you're in a high tax bracket.

Bonds are essentially **promissory notes**: In exchange for an investor's cash, the bond issuer promises to repay the face value of the bond (the **par value**) at a certain time and provide a certain amount of interest (the **coupon rate**) at regular intervals. Most bonds, but not all, can be sold prior to maturity.

While a lot of different organizations issue bonds, **governments** issue the greatest number: the federal government, which issues Treasury bonds and whose various agencies also issue bonds, and then state and local governments, which issue municipal bonds. **Corporations** also issue bonds. These are not generally as secure as government bonds; although corporate bonds from companies with top credit ratings are very secure, there are also **junk bonds** which are rated as "highly speculative" (this is because the companies that issue them have a credit rating lower than that deeemed "investment grade" by analysts). However, you can get generally higher rates of return from corporate bonds than government bonds. Also, should a company crash and burn, corporate bondholders get to carve up the company assets before the shareholders.

Buying Bonds Online

Relatively few **online brokerage houses** provide access to bonds: Out of 56 online brokerages in Xolia's Online Brokerage Decision Maker database, only 11 offered access to bonds, among them Fidelity (http://www.fidelity.com), Suretrade, and E*Trade. Although researching bonds is somewhat more complicated than researching stocks and mutual funds (partially due to sheer numbers—there are over a million bonds available, versus mere thousands of stocks and funds)—purchasing bonds is again a reasonably familiar process.

After researching your intended purchase, enter the number of bonds you wish to purchase and the bond's CUSIP number (Computerized Uniform Securities Identification Program) to identify the particular stock in which you are interested. You may then be given the option of buying **at market** (ie, the best price available) or buying **by yield** (which takes into consideration criteria such as time to maturity, credit rating of the issuer, and market conditions). Once you've entered your information, you'll confirm your order on a second screen, after which it will be executed, and your brokerage will then charge you a fee. You may also be allowed to buy US Treasuries at auction.

If you are primarily interested in **US Treasury securities**, you can deal with the government directly and online, through the TreasuryDirect program (http://www.publicdebt.treas.gov/sec/sectrdir.htm). The fees are a reasonable $25 per year on holdings above $100,000, and for less than that there is no charge. Dealing directly with government can save on fees if you are a small, individual investor.

IPOs

Initial Public Offerings (IPOs) are not often open to small investors. IPOs are underwritten by brokerages which then typically give first dibs to their larger, institutional investors or other important clients, leaving individual investors to scramble after the fact (and after the stock prices have shot through the roof). However, certain **online brokerages** (alongside their parent companies) are now underwriting IPOs, which means that individual investors with those brokers may have some access—if you meet certain brokerage requirements.

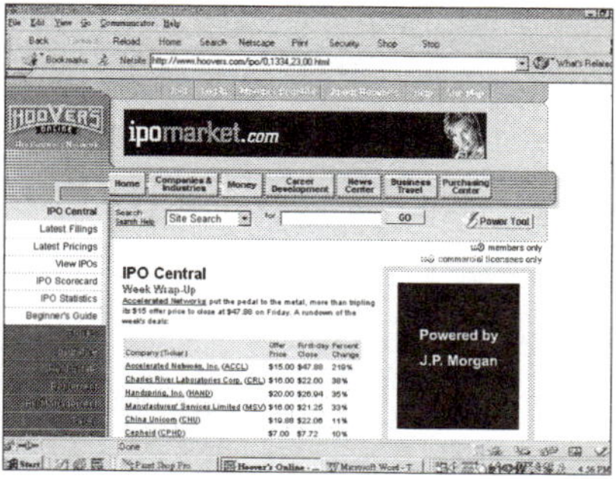

What are those requirements? It varies from broker to broker, though it usually comes down to having a lot of money to invest—typically, you have to be a preferred customer. On DLJ Direct, it means keeping an account minimum of at least $100,000 dollars. Charles Schwab requires $500,000. If you're on E*Trade, you don't need to have a lot of money—but you have to make at least 75 trades per quarter. In short, online brokerages that do allow their members to invest in IPOs are like any other brokerages in this regard: They save these deals for their best customers.

Don't get too depressed if you don't meet the criteria to participate in IPOs. Despite the spectacular performances (and subsequent huge news coverage) of certain IPOs in the Internet era, most IPOs don't debut like a rocket off a launch pad—and many of those that do fall back to earth within months, weeks, or even days. Most IPOs are stock offerings for young and untested companies—this makes them, by definition, highly speculative investments. Long-term investors, who are interested in performance over time, will probably not miss having these stocks in their portfolio right out of the gate.

Investors who are interested in **IPO information** will get their fill at IPO.com (http://www.ipo.com/), Bloomberg's IPO Center (http://www.bloomberg.com/markets/ipocenter.html), and Hoover's IPO Central (http://www.ipocentral.com, AOL Keyword: IPO). Each of these features information on the latest IPOs, information on upcoming IPOs, and information both on the companies being offered and the underwriters of the initial public offer. Online brokerages that underwrite IPOs (other than the three mentioned previously) include Ameritrade, Fidelity, Web Street, and Morgan Stanley Dean Witter.

Penny Stocks

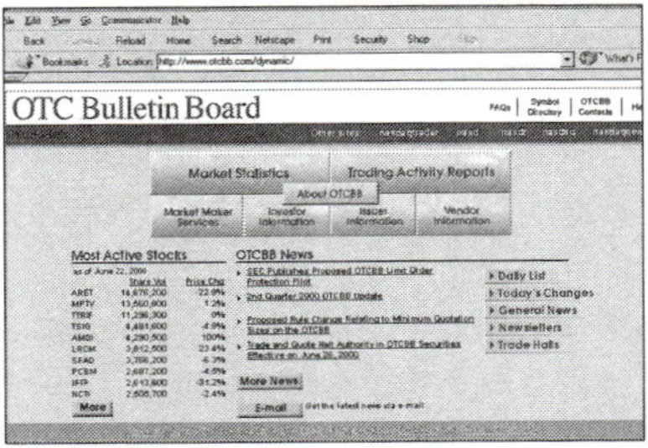

Penny stocks are defined as any stock that trades for $5 a share or less. The majority of these stocks are not listed on the New York Stock Exchange or the NASDAQ, but are traded "**over the counter**" and can be tracked online through the **Over the Counter Bulletin Board** (http://www.otcbb.com), or offline through "**Pink Sheets**" distributed to brokers. Some but not all online brokerages offer penny stocks, and many of those only allow broker-assisted trades.

Penny stocks can be initially appealing to investors; thanks to their low share price (sometimes—and true to their name—just pennies per share), it's possible to buy a lot of shares for not a lot of money. A lot of people seem to think it's better to have 200 shares of Bob's Gasket Company at 50 cents a share than one share of Coca Cola at $100. Well, maybe.

Penny Stock Characteristics

Lots of shares notwithstanding, penny stocks tend to be a bad investment idea for a number of reasons. First is that a high number of penny stock companies are **penny stocks for a reason**: Poor management, bad products, undercapitalization, or plain old incompetence has driven these stocks into the ground. Sure, if the stock goes up mere pennies you can double your investment. But it's as likely not to, and if no one wants to buy your penny stock from you (as is very possible—penny stocks are thinly traded) you'll be stuck holding the bag.

Second is the fact that even well-managed, well-run penny stock companies are **susceptible to fraud**—it's easy for unscrupulous investors to hijack the stock and drive the price up or down for their own purposes, leaving legitimate investors dazed and confused.

For example, con artists create **scam companies** (or hijack the stock of real companies) and then perform "pump and dump" operations, in which they artificially inflate the value of a company stock through fraudulent means and sell their stocks at a high point, leaving real investors to take a financial bath when the stock drops back to its natural (and low) level. If you ever get a call about a great stock you've never heard about from a broker who wants you to send money right now, hang up the phone. If anyone sends you an email with the same sort of message, delete it. Penny stock opportunities that sound too good to be true almost always are.

If you want to go ahead and invest in penny stocks, at least do yourself a favor and avail yourself of your online brokerages' **research tools**, or visit the SEC home page (http://www.sec.gov) and search for the companies you are looking at in the agency's company database. And remember that penny stocks are highly speculative and risky investments: Invest in them if you have money to spare, but keep your retirement nest egg in blue chip stocks.

11

Taxes Online

THE GLAMOR CHAPTER

You've done your research, made your trades, reaped your profits. It's time to pay your taxes. Not even the Internet can help you avoid them—though if you're looking for help or information, or a way to fill in and submit the forms, it's up for the job. Taxes are the last great financial frontier on the Net, and in the last year or so there has been an explosion of services available for taxpayers. You can do it all online—even file your taxes and get your return.

The Net can also help with tax planning. You may be of the persuasion that the only time to think about taxes are the few weeks leading up to April 15. That's the sort of thinking that will ensure the government gets to keep more of your money than it should; the time to think about taxes is while there's still time to plan, save, and benefit. This chapter shows how you can get into serious tax planning online and prepare for your filing, and then walks you through doing your taxes on the

Web. It's all a lot simpler than the days when you had to do your taxes with a pencil, a calculator, and a large pot of coffee.

First Steps: US Tax Fundamentals

Here's the sad fact: Many of us don't even know the basics of our own tax situation. We don't know how to fine-tune payroll exemptions to keep more money in our pocket, or how to file estimated taxes on self-employment income to avoid penalties, or whether it's better to file as "single" or "head of household," or which form to complete: the 1040-EZ, 1040-A, or the standard 1040. It's a lot to keep track of, but doing it right can mean the difference between owing money on your taxes and getting something back.

Basic Information and Tutorials

Fortunately, there is some excellent **information online** on tax fundamentals, including basic tutorials that you can fine-tune to your needs. One of the best is **Intelligenttaxes.com** (http://www.intelligenttaxes.com, AOL Keyword: Intelligenttaxes). This is a full-service tax site, with forms, resources, and so on, but to start off with, just click through to the site's "Basics" area (the link is at the top of the page in the shape of an apple). You'll see a five-section tutorial that hits all the highlights of doing one's taxes from the cradle (tax deduc-

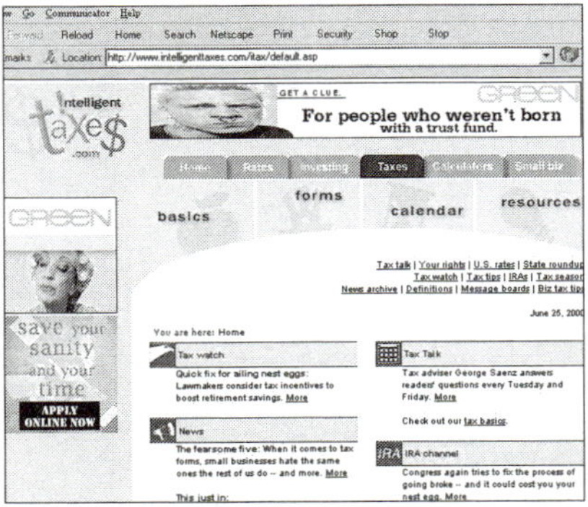

tions and credits for children and other dependents) to the grave (strategies for avoiding Uncle Sam's heinous estate tax). It'll get you right with your present tax situation and will help you get a grip on what you can expect for your future, and it's written in a straightfoward style.

Another good and somewhat briefer tutorial can be accessed at the **Money magazine** site, in the Money 101 section (http://www.money.com/money/101/). And if investments and their attendant capital gains are part of your tax picture this year, try **Smart Money**'s Tax Guide (http://smartmoney.com/ac/tax/), which features specific information for investor tax breaks and capital gains.

On **America Online**, AOL's tax site (AOL Keyword: Taxes) features links to both Intelligenttaxes.com and the Money 101 information. You'll find the link in the box at the bottom left corner of the area. As this site is also the omnibus site of AOL's tax information, we'll be coming back to this area in the next section.

In-Depth Tax Information

If you feel comfortable with the basics of your tax situation and are instead looking for in-depth information on particular topics, there are a couple of sites that will fill your bill. The first of these, naturally enough, is the Tax Information page at the **Internal Revenue Service** site (http://www.irs.gov/ind_info/index.html). Here you'll find a wide range of information on just about all specific tax questions and concerns, including recent tax changes, updated credits and exemptions, along with interactive tests to see if you are eligible for certain deductions or exemptions. All this information is straight from the source, but be warned that it's not brilliantly organized—the IRS site is friendly looking at the top but gets murky right under the surface.

If you know the tax subject you're looking for, you'll find a somewhat more intelligently laid out repository of information at **WorldWideWeb Tax** (http://www.wwwebtax.com/). Click on the "Master List" button at the top of the page, and you'll be presented with an alphabetical list of over 1500 pages, covering nearly a thousand separate tax topics. Topics don't quite go from A to Z (the last listing is for "Worthless Securities"), but it has well-researched articles on almost every subject on your federal taxes. It also features thumbnail information on the taxes of all fifty states.

If you're truly a tax whiz or a glutton for punishment, you can peruse the entire **United States Internal Revenue Code**, as provided by Cornell University's Law School (http://www4.law.cornell.edu/ uscode/26/). A search engine is provided: Enter a subject and it provides you with chapter and verse (or more accurately, title and section) pertaining to your query. The obvious warning here is that the US tax code is written in language unused by normal humans.

Expecting some **legal issues** with your taxes? You're probably best off contacting a tax lawyer. However, you could start your legal research with **Nolo.com's tax law encyclopedia** (http://www.nolo.com/encyclopedia/tax_ency.html). You'll find basic information on some common legal issues involving taxes, including audits, back taxes, and (gulp) tax fraud.

Tax Preparation Resources

You've fine-tuned your tax profile so that when tax time comes, you won't have to pay any more than you absolutely have to. Fine. But eventually you have to tally up the taxes and pay what you owe. For these trying times, there are several options to choose from online.

Omnibus Tax Sites

Yahoo!, the leading directory on the Web, has a tax center (http://taxes.yahoo.com/) that is both well-stocked and free of

Charge Your Taxes? A Bad Idea

Uncle Sam these days allows taxpayers to pay what they owe with plastic: You can charge your indebtedness to your credit cards. While this certainly is convenient, it's also a tremendously bad idea—if you plan to carry a balance. The reason is simple: The average credit card has an interest rate between 15 and 19 percent, which makes it just about the most expensive loan you can have. You'll end up paying what you owe on your taxes plus a large additional chunk (none of which is tax deductible).

If you know that you're going to owe more than you can pay, try getting a bank loan instead (which won't have a great interest rate either, but should be better than that of a credit card). You can also request that the IRS let you pay your taxes in an **installment plan** (you'll use Form 9465); tell the IRS how much you'll pay each month and on what date, and they'll approve or deny it within 30 days. There's a filing fee, plus interest and late payment fee, but they may also be cheaper than your credit card interest will be.

In short, pay with a credit card only as a last resort, and make sure you know what your other options are first.

annoying bells and whistles. It features tax information and tools provided by the tax preparation firm **H&R Block**, and includes a refund estimator (which will also determine what you owe if that is the case), a tax prep checklist, a solid tax guide, and a wide range of tax tips on specific issues ranging from credit to retirement planning, tax calculators, and finally a collection of links to relevant tax sites on the Web. The site also features federal and state tax forms, as well as the ability to file your taxes online with the TaxCut Web software (a subject which

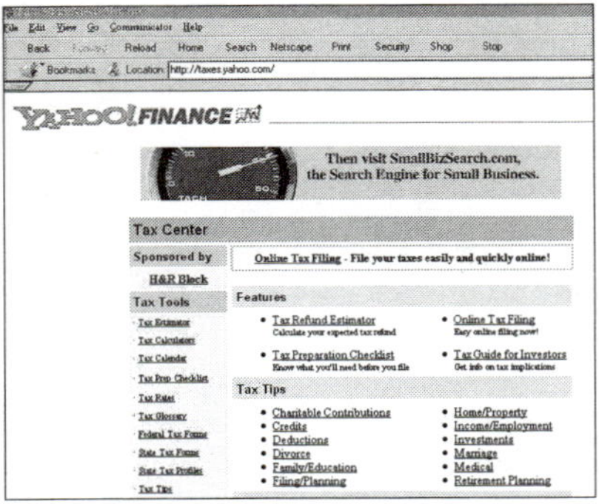

will occupy its own section later in this chapter).

H&R Block also provides tax information for **Snap.com** (http://home.snap.com/LMOID/resource/0,566,-1355,00.html), as well as its own Tax Center (http://www.hrblock.com/tax_center/index.html). The H&R Block site also advertises a help phone number ($2.49 a minute) and a locator for its local offices.

America Online has no fewer than four omnibus sites for taxes. The one on the service itself (AOL Keyword: Taxes) includes tax calculators and estimators, tax tips and strategies, lots of links to other tax-oriented sites, tax forms, and online filing provided by TurboTax. It also features a repository of tax questions answered by CPAs and tax experts from TaxLogic.com. A second AOL tax site is located on the AOL Web site, under the site's "Time Savers" category (http://www.aol.com/timesavers/tax.adp). And two further tax sites can be found at the sites of AOL subsidiaries **Netscape** (http://personalfinance.netscape.com/finance/taxes/) and **CompuServe** (http://www.compuserve.com/gateway/personal_finance/taxes.asp). All these feature tax strategies, online tax forms, tax estimators, and tax site links; the Netscape site also has a TurboTax online filing link.

TurboTax is also at the heart of the **Quicken.com** tax area (TurboTax and Quicken both being financial products offered by software maker Intuit). Quicken.com's site (http://www.quicken.com/taxes/) offers the usual tips, information, and forms, as well as some specialized tools aimed at the tax-savvy investor, including several tax calculators to estimate taxes from investments, and articles on tax-smart investing ideas.

And of course, let's not forget Uncle Sam himself: the **IRS site** (http://www.irs.gov/). As you might expect, this features every US federal tax form known to humanity and furnishes quite a lot of information on other subjects, including "plain English" interpretations of the tax code and information on "e-filing" (the IRS term for filing electronically or over the phone). It also provides electronic versions of its publications. As mentioned earlier, the site isn't as people friendly as it could be. It features a "search" function, but given the vast amount of information on the site, if you're not specific on what you want, you'll end up with a long list of information to wade through. If you're in the initial stages of planning, hit some of these other sites first.

A note on the **IRS forms and publications** you can download: They are commonly provided in Adobe Acrobat format (*.pdf), so in order to read or print them, you'll need the **Adobe Acrobat** reader. It's available off the Adobe Website (http://www.adobe.com/).

Maybe the best news is that all of these omnibus sites carry **Form 4868**—the form you file for an extension.

Tax Preparers

Neither the time nor the inclination to do your taxes yourself? Fortunately, **tax preparation sites** online can connect you to local accountants and tax pros who will do them for you, or will actually do them for you online. Many of these sites participate in the **IRS "e-file" program**, which means that your taxes will be filed electronically, and your refund (should you get one) will be processed and in your hands more quickly, all the better to spend on frivolities.

Looking online to find someone local to prepare your taxes, you might start off at **taxprofessionals.com** (http://www.taxprofessionals.com/). This site, affiliated with the National Association of Tax Practitioners, lists accountants and tax preparers in all fifty states and DC as well as selected territories and foreign countries. However, the site offers no warranties on the quality of the preparers; it's merely a directory.

Prefer a name brand you've seen on TV? As already noted, **H&R Block** features a local office directory at its Web site; another national chain you've probably heard of is the **Jackson Hewitt Tax Service** (http://www.jacksonhewitt.com), whose Web site also features a locator for its more than 3000 offices in 45 states and DC. Both H&R Block and Jackson Hewitt are participants in the IRS "e-file" program, which means that although your taxes are done by a local preparer, they're filed electronically.

Both firms also offer **advances on your refund**, through something called a "refund anticipation loan"—a loan based on the amount of cash you're getting back from Uncle Sam. While this may sound ideal for those of you who just can't wait to spend that cash, it is a real **loan**, which mean certain

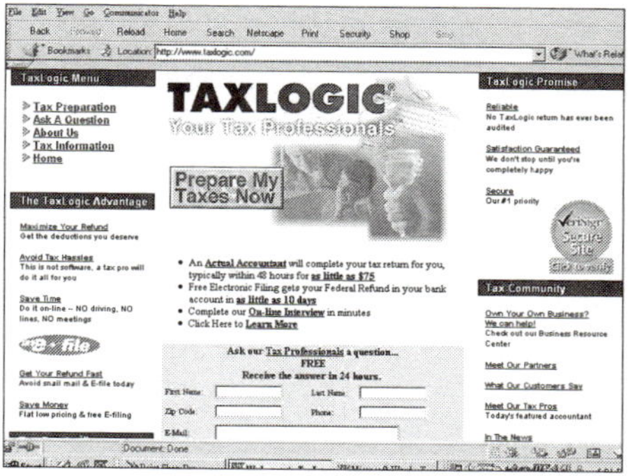

charges and restrictions apply. Check out the pros and cons of these refund advances in our sidebar overpage.

It's not only the big franchise tax preparers that can "e-file" your return; the **IRS** keeps a list of tax preparers who participate in the program at its Web site (http://www.irs.gov/elec_svs/ero/indiv.html). Just enter your zip code, and out comes a full list of authorized IRS e-file providers near you.

And if you prefer not to leave your home you might appreciate the services of **TaxLogic.com** (http://www.taxlogic.com, AOL Keyword: Tax Logic). For a fee starting at $75 (more for the self-employed and landlords), TaxLogic has a human tax preparer work on your taxes based on information you provide in an online questionnaire. Additional questions, if any, are mailed within 24 hours; the whole process is typically completed within 48 hours. They will then provide the form for downloading, or will file it for you online.

Downloadable Tax Software

Besides the options of working out everything with a pencil and a calculator, or having your taxes done for you by a pro tax preparer, there's a middle ground that works well for many taxpayers: **Tax software**. Today's tax software does more than simply crunch your tax numbers like a calculator and then print out your forms. The most popular tax programs walk

"Instant" Refunds: Why the Rush?

Several tax preparers, online and off, offer taxpayers the chance to get their refunds early, through "**refund anticipation loans**." The idea is that the preparer does the taxes and hands over the refund long before the IRS would—minus a processing fee and finance charges, of course. Instead of waiting weeks, the refund can be in your hands in 48 hours or less.

The main problem is that fee, which, depending on the company and the size of the refund, can be a disproportionately large chunk of the total refund—over $100 at some places. While it's tempting to have eighty or ninety percent of your refund the day after tomorrow, you have to ask if it's that much better than having all of it a few weeks down the road. Another bump: First-time users of the service can initially only get up to $500 of their return from the preparer; the rest comes a week later at best. And if the refund turns out to have been issued in error, you're responsible for the money you've spent.

Instead of getting an "instant" return, it's a much better idea simply to **speed up your refund**: First, file electronically, which can trim a month off your return waiting time. Second, opt to have your refund electronically deposited into your bank account, which can usually shave off another week. Third, file early; the sooner you file, the sooner your return will be in your hands.

taxpayers through the entire tax process, profiling you through an "interview" session and helping you to discover and take advantage of deductions, credits, and other tax relief measures you had probably never heard about. The major software programs will also file your claim electronically, so the entire process can be a paperless and relatively painless experience.

Tax software isn't going to be the best thing for every one;

people with a particularly complex tax profile are probably better off seeing a live tax preparer, who will be able to tailor tax advice and strategies to that particular profile. But your "average Joe"—someone with a full-time job, a family, savings, and some investments—will get good mileage out of these programs. The programs will also import any financial information from other financial programs you use, such as Quicken or Microsoft Money, to streamline your tax process.

The most popular tax software programs are Intuit's **TurboTax for Windows** (and its Macintosh sister, **MacInTax**) and **Kiplinger's TaxCut**, which is available in both Mac and Windows. Both of these programs are readily available at any computer retailer or on most online software retailers. Or they can be downloaded online. TaxCut programs are available for download at their Web site (**http://www.taxcut.com**). TurboTax is likewise available for download at its own Web site (**http://www.turbotax.com**), as is MacInTax (**http://www.macintax.com**).

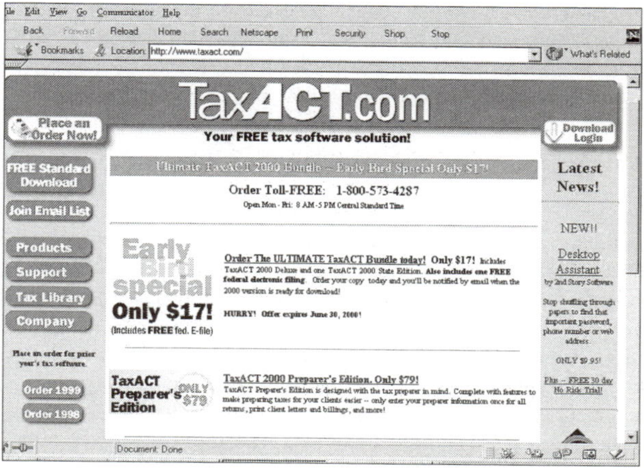

Two points: First, all these software programs cost money, ranging from about $15 for basic federal return software to $70 for packages that combine federal and state tax programs as well as home and small business tax programs. (Good news: The cost of these programs is itself tax-deductible). Second, each of these programs is about thirty megabytes, so if you're on a slow Internet connection (28.8 or slower), you'll be downloading for a while and might prefer to buy from a retailer.

Some other tax prep programs are available exclusively online—and for a lot less. CCH Incorporated's **CompleteTax** (http://www.completetax.com), for example, will walk you through your tax situation and process both your federal and state taxes beginning at $7.50. You can then print your forms or have them filed electronically through CompleteTax. Or the basic federal tax program **TaxAct** (http://www.taxact.com) is available as a free download—though in return, you'll have to wade through ads hawking TaxAct's Deluxe Edition, which is available for $10. Other tax products from TaxAct, including state forms, cost additional cash.

Be aware that with all these programs, **some states may not be available** to be filed online. Check with the individual programs to see if your state makes the tax cut.

Preparing and Filing Taxes Online

Another option is to use an exclusively **online program** to prepare and file your taxes—accessing a Web site rather than downloading software onto your computer. Such online programs are similar to the traditional tax software that you install: The programs handle the number crunching and guide you through a series of questions designed to produce accurate tax returns, which are then filed electronically. The industry leaders **TurboTax** and **TaxCut** have the largest presence, with online versions of their tax software on their own sites and

The Costs of Filing Online

One big attraction in using an online tax program and filing online is that it's inexpensive. Both the **TurboTax** and **TaxCut** programs **charge $9.95** for preparing and/or filing your federal and state taxes, whether you access them through their own sites or through their affiliate sites such as AOL (for TurboTax) or Yahoo! (for TaxCut). You'll pay by credit card.

In both cases, however, if you can file an 1040-EZ form (which means you make $50,000 or less and are using your standard deductions instead of itemizing), you can **file for free**. If you use a 1040 form, but your adjusted gross income is $20,000, you can also use TurboTax free.

Can't use the 1040-EZ, make more than $20,000, but still don't want to pay a dime to do your taxes online? Head over to **H.D. Vest Financial Services** (http://www.hdvest.com/), which offers to let you prepare and file your taxes online absolutely free. In exchange for the free service, you'll get a banner ad for other (chargeable) H.D. Vest products on every page of your online tax process. That's a lot of banner ads. Be that as it may, the H.D. Vest tax program runs and is laid out very much like the TurboTax and TaxCut online products; you should have no problems doing your taxes with it.

These three are not nearly the only providers of online tax preparation and filing; just the largest. You can find a more definitive list at the IRS site (http://www.irs.gov/elec_svs/company.html). Find the product you're most comfortable with, at the price that's right for you, and dig into your taxes.

licensed to other sites, but several other companies are also offering online tax prep and filing online, at costs that range from reasonable to entirely free.

Pros and Cons of Online Tax Programs

These online tax programs have good and bad points, neither of which should be overlooked by anxious taxpayers. In the plus column, they take up no space on your computer: All you need to access them is a reasonably up-to-date Web **browser** (Netscape/ Microsoft browser versions 4.0 or higher). They are also cheap to use—in fact, in most cases the software is free; charges come only when it's time to file your return online. So you can "tour" the program without cost to see if you like it. And filing electronically, as with other tax software, any returns you're owed will be speedily processed.

The downside can be summed up in one word: **access**. You have to be online to access your information. Less obviously, the number of people accessing the Web and particularly the Web site your taxes are on will affect your ability to pull up your information—if the server is being hit with thousands of requests per second, or if the Web is busy in general, your information will come in very slowly ... or not at all.

This is a potentially serious problem the closer it gets to April 15, as thousands of late filers attempt to slam their returns into the IRS electronic mail slot before midnight. If you've got your taxes in order in February and are ready to file, doing your taxes online should present no problem.

Whenever, and as ever, you need to make sure the tax service provider is using **secure Web pages** while you're doing your taxes online—after all, you are passing along some fairly detailed personal information.

Online Tax Preparation: A Walk through

You've decided to use an online tax prep and filing program. Here's a quick walk through of what you can expect, using as models the **TurboTax** and **TaxCut** programs.

Preparation

Before you begin the online tax process, you'll need to get together the same **forms** as if you were filing conventionally. These include your employment forms (W-2s for those employed by someone else; 1099-MISC and K-1s for the self-employed), homeowner forms (1098 for mortgage interest; 1099-S if you've sold a house), and the various 1099 forms associated with investment, dividend, and interest income. You'll also need your information on the **deductions** you wish to take, including retirement vehicles like an IRA or a home office deduction if you're self-employed, information on charitable contributions, and information on any deductible financial liabilities, such as school loans. And of course, you'll need your own data and that of anyone who shows up on the return: Names, dates of birth, and social security numbers.

Signing on

Once you've decided on a tax product to use, you'll be required to **sign in** to the program's system; this will allow the program to keep track of who you are, and allow you to return to your tax preparation should you have to sign off and then sign on again at a later point. This process will require you to read and accept a usage agreement (ie, fine print). You should actually read this.

After you agree to the fine print, you'll be allowed to enter a user name and a password, so you can access the system. At this point, you should be in a secure Web area (with a closed "lock" icon showing on your browser). If you're not in a secure area at this point, try another program provider.

What's On Screen?

Once you've begun the tax program, you'll find that your Web browser's screen is divided into three main parts. The first and largest part is where you'll **enter information** for the questions that you are asked—name, income, amounts of deductions, and so on. After you fill in the information, you'll click "done" (or "forward" or "yes") and another page will be generated with new questions to answer. You'll also be able to navigate backward through the questions to fix or update any questions you've already answered.

A second portion of the screen (typically running down the right side) is a **"help" area**, which provides information on the questions in the main section. For example, if you've been asked if you've received a 1099-S form, the help area will give you options to find out what a 1099-S is used for, and what sort of income that is reported on a 1099-S has to be entered into your tax return. The third portion, usually running across the top, serves as a **navigation tool**, allowing you to move quickly from one major portion of your return to another.

Additionally, in both TurboTax and TaxCut, a **running tally** of your tax indebtedness is kept in the top right corner of the screen, so you can see every step of the way how much tax is being piled on, or taken off through deductions. This is a good way of seeing how deductions and credits work to reduce your tax bill.

Filing Online

The tax program breaks your information into a number of general groups, including personal information, income, deductions and credits, and miscellaneous. After you've entered all your information, you'll be given a chance to review what you've inputted and correct any errors. You should then print your return for your records.

This done, you're ready to **file your return**. The online versions of TurboTax and TaxCut can both file online; additionally, you can set up to send money you owe (or receive money you're owed) online. If you **owe taxes**, you can have the sum taken directly from your bank account, or you can charge your taxes to your credit card. Or you can simply opt to send a check, like you usually do. Paying your taxes online with a credit card may seem like a good idea, but it's probably not. Check out the sidebar on p.165.

If you're **expecting a return**, you have the option of having the IRS cut you a check or deposit the refund directly into your bank account. You may also have the option of getting an "advance" on your loan from your preparer, for a fee (see the sidebar on p.170).

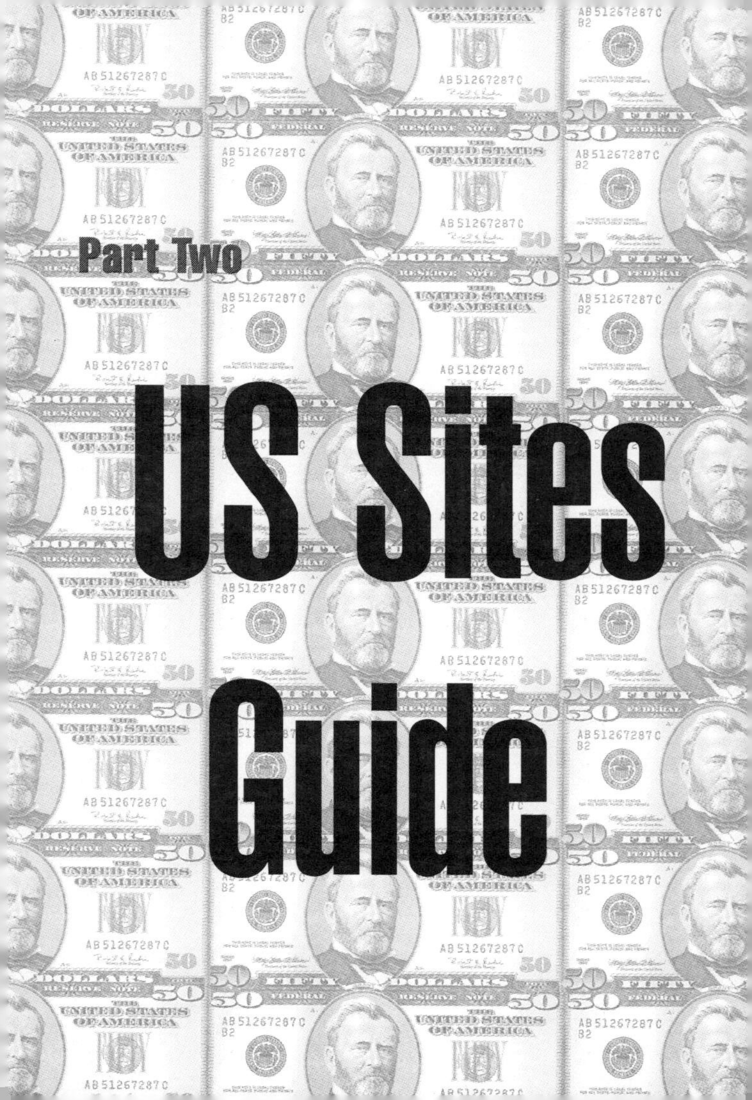

Part Two

US Sites Guide

Star Web Sites

A select number of Web sites in this US directory have been tagged with a star icon (✪). They are—at time of writing—the top recommendations in their respective categories. The **starred information sites** are likely to be ones you'll want to return to often; the **starred businesses**, even if they don't suit you personally, should provide benchmarks for measuring your own final choices.

Banks and Bills

Banks p.181, Bank-Related Sites p.190,
Government Bank-Related Sites p.192,
Bill Payment and Other Money Services p.193.

Banks

Here's a sampling of banks available online—some national, some serving a select clientele, all (unless noted) accessible through the Web. As with all site reviews in this guide section, comments reflect what's on offer at time of writing; obviously things change fast and often in this sector. And note that these listings are only the tip of the iceberg; to find out how to locate any bank see Chapter One of this book and visit Yahoo's Complete Banks Listing at:

http://dir.yahoo.com/Business_and_Economy/Shopping_and_Services/Financial_Services/Banking/Banks/Complete_Listing/

American Bank Online

http://www.pcbanker.com/

American Bank claims that their checking accounts offer the best interest rates available: 6.25% as of this writing (the catch: they're for accounts with less than $10,000 in them). Overall costs are low, but service can be spotty.

American Express Personal Membership B@nking

http://home.americanexpress.com/banking/

For Amex card holders who don't mind putting all their money in one place, this site offers above-average rates on interest checking and on CDs.

AmSouth Bank

http://www.amsouth.com/

Highly ranked by Gomez.com for customer confidence, this site offers online trading as well as banking. It is a little difficult to navigate around.

Bank of America

http://www.bankofamerica.com/

Bank of America offices stretch from sea to shining sea and now into cyberspace, too. They offer a pretty comprehensive range of services online, from regular checking and savings to a bank specifically designed for military folk. Plus small business services, investment products, etc.

Bank Atlantic

http://www.bankatlantic.com/ AOL: BofA

Selling points for this bank include free Bill Pay for three months with an interest checking account and something called a "Virtual Safe Deposit Box"—online storage for your files (in case your computer implodes, presumably).

Bank CaroLine

http://www.bankcaroline.com/

This bank's homepage features a cutesy mascot named—yep—CaroLine (a computer monitor with old lady glasses). Probably more attractive is the rate on interest checking, which can reach up to 6% with free Bill Pay thrown in.

BankDirect

http://www.bankdirect.com/

BankDirect offers unlimited Bill Pay and high interest checking, attractive CDs and money market accounts, and frequent flyer miles from American Airlines for opening accounts and keeping certain balances. Interesting.

BankOne

http://www.bankone.com/

BankOne runs online-only Wingspan Bank, but also provides an online service for its regular customers under its own name. It is generally easy to use and offers bill presentment with selected companies.

Bank United

http://www.bankunited.com/

Bank United offers online accounts without monthly service charges (after an initial $9.95 set-up fee), free checking and free Bill Pay for three months.

BB&T

http://www.bbandt.com/

Basic online bank offerings: rather than working through the Web, BB&T offers its own brand of online banking software known as Home ATM as well as offering access through Quicken and Microsoft Money.

Chase Manhattan

http://www.chase.com/

Chase's site is well designed, easy to navigate, and lets visitors look up a number of informational and educational materials as well as the usual financial stuff.

Citi f/i

http://www.lite.citifi.com/ AOL: Citi

Citibank's "online only" bank (the company also has online bank offerings under its traditional name) offers free bill payment, ATM refunds, an online discount brokerage, and a reference library.

Citibank Direct Access

http://home.da-us.citibank.com/hb/ AOL: Citi

If you already have a Citibank account, this is where you'll go to bank online. It offers free Bill Pay and transfers and no monthly fee.

Citizen's Bank

http://www.citizensbank.com/

The good news: Online banking is free if you have a Circle Gold account with Citizen's Bank. The bad: To get a Circle Gold account, you have to have a $35,000 balance. Details, details.

CompuBank

http://www.compubank.com/

Offerings here are limited to savings, checking, money markets, and CDs, but this limitation is made up for by the fact that most services provided to personal accounts are free.

Directbanking.com

http://www.directbanking.com/welcome.htm

Quirky Web site design but surprisingly full-featured for a small bank: offerings include a brokerage, business banking, and even insurance.

Dollar Bank

http://www.dollarbank.com/dollarbank/

This bank's been around since 1855, when a dollar was a dollar. The site design is a little sparse, but the bank gets high marks for customer service.

E*Trade Bank

http://www.etradebank.com/

The online bank companion to (you guessed it) the E*Trade online brokerage site. Well-integrated with the brokerage site (your brokerage and banking accounts can be linked), this is also a full-featured bank in its own right, including loans, mortgages, credit cards, and free Bill Pay.

Everbank

http://www.everbank.com/

Everbank's site design is a little screamy (too many exclamation points!!), but it offers a good set of high rates and low fees, and its Evermoney e-checking account offers 6% apr and free Bill Pay.

Fifth Third Bank

http://www.53.com/

Fifth Third Bank offers a full range of financial products and good rates for a 'real world' bank. However, the Web site can be very slow to get around.

First Internet Bank of Indiana

http://www.firstib.com/

Is there a Second Internet Bank of Indiana? Probably not, but this one offers enough nice features to make up for the loss, including the ability to make deposits into a MAC-branded ATM and to view digital copies of checks. Slick.

First Union Bank

http://www.firstunion.com/

You may remember this company's entirely freaky television commercials, with people's faces breaking off and bankers in bowlers scaling skyscrapers like the Matterhorn. This bank offers lots of resources from Bill Pay to brokerage, and also features bill presentment.

Firstar

http://www.firstar.com/persfin/persfin.html

Firstar offers a nice selection of financial products, including insurance and Bill Pay, but it's easy to get lost in the site design if you're visiting for the first time.

G&L Internet Bank

http://www.glbank.com/

G&L is a bank specifically designed for the financial needs of gays and lesbians. Site offers a good range of services including home and vehicle loans and good rates on CDs.

Guaranty Federal Bank

http://www.gfbank.com/

This site was extremely slow to access and scant of information and services, and the banking online requires special software. But folks who stick with it can get online banking without monthly charges and Bill Pay for a low monthly fee.

Harris Bank

http://www.harrisbank.com/

A nicely designed site and a good set of online banking options make this bank and its site worth a visit: The site not only offers financial and banking information, but also provides breaking news and other features.

Hibernia National Bank

http://www.hibernia.com/

Located in that Celtic stronghold, Louisiana, this bank strives to offer its customers a full range of financial services, including banking, investing, insurance, and loans. It also features a "marketplace" where small business folks can get assistance getting their businesses online.

Huntington

http://www.huntington.com/

Huntington's site offers a rich and easy-to-use set of features, as noted by Gomez.com, which ranks it in the top ten in terms of onsite resources and in the top five for ease of use. However, it is more expensive to use than many online banks.

✪ KeyBank

http://www.key.com/

An incredibly user-friendly banking site that offers a really nice array of banking and investment options (and also includes online shopping from its site), KeyBank seems designed to put visitors at ease right away. The only drawback is that it is one of the more expensive online offerings.

LaSalle Bank

http://www.lasallebank.com/

LaSalle's site design seems to consider online banking as an afterthought, but at least there is a complete set of services available, including an online brokerage through SpeedTrade. The site is also a little slow to load in.

M&I Bank

http://www.mibank.com/

M&I Bank is trying to establish its online credibility not only with banking and financial services (presented in an aggressively cute design) but also with a Web portal, "MiWeb World," specifically designed for M&I Bank members. While AOL's probably not losing sleep, it's not un-useful.

Mellon Bank

http://www.mellon.com/

Mellon Bank's homepage exudes a "we have so much money we don't care if we get yours" vibe, but once you get past that you'll find a substantial range of services, including a Tax Center and a page for special discounts and services available only through the Web site.

National City

http://www.national-city.com/

By contrast, this is a Web site that reaches out and makes you feel like it wants your business. User-friendly menus lead to a nice complement of information, and while the services provided are fairly standard, the helpful feeling the site exudes is a boost.

nBank

http://www.nbank.com/

Here's an interesting deal: Sign up for checking and get an ISP as part of the deal (actually, it's sign up for the ISP and get a free checking account, but either way). Whether consumers really need an Internet account to go with their checking or not, nBank also provides pretty good rates on its interest checking (5.5% at this writing) and CDs.

NetBank

http://www.netbank.com/ AOL: Netbank

NetBank claims to be the biggest Internet bank and was recently awarded a number-one ranking from Gomez.com for its onsite resources, which include credit cards, brokerage services, leasing services, Bill Pay, and even safe deposit boxes (the virtual kind). Online Bill Pay is free with interest checking (which provides a respectable 4% at this writing).

People's Bank

http://www.peoples.com/

The People's Bank site is cute, with happy little icons that wink at you, but offerings are basic, both in type and in quantity. However, an interesting gimmick is a feature that lets you chat live with an actual bank employee (presumably they prefer you to focus on banking-related questions).

PNC Bank

http://www.pncbank.com/

PNC doesn't make it easy to find its online banking offerings (you have to click down a couple of levels), and other options covered on the site (investment, insurance) aren't always accessible or able to be applied for online—there is online shopping, however. Whew!

✪ Security First Network Bank

http://www.sfnb.com/

This bank is Gomez.com's number-one site overall as of this writing, an award merited by providing the best of online-only banks (high rates on interest-bearing checking and CDs, good deals with online Bill Pay, ATM rebates) with the best features of traditional banks, namely, stability (it's owned by the Royal Bank Financial Group, with $180 billion in assets) and customer support. Good range of services and support. Kind of a goofy-looking site, though.

Summit Bank

http://www.summitbank.com/

A good range of finance services (you can bank and apply for loans and credit cards from the site), but the banking services themselves seem simplistic and probably better for folks who only need the minimum of online access.

TD Waterhouse Bank

http://www.tdwaterhousebank.com/

Another bank opened to support brokerage customers (like E*Trade Bank), TD Waterhouse offers services that are designed to dovetail into the needs of the brokerage's customers. Although the banking and brokerage accounts are well-integrated, the bank provides only basic offerings in areas like personal loans (credit cards, mortgages, and home equity loans are about it).

Union Bank of California

http://www.uboc.com/ AOL: Union

When you sign up for online banking at Union Bank, they'll credit your account 50 smackeroos—so long as you also use their online Bill Pay account. There's always a catch. The offerings on this site are fine, but the design is poor; the front page in particular looks like a wall intended to discourage you from diving in any further.

USABankshares.com

http://www.usabancshares.com/

The online bank with the rock'n'roll attitude—literally: It's the bank that partnered with David Bowie for his online bank (http://www.bowiebanc.com). Refreshingly, it seems to be designed for people who want to bank online but don't have a lot of money: With no monthly fees and a minimum account balance of $1, its banking costs are some of the lowest around, while the returns on CDs and interest checking are very good. There's also free online Bill Pay. A good deal if you don't have a lot to start.

USAccess Bank

http://www.usaccessbank.com/

USAccess offers good rates on CDs and interest checking but has a limited range of financial products (credit products are confined to mortgages and credit cards).

Wachovia

http://www.wachovia.com/

Wachovia is a nicely put-together site that makes most things easy to find and use, and features a nice collection of calculators and articles on money and investing in its Personal Finance Resource Center. The online banking area is reasonably fleshed out as well.

✪ Wells Fargo

http://www.wellsfargo.com/ AOL: Wells Fargo

This massive site is packed to the rafters with all sorts of financial products and services. The online banking component is fleshed out and easy to use, and most any service the bank offers traditional customers it also offers online. Probably the best Web site out there from a traditional bank.

Wingspan Bank

http://www.wingspanbank.com/

This online-only offering from Bank One is a pretty good bank in its own right, with a solid array of financial options including a brokerage, free Bill Pay, good rates on CDs and loans. Plus the site itself is pretty easy to move around in.

Bank-Related Sites

✪ Bankrate.com

http://www.bankrate.com/brm/default.asp AOL: BRM

An essential site, Bankrate provides the state of play on which banks are offering the best rates on savings, checking, CDs, money markets, mortgages, home equity and car loans, credit cards, and ATM fees. You should consult this site before you make a choice about your banking.

BankWeb

http://www.bankweb.com/

BankWeb claims the title of "Most comprehensive directory of banks on the Internet!" Its mother must be proud. The site in fact links out to nearly 3000 banks in the US and abroad, relevant federal sites, including the FDIC, the Federal Reserve Board, and all the Federal Reserve Banks, and to national and state banking associations.

BanxQuote

http://www.banx.com/

This site will give you information on what rates banks are offering for mortgages and auto loans, as well as suss out a bank's current rates for CDs and other investment vehicles. Also provides information on the latest bank rates, economic indicators, and exchange rates. The site's a little spare, but useful.

CreditUnions.com

http://www.creditunions.com/data/

Rather keep your money close than give it to a stinkin' multinational? A credit union may be a viable alternative. This site helps you find credit unions near you, and provides a full report on any credit union in its database (of which there are over 10,000).

Financial Services Center

http://www.bankonline.com/

A directory of banks that offer online banking and Bill Pay, this site also provides links and information on investments, financial planning, loans, and insurance. Useful, but also a tad chintzy.

Internet Bank Report

http://www.internetbankreport.com/

Offers comparisons of leading Internet-only banks as well as news relevant to them. Also lists specials that Net-only banks are running, so if you're shopping for deals, it could be useful.

Maxrate.com

http://www.maxrate.com/

Here's an interesting idea for a site: You go online and say "I've got money to invest in a CD," and the banks come to you and compete for your business by offering their best rates. That's the basic idea (the reality is, inevitably, slightly more complex).

Money-Rates.com

http://www.money-rates.com/

Who's offering the best rates on what? Money-rates.com provides the scoop on the best CD, bank, and consumer rates, and clues you into the latest rate-related news and events.

Online Banking Report

http://www.onlinebankingreport.com/

An online magazine that tracks and reports on online banks. Informative but not cheap: It costs $695 a year for a subscription (and you don't even get a cool football-shaped phone).

Rate.Net

http://www.rate.net/

Claims to be the largest index of financial institutions on the Net, tracking 11,000 institutions and over 100,000 rates every week, including savings, mortgage, auto and equity loans, and credit cards. The site lists top ten rates nationally and in each state so you can find the most competitive rates nearby. It's not brilliantly navigable, but the information is solid.

Shoprate.com

http://www.shoprate.com/

Like Maxrate.com, this site matches your money to the bank that's willing to offer you the highest rate on a CD. It also throws in financial news as well, perhaps to give you something to read while banks are fighting over your cash.

Government Bank-Related Sites

Board of Governors of the Federal Reserve Board

http://www.bog.frb.fed.us/

Think of this as Alan Greenspan's homepage. Site includes press releases, speeches, and testimony, just in case you want to relive Greenspan's "Irrational exuberance" moment.

Federal Deposit Insurance Corporation

http://www.fdic.gov/ AOL: FDIC

The guys that bail you out when the bank robbers hit your local branch office. Their site has answers to your pressing questions about how your money is insured and also provides data on banks and helpful consumer information.

The National Credit Union Administration

http://www.ncua.gov/

Web site of the agency that supervises and insures America's credit unions. The site looks like it was put together by a couple of not-so-talented teens during detention, but features a listing of all the credit union Web sites in the US. It also features news and reference information relevant to credit unions.

Office of the Comptroller of the Currency

http://www.occ.treas.gov/

This is the guy responsible for all the banks in the US and his Web site has a section on Internet banks, what it takes to start one, and what services can actually legally be provided over the Net.

Office of Thrift Supervision

http://www.ots.treas.gov/

These guys are responsible for regulating savings banks and savings and loans (yeah, great job in the 1980s, guys!).

Bill Payment and Other Money Services

If you prefer not to pay your bills online through your bank or through another financial institution online, here are some alternatives.

CheckFree

http://www.checkfree.com/

This Bill Pay company can direct you to one of the various banks or online sites that use it to process their Bill Pay services, or you can elect to use them directly for a fee of $12.95 a month for 35 bill pays, with additional bill pays costing more.

PayMe.com

http://www.payme.com/

Use your credit card to send money to someone through the Net and email. This isn't a Bill Pay service; rather a service that lets you make one-time payments. It's useful for stuff like online auctions or to send cash to a pal (note that when you use your credit card to do this, it's going to be put down as a cash advance).

PayPal.com

http://www.paypal.com/

Another service that allows you to send one-time payments to someone else via email and the Net.

PayMyBills.com

http://www.paymybills.com/index.html

Bills get sent to PayMyBills; PayMyBills alerts you, you pay the bills electronically. At the end of the year, you get an archive of every bill you pay (they also scan them in so you can see them). This has to be tied to your bank account, incidentally; PayMyBills does not support drawing money from your credit cards (which is just as well). Current price for this is $8.95/month.

Paytrust

http://www.paytrust.com/

Works on the same principle as PayMyBills: All your bills are handled, collated, and paid electronically. This is also tied into your bank account and costs $8.95 a month.

US Sites

Brokerages

Online Brokerages p.195, Exchanges and Indexes p.205, Day Trading and Software Sites p.206, Trading Information Sites p.207, Trading-Related Government Sites p.209.

Online Brokerages

As with banking, this is only a cross-section of brokerage options, but it's a fair cross-section: These brokerages cover the full range of costs, services, and offerings available in the online space. Be aware that the vast majority are discount or deep discount brokers, which means that when it comes to trading, you're on your own. Read more about this in chapters nine and ten. Prices cited for trades reflect market orders of 1000 shares or less unless specified otherwise.

1800DayTrade.com

http://1800daytrade.com/

Site designed for day traders, with NASDAQ Level II quotes access, after-hours trading and remote trading options. Level II quotes are "free" if you have $25 in your account or make more than 50 trades a month.

A.B. Watley

http://www.abwatley.com/

This site features trading for average investors with its "WatleyTrader" option, while its "UltimateTrader" option is designed specifically for day traders and other heavy hitters. It puts information in front of you right away, and at $9.95 per market order, it's fairly cheap, too.

American Century

http://www.americancentury.com/index.jsp

American Century is better-known for its mutual funds than its brokerage, and its brokerage reflects that tilt, with access to over 9000 mutual funds, hundreds of which feature no transaction fee. Its $24.95 trading fee is on the higher end, however.

American Express Online Brokerage

http://br1.americanexpress.com/amex/bu/fd/cda/main/1,1484,L-2,00.asp

American Express are serious online players (they also have a bank), and this brokerage site is pretty good, with a range of mutual funds and middle-of-the-road prices for stock trades. Members can buy stocks for free when they keep $25K in their accounts; at $100K they can sell for free too. Members also have access to Amex financial advisors, either on the phone or in person.

Ameritrade

http://www.ameritrade.com/ AOL: Ameritrade

One of the lowest cost brokerages ($8 equity trades), Ameritrade also offers IPO access, after-hours trading, and access to over-the-counter or "penny" stocks. The site is easy to get around in, and its demo for potential investors is one of the best.

Bank of America Investment Services

http://www.bankofamerica.com/investments/index_frame.cfm

The investment arm of (no surprise here) Bank of America. The brokerage layout is bare bones and not all that fabulous to get around in, nor is the trading fee of $24.95 anything to get worked up about. But for someone who already has a B of A account, it's an easy way to get set up for trading online.

Bidwell & Company

http://www.bidwell.com/

Trades begin at $12, and the site is simple to use and easy to get around in, if not as complete in investment research offerings as some other online brokerages. However, the company offers excellent customer service.

Brown & Company

http://www.brownco.com/

If all you want to do is to make cheap trades, and to heck with a lot of research tools, and you meet the site's reasonably stringent requirements (which includes a $15,000 minimum initial deposit), you can make trades here for as little as $5. Oh, and they all but require you to open a margin account. Not a site for novice investors, obviously.

Bull & Bear Securities

http://www.bullbear.com/

This site assumes you know what you're doing, as it's a little light on educational materials and market resources. Trades start at $19.95, but the site also offers "Wall Street Rewards," a premium program that provides things like discounts and air miles based on number of trades and account balances.

Citicorp Investment Services

http://www.citibank.com/us/investments/products/onl_idx.htm

Designed specifically with Citicorp customers in mind (you have to be a Citibank customer to have access to the investment services), the site doesn't have much in the way of resources, nor is it all that easy to use. Guess they're not working that hard to attract new customers.

CompuTEL Securities

http://www.computel.com/

A site that caters to investors who need a little something extra: after-hours trading, direct access to an ECN (to ensure rapid trades) and access to investment professionals for large or otherwise tricky trades. $9 trades are really $11.50 because of "service fees," although that's still pretty low.

CyBerCorp.com

http://www.cyber-brokerage.com/

Brokerage site for day traders. Users employ the CyBerTrader software for their rapid trades and have access to NASDAQ Level II quotes, and ECNs and market makers for fast executions. The site also offers other software designed for people who trade fast and frenetic, as well as a 12-hour trading day, from 8am to 8pm. The software and the site are not for amateurs.

Datek Online

http://www.datek.com/

Datek offers extended hours trading from 8am through 8pm, as well as trades for $9.99, and allows quick access to trading, endearing it to traders who want to make a lot of trades but aren't quite ready to step up to day trader status. Recently rated the number-one broker by theStreet.com.

DLJDirect

http://www.dljdirect.com/ AOL: DLJ

Not exactly cheap ($20 a trade), but offers after-hours trading and the full range of tradeables, including mutual funds, options, penny stocks, and IPOs.

Dreyfus Brokerage Services

http://www.edreyfus.com/

Not entirely surprisingly, Dreyfus provides a good range of mutual fund offerings for investors (including funds that are not their own), but the rest of their brokerage services are pretty basic, not withstanding after-hours trading. Trades $15 each, pretty much middle of the road.

✪ E*Trade

http://www.etrade.com AOL: Etrade

The number-one ranked online brokerage by Gomez.com as of this writing, and with good reason: E*Trade offers just about every investment possibility going, from IPOs (for its Platinum members) down to penny stocks. The site offers a nice brace of research and education tools, clear and concise help, and a whole range of financial services, including a bank. It even caters to the active trader crowd with NASDAQ Level II quote access. $14.95 market trades.

FBR

http://www.fbr.com/

FBR's corporate parent underwrites IPOs and makes up to 50% of that underwritten stock available to its online investors, so if IPOs are your thing, this might be of interest. Otherwise the brokerage is average in terms of both offerings and trade price.

Fidelity Investments

http://personal400.fidelity.com/

Fidelity is on the upper end both in cost of trades ($25 for market orders, but $14.95 if you trade a lot) and in account opening minimums ($5000), but otherwise is just peachy, with a full range of investment offerings (mutual funds, options, IPOs, etc) and educational/research materials. Fidelity's PowerStreet Pro accounts also get NASDAQ Level II quote capability.

Firstrade

http://www.firstrade.com/

Way cheap ($6.95 market trades), and offers the ability to execute rapid trades for fast-moving active traders. Flip side of this is that the research and education materials are sparse.

InvesTrade

http://www.investrade.com/

A deep-discount brokerage with an impressive selection of investment choices, including IPOs, bonds, and options. Its $7.95 market orders are near the bottom in terms of costs, and it offers a fair selection of no-load mutual funds as well.

JB Oxford

http://www.jboxford.com/

If you keep a $2000 minimum with JB Oxford, they'll throw in free Internet service (of course, if you didn't already have Internet service, how would you get to their Web site?). A decent spate of offerings and a trading fee ($14.95 market orders) that's right down the middle.

KeyTrade Online

http://www.keytradeonline.com/

KeyTrade Online offers lower-than-average rates ($12 a trade, both market and limit orders), and a good range of investment options (no bonds or IPOs however). The site also offers a nicely packaged suite of educational materials in its "KeyTrade University" area. Not bad for beginning investors.

Merrill Lynch Direct

http://www.mldirect.ml.com/

Merrill Lynch Direct will cost you: It requires $20,000 to open an account, and will set you back $29.95 for both market and limit orders. In return you get Merrill Lynch's investor analysis, access to the IPOs the company underwrites, and a wide selection of funds from Lynch and others.

Morgan Stanley Dean Witter

http://www.online.msdw.com/

Formerly Discover Brokerage (they were the guys with the commercial where the tow truck driver owned his own country), this site has high trading fees ($29.95 for market and limit orders) but is otherwise very good, with the whole range of stocks, funds, bonds, and IPOs, as well as research and tools to help you find the right investibles. You can also pop by the real-world branch offices when you want.

Mr. Stock

http://www.mrstock.com/

Not a kids' education television show ("Hey kids! It's Mr. Stock!"), Mr. Stock is a brokerage that is primarily focused on the buying and selling of options, and can handle obscure option trading maneuvers other brokerages can't or don't. The trade-off is that other offerings are only so-so. If you're into options, however, this is the place.

My Discount Broker

http://www.mydiscountbroker.com/

This chummy site has decent trading fees ($12 for market and limit orders) and online or broker-assisted offerings in every category but IPOs. It also does not require a minimum deposit in order to open an account. Finally, the educational section (which borrows articles from *SmartMoney* magazine) is really very nice.

National Discount Brokers

http://www.ndb.com/

Active traders will really like NDB's policy of letting investors make multiple same-day trades of a stock with only one commission fee. The site has good offerings in trading and in education and research, and an average trading fee ($14.95 market order).

NetVest

http://www.netvest.com/

NetVest trades everything online but bonds (you have to go through a broker for those) and is particularly proud of its mutual fund selection, with 6000 funds, over 600 of which have no transaction fees. Fees are average. Site is well put together, and it's easy to find information on any subject thanks to a menu that's permanently down the side of the page.

Quick & Reilly

http://www.quick-reilly.com/

Quick & Reilly offers a good range of investment choices and 24-hour customer service, average fees, and does not require an initial deposit for cash accounts. As it is linked to Fleet Bank, the bank's online customers may also access their banking and Q&R brokerage information at the same time.

✪ Charles Schwab

http://www.schwab.com/

Although their fees are not cheap ($29.95 market and limit trades) and you need $5000 to get in, Schwab offers it all, particularly a fabulous selection of mutual funds, many of them no-load or no-commission. Schwab is also rated number-one in relationship services by Gomez.com, and number-one overall by *Forbes* magazine.

Scottrade.com

http://www.scottrade.com/

One of the lowest of the low in terms of trading fees ($7 market orders), Scottrade also requires a low deposit to get started ($500). Offerings are good, although broker assistance is required to trade penny stocks and bonds.

Siebert.Net

http://www.msiebert.com/

This site makes rather too much out of Muriel Siebert, the firm's founder (her face is plastered on the site about as often as Mao's is in China), but the offerings, which include IPOs, are nothing to sneeze at, and the site also offers after-hours trading and a goodly amount of research materials. Accept Muriel as your maximum leader and your trades are $14.95 for market and limit orders.

Stockwalk.com

http://www.stockwalk.com/

Stockwalk is offering some aggressive deals to draw in investors; at the time of writing, it was offering lines of credit to get folks up and trading within a few minutes of sending in an application, and dropping the minimum required deposit. The site's investment and research offerings are fine but nothing special, and the $18.95 fee for market and limit orders (up to 5000 shares) is average.

Suretrade

http://www.suretrade.com/

Suretrade offers a nice complement of investment options (stock, funds, bonds, IPOs), with no minimum deposit for cash accounts and a low trading fee of $7.95 for market orders ($9.95 for limit orders). The company also offers 24-hour customer service. A good deal, even if their TV commercials are annoying.

✪ TD Waterhouse

http://www.tdwaterhouse.com/ AOL: Waterhouse

TD Waterhouse offers over 9000 mutual funds, one of the most complete fund offerings out there, and a nice suite of educational and research tools and information to go with its lower-than-average $12 market and limit order price. The company also offers 24-hour customer support—and branch offices for face time with real humans.

Trading Direct

http://www.tradingdirect.com/

Trading Direct is oriented to the active trader, with low fees ($9.95 for any sort of stock trade done online) and no account minimum to start. On its site, Trading Direct notes in several places that it does not allow you to purchase stock valued under $1, but will allow you to liquidate stock worth less than that. What a relief. Offers bonds, but these must be broker assisted.

UMC Online

http://www.umcstock.com/

UMC might be interesting to folks who want to work OTC (or "penny") stocks, as it takes no commissions on certain of these stock trades. Otherwise, the site offers average trading fees ($14.95 market orders) and average services.

USRICA

http://www.usrica.com/

You can't do a whole lot with USRica—it only offers stock trades—but it does allow you to do that for a very interesting price: $29.95 a month for unlimited Internet trades (for trades of 100 shares or more). Each trade has a $2.50 "service charge" as well, but if you're planning to make a lot of trades each month, that's still pretty attractive. Trades are otherwise $9.95 per trade, or $4.95 if the order is for 500 shares or more.

Vanguard

http://www.vanguard.com/vbs/online/online.html

Vanguard features good planning and educational tools and after-hours trading and offers a wide range of funds, both its own and others, through its FundAccess service. Trades are $20 for market and limit orders.

Vision Trade

http://www.visiontrade.com/

Vision Trade adds a personal touch by assigning subscribers a broker to help them with trades when needed. Trades are $14.95 for up to 2000 shares and there is no opening minimum for cash accounts.

Wachovia

http://www.wachovia.com/

Definitely not cheap ($29.95 per trade), but on the other hand, Wachovia doesn't require a deposit to open a cash trading account. Offers stock, funds, and options online, bonds with broker assistance. Wachovia also offers online banking, so all your money can be managed in one place.

WallStreet Electronica

http://www.wallstreete.com/

WallStreet Electronica wants its members to trade a lot, as evidenced by the credits of 15 and 20 percent it gives on trades when commission fees top $1000 and $2000, repesectively, within a certain time period. The site is also highly ranked in terms of services and product offerings by *SmartMoney* magazine. Also offers a Spanish-language mirror site.

Wang Investments

http://www.wangvest.com/

Wang offers some great prices ($8 for market orders of 999 shares or less, just $5 for market orders of 1000 shares and over), and a decent range of products is available for investment (bonds must be assisted by a broker). It offers a brokerage in Chinese as well.

Web Street Securities

http://www.webstreetsecurities.com/

Planning to buy or sell a big chunk of a NASDAQ stock? Web Street will let you buy or sell 1000 shares or more of a NASDAQ-listed stock for free (as long as the stock is trading for more than $2). Buy into a mutual fund with more than $500, and it's likewise free. And there's no minimum to open. And the site further enhances its attractiveness to active traders with NASDAQ Level II quote access.

WellsTrade

http://wellsfargo.com/wellstrade/

Wells Fargo offers an excellent online banking site, but the brokerage offering is playing catch up. It has high trading fees ($29.95), but offers good integration with the banking end of the online experience. Useful for existing Well Fargo customers; other folks can find the same service cheaper elsewhere.

Wingspan Investment Service

http://www.wingspan.com/

Wingspan's investment strength seems to be in mutual funds: The site offers 7300 of them and allows investors to use "dollar cost averaging" in purchasing. Other investment offerings are pretty standard, and the fees ($19.95 for market and limit trades) are nothing special.

Wyse Securities

http://www.wyse-sec.com/

Wyse is cheap—$7.95 for market and limit orders of any size— and multilingual, with information in Spanish and Chinese on the top pages. Offerings are the usual, but the cheap trade price will appeal to many.

Exchanges and Indexes

American Stock Exchange

http://www.amex.com/

News and market information relating to the AMEX. There's also information on AMEX financial products, such as Spiders, Diamonds, and Triple Qs, financial trusts that closely follow the S&P 500, Dow Jones Industrial and NASDAQ indexes respectively.

Dow Jones Indexes

http://averages.dowjones.com/

Sure, you can find the Dow Jones Industrial averages anywhere. But what about the Dow Jones Sustainability Group Index? Or the Dow Jones Islamic Market Index? Or the...well, you get the idea.

NASDAQ

http://www.nasdaq.com/

Official site for the highly influential stock market, featuring market news and quotes for stocks traded on the NASDAQ.

New York Stock Exchange

http://www.nyse.com/ AOL: NYSE

The official Web site for the most important stock exchange in the world, this features market information, data on listed companies and members and regulation. You can also view panoramas of the NYSE trading floor.

Pacific Exchange

http://www.pacificex.com/

The San Francisco and LA-based stock market rates number three in the US. It lists 2500 stocks, bonds, and other securities.

Yahoo! Index of Stock Exchanges

http://dir.yahoo.com/Business_and_Economy/Finance_and_Investment/Exchanges/Stock_Exchanges/

Links to stocks exchanges all over this gassy globe of ours. For when you're wondering how the Bolsa de Valores de Lima is doing right about now.

Day-Trading and Software Sites

eSignal

http://www.esignal.com/

Day-trading software that features real-time streaming quotes, news updates, intra-day and multiday charts, and other essential stuff for hyperactive traders.

The Executioner

http://www.executioner.com/

This dramatically titled day trading software and brokerage features real-time quotes (including NASDAQ Level II) and fast order executions. Software is fairly expensive but like many of these software/brokerage combos, some fees are rebated with high usage.

Princeton DayTrading

http://www.princetondaytrading.com/

This day-trading brokerage offers course for beginners on how to day trade, including stock market and technical analysis, and basic computer and Windows skills. However, if you actually need the latter, you probably shouldn't be day trading online.

SpeedTrader

http://www.speedtrader.com/

Day-trading software and brokerage. For a monthly fee, the software provides NASDAQ Level II quotes, intra-day charting, and more; brokerage offers fast trades at $14.95 a pop.

TradeCast

http://www.tradecast.com/

Tradecast prvides day-trading software and brokerage. The software (which isn't cheap) offers NASDAQ Level II quotes and dynamic steaming data; brokerage connects with ECNs for fast trades.

Trading Information Sites

Bonds Online

http://www.bondsonline.com/

Links to various sites that provide news, bond rates, and yield information. Be aware that a lot of the sites linked to will try to sell you information for money. The cads.

Brill's Mutual Funds Interactive

http://www.brill.com/

Covers the gripping world of mutual funds with news reports and features, provides links to the Web sites of fund companies, and offers educational materials.

Chicago Board Options Exchange Options Education

http://www.cboe.com/education/

Everything you ever wanted to know about buying and selling options but were too thoroughly confused to ask. Not a simple read, but then trading options isn't simple either.

Find a Fund

http://www.findafund.com/

Scads of fund lists arranged by name, category, and ticker symbols, tools to compare funds, educational resources, and category averages.

FreeRealtime.com

http://quotes.freerealtime.com/frontpage/

Can you guess what kind of financial quotes FreeRealtime.com provides? If you said "why, free real time quotes, of course!" you are a person of rare insight. The site also provides other market research and message boards. It is (of course) free but requires registration.

FundSpot

http://www.fundspot.com/

News and educational resources on mutual funds, links to about 1000 fund screens, and an extensive listing of fund companies.

InvestingInBonds.com

http://www.investinginbonds.com/

This educational site put out by the Bond Market Association is useful – though the articles are written with all the fire and vivacity you'd expect of bond market professionals.

The Investment FAQ

http://www.invest-faq.com/

"FAQ" is Net-speak for "Frequently Asked Questions," and this site features a good database of information to answer a good chunk of your general investment questions—everything from advice to warnings. There are even some trivia FAQs.

InvestorGuide.com Brokerage Listings

http://www.investorguide.com/Brokerages.htm

A list of brokerages that offer online services. Also features links to sites that rate brokerages, including Gomez.com.

MAXfunds.com

http://www.maxfunds.com/

Cute-looking site that aims to do for mutual funds what Motley Fool did for stocks—ie, make them hip and cool. MAXfunds in particular spotlights newer and smaller funds, which it believes can outperform older, bigger funds.

Mutualfundsnet.com

http://www.mutualfundsnet.com

This is a directory for mutual funds, which you can search by name or investment objective (for example, there's a directory of "socially responsible" funds). The site also features information targeted at mutual fund professionals.

OTC Bulletin Board

http://www.otcbb.com/dynamic/

Web site where investors can research over-the-counter or "penny" stocks; about 6500 stocks not listed on the NASDAQ, NYSE, or other markets are tracked here. The site takes pains to note that it is NOT an actual market, it's merely a "quotation medium for subscribing members." Well, okay then.

Stockpoint.com

http://www.stockpoint.com/

All stock information, all the time. Stockpoint charts markets in the US and abroad, provides information on mutual funds and IPOs, and also holds out a spread of stock news and commentary. Users can personalize the site with a portfolio option.

Trading-Related Government Sites

American Association of Individual Investors

http://www.aaii.com/

The AAII is a non-profit organization whose aim is to educate investors so they can make the right investment choices. This site is thus filled with useful information on investment basics, funds and stocks, financial planning, and more. Useful.

EDGAR Mutual Fund Reporting

http://www.sec.gov/edaux/mutual.htm

Database of SEC information on mutual funds. Bone up on a fund's activity on any date back to 1994. The reports are written in financialese but the pertinent information is there.

Investing Online Resource Center

http://www.investingonline.org/

The Washington State Department of Financial Institutions wants you to know what you're getting into when you begin investing online. Nice of them. The site is written for the average Joe and Jane and is pretty easy to wander through.

National Association of Investors Corporation

http://www.better-investing.org/

Another investing association which aims to keep novice investors from making bad choices, the NAIC site offers educational resources, links to stock research tools and to educational publications, and also features a list of the top 100 stocks held by investment clubs (number-one stock: Intel. Take that, Steve Jobs!).

✪ National Association of Securities Dealers

http://www.nasd.com/

Your online broker really should be a member of the NASD. Its site features a member directory and a well thought-out Investors Services area that provides useful information to those who want to trade, online or otherwise.

Securities Investor Protection Corporation

http://www.sipc.org/

This is the corporation that insures most reputable online brokerages. Its site includes news and information as well as a membership database you can use to determine if your brokers (or would be brokers) are members. If they're not, maybe you should reconsider.

TreasuryDirect

http://www.publicdebt.treas.gov/sec/sectrdir.htm

This site allows you to buy US Treasury securities direct from the US government, thus eliminating your brokerage middleman (and saving you fees). Not the easiest site in the world to use, but if you buy a lot of Treasuries, it's going to be worth your while.

✪ United States Securities and Exchange Commission

http://www.sec.gov/ AOL: SEC

The feds site includes the essential EDGAR database (where you can research companies), current SEC rulemaking, and an area for investor assistance and complaints. That's right, you can sic the MAN on whoever's messing with you.

Mortgages and Homes

All-in-one Sites p.212, Mortgages p.214, Home Listings p.217.

All-in-one Sites

Sites listed below will help you locate a home, find a mortgage to finance it, and maybe even get you in there. Seems a shame they can't sort out schools and doctors and fill the fridge.

HomeAdvisor

http://homeadvisor.msn.com/

Microsoft's home-buying site offers to help you find a home, sell a home, finance a mortgage, and even move your stuff from your old place to the new one.

✪ HomePath

http://www.homepath.com/

Do you know what you need to do before you go looking for a house? If you're not sure, Fannie Mae has created HomePath to walk you through it. This site is very informative and hits all the basics of looking for a new home and securing financing. The site also offers calculators (to help find out how much home you can afford) and lists Fannie Mae-owned properties for sale.

Homes.com

http://www.homes.com/

All-in-one site to locate a home, get a mortgage, and plan the move. Homes.com realty listings claim 700,000 homes for sale at any one time.

Homestore.com

http://www.homestore.com/ AOL: Homestore

Another "all-in-one" home site, Homestore will help you buy and/or sell a home, get a mortgage, and move. The site also offers decorating tips and features in-home appliances and electronics.

iOwn.com

http://www.iown.com/

This all-in-one site includes realty listings, mortgage financing, and educational materials. It also provides listings for home inspectors and a home improvement area.

Mortgage.com

http://www.mortgage.com/

One of the largest online mortgage lenders, Mortgage.com will also provide help for consumers looking for home services, moving services, home improvement, and furnishings.

Move.com

http://www.move.com/

Move.com's site offers realty listings from Century 21 and Coldwell Banker, as well as tons of information on buying or selling a house and (as you'd expect) on the actual move itself. They will even help you turn on your utilities and reroute your subscriptions to your new home. It's a zany world we live in.

Reals.com

http://www.reals.com/

A directory that covers just about every angle of the real estate universe, from real estate to mortgage loans to escrow and title, and even foreclosure.

Mortgages

1st-Mortgages.com

http://www.1st-mortgages.com/

Fill out a mortgage application here, and it is then sent to three of more than 700 mortgage companies in the site's network. These lenders will then bid for your business, and you pick the winner.

American Loan Search

http://www.americanloansearch.com/

This site provides daily mortgage rates from top lenders around the country; also car loan, personal loan, and credit card rates.

CompareMortgageRates.com

http://compareinterestrates.com/

Pick a state, then pick the type of mortgage you're interested in—this site will present you with a list of lenders and their rates, fees, and length of lock on the rate. Then you can apply with a click.

A Complete Mortgage Guide For Home Buyers

http://www.homemortgageguide.com/

A nicely done and easy-to-read explanation of the mortgage loan process, written by a mortgage officer by the 1950s movie star name of Rock Vaughan (who—fair enough—puts in a big ol' plug for himself at the end).

Consumer Information Center: Housing

http://www.gsa.gov/staff/pa/cic/housing.htm/

Handy: A site for all those helpful pamphlets that the government puts out and you are never actually able to find. Useful booklets include such titles as "100 Questions and Answers About Buying Your New Home" and "How to Buy a Home With a Low Down Payment." It's stuff you can use, and it's all free.

Countrywide Home Loans

http://www.countrywide.com

National mortgage lender. You can apply for a mortgage on their site, or use the site to find a Countrywide branch location near you. Countrywide also makes home equity loans and refinances loans.

ditech.com

http://www.ditech.com/

One of the relatively few lenders out there still handing out 125% second mortgages. Also offers traditional loans and works with people with not-so-fabulous credit histories.

Fannie Mae

http://www.fanniemae.com/

This is the company who will likely end up owning your mortgage. Fannie Mae is a quasi-public corporation whose goal is to help get Americans into homes of their own, in part by buying up mortgages so banks can have cash on hand to create more. The site tells the history of the company, its goals and practices, and also provides consumer information on buying homes.

Freddie Mac

http://www.freddiemac.com/

Set up with basically the same charter as Fannie Mae (see above), Freddie Mac keeps the mortgage market liquid by buying up mortgages from banks; it differs from its quasi-sister only in minor ways. The site offers information on the company and its philosophy and the various mortgage products available.

Ginnie Mae

http://www.ginniemae.gov/

Fannie Mae and Freddie Mac's country cousin. Ginnie Mae services mortgages insured by the Federal Housing Administration, the Veterans Administration and the Rural Housing Service. Ginnie's site covers the purpose and history of the company and also provides links to the federal agencies it works with.

HSH Associates

http://www.hsh.com/today.html

Current mortgage rates, from all across the United States, plus information on other consumer loans, such as car loans.

Interest.com

http://www.interest.com/

This neat site will help you find a mortgage lender near you (and apply for that mortgage online) and provides a good chunk of educational material for consumers, including first-time buyers or buyers with not-so-good credit.

Mortgage101.com

http://www.mortgage101.com/

A site with dozens of informative articles on every step for the mortgage and home-buying process. Also covers topics like bankruptcy, credit ratings, and second mortgages.

Mortgage Almanac

http://www.mortgagealmanac.com/

A homey little collection of mortgage-related articles written by experts. The layout is amateurish, but the information's not bad.

MortgageQuotes.com

http://www.mortgagequotes.com/

MortgageQuotes boasts of being the largest independent source of mortgage information on the Net, offering rate information from 1400 different lenders as well as market commentary.

MortgageWhiz.com

http://www.mortgage-twz.com/default_twz.asp

Co-branded mortgage provider, which links up theWhiz.com with Mortgage.com. You get theWhiz.com's home-buying articles and Mortgage.com's mortgage products.

National Association of Mortgage Lenders

http://www.namb.org/

You can use this clearinghouse for mortgage lenders to find a local lender.

National Reverse Mortgage Lenders Association

http://www.reversemortgage.org/

A directory of lenders who provide reverse mortgages—in which the equity in a home is used to provide older homeowners with cash for their various needs. The directory includes lenders both in the US and in Canada.

Priceline.com Home Financing

http://www.priceline.com/finance/mortgage/

Here's the deal: You enter in the mortgage rates and terms you want, and then Priceline tries to find a bank that will accept that criteria. If it can't, it'll still provide you with the four offers that most closely match your terms. The drawback: Priceline.com chooses the lender for you.

✪ Quicken Loans

http://quickenloans.quicken.com/ AOL: Quicken Loan

You provide information on yourself, your finances, the sort of terms you need, and the area in which you plan to buy a house. Quicken checks through its database and provides you with a list of lenders who will work with you. From there you can apply for the mortgage directly.

Home Listings

Apartments.com

http://www.apartments.com/

Looking for an apartment, not a house? This site hooks you up with renters all over the country.

Foreclosure World

http://www.foreclosureworld.net

The world's most depressing theme park? Maybe—but there are opportunities here for the unsqueamish. Foreclosure World will provide you (for a few hundred dollars) with information on properties foreclosed upon or served foreclosure papers by their banks. You can save thousands buying a foreclosed home.

Housing and Urban Development

http://www.hud.gov/

This home site for the US Department of Housing and Urban Development offers a lot of consumer information about buying and owning a home, and also offers listings for HUD-owned and other government agency-owned homes available for sale—many of which are going for below-market rates.

RealEstate.com

http://realestate.com/

A site that's oriented more toward real estate professionals than consumers, but it does feature consumer information on financing options and a directory of agents.

Realtor.com

http://www.realtor.com/

Realtor.com features 1.3 million home listings in its database (that's a lot) and will also help you locate a realtor and a mortgage lender. It's probably the best home listings site out there.

Rent.Net

http://www.rent.net/

All that stuff about mortgages and escrows and points and stuff have you running back to apartments? This site will help you find one.

Credit and Credit Cards

General Credit p.219, Credit Cards p.220,
Credit Card Info and Ratings p.223, Credit Reports p.224,
Credit Consolidation and Advice p.225, Bankruptcy p.227.

General Credit

These sites are all-in-one concepts where you can look at your overall borrowings and maybe readjust them.

Credit.com

http://www.credit.com/

An umbrella site for a number of credit-themed sites, including 4Credit.com (credit searches), Credit411.com (credit reports), and general credit information (YourCredit.com). To get much of the information you will be required to register (registration is free).

Creditland

http://www.creditland.com/

A site that links you to credit cards, home and auto loans, as well as personal loans. While overtly commercial, each of the loan areas has informational articles within them.

GetSmart.com

http://www.getsmart.com/

Omnibus credit site that aims to match you with a credit-offering company based on your needs. Covers credit cards, mortgages, and consumer loans as well as debt consolidation (for those of you who suffer from too much credit).

Credit Cards

Usual warnings: Credit cards listed here are presented to show the range available—not as recommendations of those specific cards.

✪ American Express Cards

http://www.americanexpress.com/cards/

Learn about Amex's offerings, including its gold, platinum, and blue cards, and how to manage your Amex account. The site also includes member deals and specials on Web shopping.

Aria

http://www.aria.com

Aria is a major provider of Visa cards and their site takes applications. It also offers shopping services including a "Digital Wallet" for secure online shopping.

Diners Club

http://www.dinersclub.com/

The world's first credit card. And it's still being accepted in lots of places. No, really. The site includes useful travelers' services.

Discover Card

http://www.discovercard.com/

You can apply for your Discover Card online, manage your account, go shopping with selected online merchants, and use Discover's various financial services all on this site. Isn't the Internet grand?

Elton John AIDS Foundation Visa

http://www.webapply.com/ejaf/

Every purchase with this card results in a small contribution to Elton's AIDS foundation.

First USA

http://www.firstusa.com/

Another major card issuer, First USA provides cards under its own name as well as those of dozens of universities, philanthropic groups, sports teams, and other organizations. This site includes links to those affiliate cards as well as account management and shopping.

MasterCard

http://www.mastercard.com/

Web home of the number-two credit card issuer on the planet, the MasterCard site will help you decide what kind of MasterCard you need, and then point you in the direction of a member bank to whom you then apply for the card. Site also features shopping and exclusive deals.

MBNA

http://www.mbnainternational.com/

The largest independent issuer of credit cards, MBNA issues both Visas and MasterCards. Their site offers account access and a digital wallet for secure shopping.

NextCard

http://www.nextcard.com/

Online-only Visa card (meaning it can only be applied for online, not that it doesn't exist in plastic form); you handle your account online as well. Guarantees safe online shopping. Site also offers a "Net Concierge," to fill in online forms and remember passwords (it's a digital wallet).

Official NFL Visa Cards

http://www.webapply.com/nfl/

Choose a Visa card with the logo of any one of the 31 NFL teams, plus free admission to the Pro Football Hall of Fame when you flash the card at the entrance. Finally, a reason to go to Canton, Ohio!

Pet Assure MasterCard

http://www.nacard.com/

Using this card contributes to saving animals through an organization you select. And it features Morris the Cat on the card. You love that cat!

Purina Visa Card

http://www.webapply.com/purina

This card gets you $5 off Purina products for every $500 you spend. Hint: Clip coupons.

The Rainbow Card

http://www.rainbowcard.com/

This gay-themed card allows same-sex partners to apply jointly for a card—and it makes a contribution to the Rainbow Fund with each use.

The Sinatra MasterCard

http://www.webapply.com/sinatra/

The Chairman of the Board's term may have expired, but you can relive those Rat Pack days, baby! Earn Sinatra points for Frank-themed merchandise.

Star Trek MasterCard

http://www.webapply.com/startrek/

With this card you can get 10% off admission at your next Star Trek convention OR Star Trek: The Experience at the Las Vegas Hilton, and the card offers 100% fraud protection for use on the Net. So, you know, buy those Klingon head ridges with confidence.

Visa International

http://www.visa.com

World's largest credit card company with over one billion Visa cards in existence. Site will help you get a card with one of its thousands of member banks, and also offers exclusive deals for Visa members online.

Credit Card Info and Ratings

Not sure if having Morris the Cat, Frank Sinatra, or Captain Kirk is the chief criterion for choosing your credit card? Here's where to go for the lowdown on rates—and practices.

12 Credit Card Secrets Banks Don't Want You To Know!

http://www.state.ma.us/consumer/Pubs/credsecr.htm

Learn the awful truth about interest backdating, two-cycle billing, and double fees on cash advances!

ABCguides Credit Card Rates Guide

http://asque.com/credcard.htm

Compares the rates of 190 separate cards, arranged by rates, benefits, and other criteria.

Cardratings.org

http://www.cardratings.org/

As you'd expect, this provides ratings on credit cards. Its breakdown of criteria is fairly detailed; card reviews are broken down first by reward and then by rate, and then further by type of benefit and by gold/platinum/other status. The site also gives information on credit card scams, poor credit, and numerous other subjects.

✪ CardWeb

http://www.cardweb.com/

Omnibus site offering the latest credit card news and commentary as well as surveys on rates and offerings.

Credit Card Freedom

http://www.creditcardfreedom.com/

Reviews of credit cards, facts and secrets (for example, how to negotiate a lower rate on your card), and a passel of information on debt management.

Credit Card Info Center

http://www.creditinfocenter.com./cards/

A clutch of articles designed either to dissuade you from abusing your cards, or to encourage you to at least pay attention to what you charge. Best article title: "Diary of a Mad Credit Card Customer Service Rep."

Gromco Credit Card Menu

http://www.creditcardmenu.com/

Evaluate credit cards under various criteria, read their terms and conditions, and then apply for the cards online through this site.

Student Credit

http://www.studentcredit.com/

Credit advice and information specifically tailored for college students, who are (this is experience talking here) more likely to do dumb things with their credit cards than real adults. The site also (of course) allows students to apply for cards. Remember what you've learned kids!

Credit Reports

Ever been turned down for credit or any other financing? You'd do well to invest in a personal credit report to see what's in the closet. There are three big players in the US.

Equifax

http://www.equifax.com/

Equifax offers online reports for $8 a shot.

Experian

http://www.experian.com/

A similar service, with credit reports online for $8.50.

Free Credit Analyzer

http://www.freecreditanalyzer.com/

Visit this site if you want to know about your credit rating. Enter information on income and liabilities, and out pops a number that relates to your creditworthiness. This number is informational only (you can't use it for anything), but you won't be surprised by your real credit rating.

PrivacyGuard

http://www.privacyguard.com/ AOL: CA

PrivacyGuard allows you to see what creditors are saying about you by combining credit reports from all three major credit-reporting companies into a single statement you can peruse and correct. You can choose from a quarterly subscription or buy a single report.

TransUnion

http://www.transunion.com/

The third big name in the reports business. Also charges $8.50.

Credit Consolidation and Advice

Listings below include charitable and/or non-profit organizations for advice on credit consolidation—moving around and paying off your debts—as well as folk who would like to invest in your problems. Note that debt-consolidation companies listed here have not been vetted (or, mercifully, used) by the author and are in no way recommendations. Some debt-consolidation companies have been caught doing very bad things, so before you submit an application, exercise due diligence.

American Consumer Credit Counseling

http://www.consumercredit.com/

This non-profit organization works to help people with a lot of debt consolidate and pay off their obligations. Be aware there is a small processing and monthly management fee (some credit counseling organizations charge this while others don't).

Auriton.com

http://www.debt-help.com/

The idea behind this non-profit debt consolidation organization is to help consumers with a lot of debt consolidate what they owe and make it more manageable.

Christian Credit Counselors

http://www.christianccc.org/

Not just a debt-consolidation organization, but an actual Christian ministry, this site is presumably for those whose credit troubles are bad enough to require divine intervention.

Debt & Credit Law

http://www.nolo.com/encyclopedia/dc_ency.html

Nolo.com's easy to understand legal advice concerning debt and credit is useful if you want to know where you stand legally with your creditors, as well as for general questions on credit.

Debt Wizards

http://www.debtwizards.com/

Consumer advocate site written with an amusingly prickly tone, designed to keep you from making dumb mistakes with your credit. The site looks like it was designed by a five-year-old, but the information is good and the writing is refreshing.

Debtors Anonymous

http://www.debtorsanonymous.org/

Debt addiction? Whether you believe in it or not, this group aims to help people help themselves with a twelve-step program based on the precepts of Alcoholics Anonymous.

✪ Myvesta.org

http://www.myvesta.org/

The most professional looking of the debt counseling sites, Myvesta claims to have helped more than four million people reorganize their debts. Their site has downloadable informational resources and has created special resources for debtors with particular needs.

National Foundation of Credit Counseling

http://www.nfcc.org/

On this site, the NCCC, one of the oldest debt counseling organizations (it was founded in 1951), helps you find one of its affiliated debt counselors in your area.

Victims of Credit Reporting

http://members.aol.com/victcrdrpt/index.html

Feel like you've been hosed by a credit card company, or that errors have been made on your credit report, or that your credit is otherwise messed up through no fault of your own? Join the club. This site offers tips and advice for people who think they're on the raw end of a credit deal.

Bankruptcy

It may be a solution. Here's how to find out the implications.

Bankruptcy.org

http://www.bankruptcy.org/

Informational site that helps consumers figure out if they are at risk of bankruptcy, offers stats on bankruptcy and some alternatives to filing a Chapter 7, 11, or 13.

Bankruptcy and Debt Collection Law

http://www.priweb.com/internetlawlib/311.htm

Know your rights! This directory points you in the direction of state, national, and international bankruptcy laws on the Web.

BankruptcyAssistance.com

http://www.bkhelp.com/

Helps customers file Chapter 7 bankruptcy with a minimum of fuss. Before you file, be sure to read the Bankruptcy FAQ provided on the site, which can answer a number of questions about the process.

Loans and Autos

General Loans p.228, Auto Loans p.229,
Auto Warranties p.232, Auto Prices and Tips p.232.

General Loans

This section covers general loan sites. Mortgages are covered on p.214, while specific auto loans follow these listings on p.229. Banks (see p.181) also make loans, of course.

✪ E-Loan

http://www.eloan.com/

E-Loan works with dozens of banks and lenders and offers home mortgages and refinancing, auto loans, credit cards, business financing, and home equity loans through its site.

Household International

http://www.household.com/

This provider of home loans and credit cards also offers auto loans and tax-related financial service. Auto loans and credit cards can be applied for online.

Lending Tree

http://www.lendingtree.com/

Lending Tree pits banks against each other to bid for you. You can apply for mortgages, home equity loans, and car loans, as well as receive bids for debt consolidation, small business loans, and credit cards.

Loans USA

http://www.loansusa.org/

Like other loans sites, Loan USA features home, auto, and personal loans, but it also works with folks who want loans for boats, RVs, and even airplanes, and those with credit issues in their past.

LoanWeb

http://www.loanweb.com/

Home loans, car loans, business loans, student loans, and credit cards are all on offer here, along with links for insurance, airline reservations, and home furnishings.

The Money Store

http://www.themoneystore.com/

The Money Store primarily deals with mortgages, home refinancing, and home equity loans, but they also provide small business loans, all of which can be applied for through this site.

Auto Loans

1-800-Car Loan

http://www.carloan.com/

"As seen on TV!" the site notes, as if being on TV means you're entirely trustworthy. Car Loan offers loans to people with good and not-so-good credit, and in fact claims to specialize in the latter.

1-800 Drive Today

http://www.1-800drivetoday.com/

Another site specializing in providing loans to people with a history of bad credit.

Audi Finance

http://www.audiusa.com/financial/

Lusting after that groovy-looking new TT? This is how Audi suggests you finance it.

Auto Credit Finders

http://www.autocreditfinders.com/

This site claims to find you an auto loan lender in any of the 50 states even if you have a bad credit history. It also touts being seen on TV, just in case you doubted its sincerity.

Auto Loan Online

http://www.auto-loan.com/

Another "Seen on TV" site. This one takes your application and refers you to a local dealer who specializes in "non-prime" credit customers (ie, people with bad credit).

Carlender.com

http://www.carlender.com/

This site offers the usual loans for new and used cars, but also refinances existing car loans as well.

Chrysler Financial

http://www.chryslerfinancial.com/

Chrysler's financial arm. If you want a Chrysler model but haven't found exactly the car you want, you can build your car from the wheels up here; you'll find out how much it'll cost you and what your monthly payments will be.

Ford Credit

http://www.fordcredit.com/

If you haven't driven a Ford lately, but are planning to, this is where the company hopes you do your financing. In addition to applying for a loan, the site allows you to access your account information.

Giggo.com

http://www.giggocar.com/

Loan site that also features pretty good information on both finding the right car for you and negotiating with the dealer for a good price. Giggo.com claims to be able to process your application in a few minutes and to have a check in your hot little hands the next day. Giggo.com also has a Spanish-language site.

GMAC Financial Services

http://www.gmacfs.com/

GMAC provides car loans on GM products, but also provides mortgages and home equity loans, as well as insurance for cars, boats, RVs, and other needs.

Honda Finance

http://www.hondafinance.com/

Finance that Honda or Acura—or that Honda riding mower (with twin bag grass catcher!) you've had your eye on. Well, here's your chance—kind of. You can download a finance application form, but currently have to return it by mail.

Intelligent Autos

http://www.intelligentautos.com/

This is not where KITT from Knight Rider hangs out. It's merely a site for finding and financing a car online. It is run by the folks at iLife (who also run Bankrate.com and theWhiz.com financial sites) but is not quite as well put together as their other offerings.

J.J. Best

http://www.jjbest.com/

If you want your next car to be a Tucker rather than a Kia, this is the site for you: J.J. Best specializes in financing for classic and exotic cars. Get this: Maximum car loan available: $500,000. Man.

NFSN Vehicle Financing

http://www.nfsn.com/Vehicle.htm

NFSN lists and provides links to lenders in your state and online who make loans for cars, boats, RVs, and airplanes.

PeopleFirst.com

http://www.peoplefirst.com/

This site specializes in "blank check" loans—you qualify for a loan, and People First provides you with an actual blank check that you can wave in front of a dealer to make the poor sap salivate (the check can't be made out for more than your approved loan, however). Applications can be made online, and you can have a response within minutes.

Auto Warranties

Chryslerwarranty.com

http://www.chryslerwarranty.com/

Extended warranties for Chrysler cars. This site is provided by an individual dealer, and not Chrysler (or DaimlerChrysler) itself.

Ford Warranty Central

http://www.fordwarrantycentral.com/

Extended warranties on Ford cars. The warranties are sold by a Ford dealership (in Iowa), not the Ford Motor Company up in Dearborn.

ToyotaWarranty.com

http://www.toyotawarranty.com/

Sells extended warranties for Toyota cars. Warranties once more offered through a dealer and not the company itself.

WarrantyCentral

http://www.gmwarrantycentral.com/

Sells extended warranties for GM cars. These warranties are not sold by GM directly, but by a GM dealership.

Warranty Direct

http://www.warrantydirect.com/

Offers extended warranties for all sorts of vehicles: Cars, boats, motorcycles, and RVs.

Warranty Gold

http://www.warrantygold.com/

Extended warranties on cars, boats, motorcycles, and RVs.

Auto Prices and Tips

Before trawling the net for dealers—and they are legion—here are some sites for tips and information to help you get the best car out there at the best possible price.

Absolute Autos

http://www.absoluteautos.com/

Learn the price of a new or used car, with or without various options added. The site also provides links to financing, lemon checks, and extended warranties.

Car Buying Tips

http://www.carbuyingtips.com/

Very helpful site with a hell of an attitude; too bad it looks like it was designed by a chimp. The site's author, Jeff Ostroff, spills the beans on all the sneaky things dealers do to rip you off when you go to buy a car. Fun to read, good to know.

Carfax

http://wsf.carfax.com/

This is a useful service: Carfax researches the title history of any car and lets you know what horrible things have happened to it that the current owner or dealer won't tell you. A basic lemon check is free; a more detailed and useful report is $14.95 (you can also get unlimited reports for 60 days for $19.95).

CarPoint

http://carpoint.msn.com/

Come on down to Honest Bill's Car Emporium! Microsoft's consumer car site tries to cover the entire car experience with new car pricing services, advice on new and used car shopping, and car reviews and features.

Cars.com

http://www.cars.com/

Monster site that includes just about everything relating to cars, with cars, car loans, and insurance all available. The site also lists current car deals and specials and features scads of research tools as well as the latest auto news and information, including previews on upcoming models.

Consumer Protection: Cars

http://www.ftc.gov/bcp/menu-auto.htm

The Federal Trade Commission hates it when someone gets scammed by a car dealer (it's more work for them), so they provide helpful advice on avoiding being ripped off. Topics here include: "Car Ads: Reading Between the Lines" and "Look Before You Lease Alert."

✪ Edmunds

http://www.edmunds.com/

Comprehensive site that will provide you with information on how much the shiny new car you're looking at actually cost the dealer (and thus, how much the dealer is attempting to soak you for). Site also features car reviews, message boards, and information on the special deals car dealers get from manufacturers in order to move product.

Kelley Blue Book

http://kbb.com/

When dealers and others talk about "blue book price," this is the book they're talking about. Kelley's site offers definitive information on the dealer cost of a new car and the resale value of used cars; the site also features reviews of new cars, motorcycle retail and trade-in value, and general research on the car-buying process.

Financial Intelligence

Online Financial Magazines p.235,
Online Financial Newspapers p.238,
Online Financial Sites p.241.

Online Financial Magazines

Sites in this section are the online counterparts to magazines that are also published in regular print editions. Some are free access; others require a paid subscription or just free registration so that you're making a contribution to their database.

Barron's Online

http://www.barrons.com/

The complete *Barron's* magazine—accessible on subscription. Its online sub is bundled with the *Wall Street Journal*'s, so if you subscribe to one, you'll get both.

Black Enterprise

http://www.blackenterprise.com/

Financial news, commentary, and features for the African-American professional. The site also offers a business directory and a stock purchasing center.

Business 2.0

http://www.business2.com/

Business magazine focusing on all those groovy Net entrepreneurs and the things they're doing in the wired world.

BusinessWeek Online

http://www.businessweek.com/ AOL: BW

BusinessWeek Online offers some of the magazine's content for free, but most of it has to be paid for with a subscription (AOL members can read the whole magazine for free through AOL's BusinessWeek site). However, there's enough free content here to make it a worthwhile stop for non-AOLers.

eCompany Now

http://www.ecompany.com/

Follows the ups and downs of the ebusiness world. Site features magazine articles plus Web-only content that relates to those articles and a guide to Net-related businesses.

The Economist

http://www.economist.com/ AOL: Economist

News of the financial world from that marvelously dry British perspective. *The Economist* talks about business globally, and also wanders away from the financial markets to talk about the world in general. Because, you know, it's not all about the Benjamins.

Family Money

http://www.familymoney.com/ AOL: Family Money

The family that invests together, gets rich together. Content focuses on how to handle domestic finances, save for school and retirement, and still have enough left over for a life. Daily updates on the Web.

Fast Company

http://www.fastcompany.com/homepage/

Magazine of record for the New Economy. The site features current magazine articles, repackaged in innovative themes, and tons of Web-only stuff. The magazine's archives are also online, all the way back to the first prototype in 1993. Those were the days.

Forbes.com

http://www.forbes.com

Forbes.com includes the articles from the week's magazine, as well as content from Forbes ASAP and Web-only material. *Forbes*' lists of the richest people are also here, just in case you thought you were doing pretty well with those investments.

Fortune.com

http://www.fortune.com/fortune/ AOL: Fortune

Missed the Fortune 500 issue? The list is here, plus the contents of the latest magazine issue, rearranged into Web-friendly categories and mixed in with online-only content.

Futures Magazine

http://www.futuresmag.com/

Magazine for people who invest and obsess over financial futures (the options, not the temporal state).

Green

http://www.greenmagazine.com/

Financial advice with Xer attitude. The Web site provides investing advice, examines the job scene for young professionals, covers issues from home buying to budgeting, and features occasional interviews with the rich and/or famous to find out where they stash their cash. Fun read.

Individual Investor

http://www.individualinvestor.com/

This site's clearly designed to sit on your desktop 24/7. It's packed with news, commentary, market tracking, links to message boards, investing tutorials, and more. A little like drinking from the firehose.

IndustryWeek

http://www.industryweek.com/

Financial news and information for those who work with actual things. You know, like assembly lines and stuff.

Kiplinger's Personal Finance

http://www.kiplinger.com/magazine/maghome.html

Web site features highlights from the current print magazine as well as collections of *Kiplinger* articles in several financial categories.

Money.com

http://www.money.com/money/ AOL: Money

Money.com's site is packed with Web-oriented content, including daily financial advice by Jean Sherman Chatzky, "Money 101" financial tutorials, and Web tools to track stocks and build portfolios.

Mutual Funds Online

http://www.pathfinder.com/mfmag/index.html

Mutual fund news and commentary from the magazine plus a lot of daily-updated content, including the best (and worst) fund of the day.

Red Herring

http://www.herring.com/

Hard-core tech business news. Sections include news on venture capital and startups, IPO news, and investor issues. Required reading for anyone who still dreams of start-up billions.

✪ Smart Money

http://www.smartmoney.com/ AOL: Smart Money

Wall Street Journal's magazine of personal business jumps successfully into Web form with great areas for financial planning, investments, and online forums. Includes a fine collection of basic information for starting investors plus constantly updated news.

Worth Online

http://www.worth.com/

Content from the magazine plus content from other *Worth* products. Requires registration, but it's free.

Online Financial Newspapers

This is a pick of the majors and specialists—but pretty much every newspaper that's online posts its finance section. For an exhaustive list of these, both in the US and elsewhere, check the American Journalism Review directory:

http://ajr.newslink.org/biznews.html

Chicago Tribune Business

http://www.chicago.tribune.com/business/businessnews/

Chicago is of course home to the Chicago Mercantile Exchange. This section features latest national and local business news.

Detroit Free Press Business

http://www.freep.com/business/index.htm

Business news from Motor City.

✪ Financial Times

http://news.ft.com/ AOL: FT

Hey, did you know that there's actually business outside of the United States? No, really, it's true. The *Financial Times* is easily the best source of information for business with an international beat, and covers both business news and general world news as it happens online. Should be on your reading list.

Houston Chronicle Business

http://www.chron.com/content/chronicle/business/index.html/

Business as it happens deep in the heart of Texas.

Los Angeles Times Business

http://www.latimes.com/business/

The glamour, glitz, and depressing financial realities of the movie industry are chronicled here.

Mercury Center Business

http://www.mercurycenter.com/business/

Front-line Silicon Valley news and events from the *San Jose Mercury News*.

Miami Herald Business

http://www.herald.com/business/

Business news with a south Florida spin.

New York Times Business

http://www.nytimes.com/yr/mo/day/business/ AOL: NYT Business

News from the financial center of the known universe. The *Times* requires you to register to enter the site, but registration is free.

Philly.com Money

http://money.philly.com/

Incorporating business news from the *Philadelphia Inquirer* and the *Philadelphia Daily News*.

Seattle Times Business

http://www.seattletimes.com/news/business/index.html

Keep up with what that sneaky Gates character is up to these days.

SF Gate Business

http://www.sfgate.com/business/

Business by the Bay.

USA Today Business

http://www.usatoday.com/money/mfront.htm

Feel like you're reading business news at an airport, right from the comfort of your own home.

✪ Wall Street Journal

http://interactive.wsj.com/home.html

The newspaper of record for the financial world. The *Journal* knows that people want it, which is why it charges a subscription fee for access. With the fee, however, comes an additional subscription to Barron's Online.

Washington Post Business & Technology

http://www.washingtonpost.com/wp-dyn/business/

Not only is Washington the capitol of the United States, it's also home to one of the largest tech markets in the country (AOL and MCI Worldcom are both there).

Online Financial Sites

In addition to Web-only sites, this category also includes sites tied to television, radio, and books.

AARP Money and Work

http://www.aarp.org/indexes/money.html AOL: AARP

Financial advice and planning for the over-50 set from the American Association of Retired Persons.

ABCNews Business

http://abcnews.go.com/sections/business/

The latest business news from broadcaster ABC. Site includes streaming video reports and content specifically written for online.

Armchair Millionaire

http://www.armchairmillionaire.com/ AOL: Armchair Millionaire

How to become a millionaire without trying too hard. The Armchair gurus emphasize a "slow but sure" investment plan to help their members retire well.

BBC World Service: Business

http://www.bbc.co.uk/worldservice/business/index_stat.shtml

Listen to all your global business news read to you in an efficient, clipped British accent.

Best Calls

http://www.bestcalls.com/

Best Calls broadcasts and archives conference calls from companies announcing earnings and reporting business news. Registration is required but is free.

BET Money

http://www.bet.com/MONEY/

Latest financial news, feature information, and advice from Black Entertainment Television's Web portal.

Blackstocks.com

http://www.blackstocks.com/

Investment news and advice and strategies for African-American investors. Also includes information on publicly held African-American-owned corporations.

Bloomberg.com

http://www.bloomberg.com/welcome.html AOL: Bloomberg

One of the largest financial news services. In addition to the latest news off the wire, the site features streaming video and audio, as well as charts and tools for investors.

Bridge Information Systems

http://www.bridge.com/

Bridge provides comprehensive financial news and information to its various business clients. The Web site features the latest business news from Bridge as well as registration for PersonalBridge, a news package tailored to the registrant.

Briefing.com

http://www.briefing.com/

This promotes itself as the leading provider of live market analysis on the Net. The site features three levels of access; the free level includes live market coverage, while the paid tiers provide live coverage in specific market categories.

BubbleEconomy.com

http://www.bubbleeconomy.com

Its motto: "Prepare for the Pop." A site for everyone who firmly believes that the good times can't last. Site aggregates news and information relating to business on the downside. Not the place to be if your stocks took a bath today.

CBS MarketWatch

http://cbs.marketwatch.com/news/newsroom.htx AOL: Marketwatch

CBS's financial Web offering is a very useful collection of original stories and news on what's happening in the financial world. Like other broadcast counterparts it offers video and sound clips, but the emphasis here is on solid written content.

ChinaWeb

http://www.chinaweb.com/

So, what are they doing over there in China right this very moment? ChinaWeb covers it—the business and investing news end of it, at least.

CNBC.com

http://www.cnbc.com/

Online counterpart to the financial-mad online network. The site is packed to the gills with news (from MSNBC) and market analysis from CNBC's stable of talking heads. CBNC's site also features clips from the day's shows.

✪ CNNfn

http://www.cnnfn.com/ AOL: CNNFN

CNN's financial news site has news, stock information and analysis tools, consumer strategies, program schedules, and entire TV shows and segments available to watch in a tiny-postage-size window on your computer.

Consejero.com

http://www.consejero.com/

Financial news, advice, and planning, all in Spanish language.

DowJones.com

http://dowjones.wsj.com/p/main.html

If you want *Wall Street Journal* content but don't want to spring for the online subscription, DowJones.com provides *Wall Street Journal* highlights as well as other news and market information provided by the Dow Jones news service.

European Investor

http://www.europeaninvestor.com/

Have stocks back in the old country? This site tracks what's going on over there on the other side of the Atlantic, with the latest news and the option to follow the European markets in real time.

401(k).com

http://www.401k.com/

You probably use a 401(k) to invest for retirement (and if you don't you should); this site provides you with ideas and tips to maximize your 401(k) return so you can retire happily. Run by Fidelity Investments, so expect a little Fidelity shilling now and again.

Fox Market Wire

http://www.foxmarketwire.com/

Fox News business offering on the Web. It has a tabloid feel, but then what else do you expect from Fox?

GainsKeeper

http://www.gainskeeper.com/

Portfolio tracking service that will also keep track of your capital gains tax liability, so you won't have any surprises when it comes time to file next April—you can just print out an attachment to your forms. Costs $35 a year.

Gay Financial Network

http://www.gfn.com/

The financial world from the gay and lesbian point of view: Beyond the straight financial news, GFN offers stories, features, and advice specifically addressing issues that gay men and women have in finance and investing.

Gay.com Finance Channel

http://content.gay.com/channels/finance/

Another site that provides business and financial news and commentary with a gay and lesbian spin. Also covers workplace and investing issues.

✪ Gomez.com

http://www.gomez.com/ AOL: Gomez

One of the essential sites. Gomez.com rates online brokerages, online banks, credit cards, online mortgage lenders, and homefinder sites, and throws in a passel of online travel and shopping sites to boot. Gomez.com's set of criteria works to ensure that you can find a site that works for you in any of these categories.

Hoover's Online

http://www.hoovers.com/ AOL: Hoovers

One of the leading sites that offers company reports—enter a stock symbol and you'll get a capsule report and the company's financials for free, and a full report if you subscribe. The site also offers a (free access) news center.

IndexFunds.com

http://www.indexfunds.com/

A site devoted to the noble index fund, that fund which reflects the market, and offers news and commentary as well as a list of index funds currently available.

InvestorGuide.com

http://www.investorguide.com/

"The only investing site you need" is a dangerously self-confident claim. Nevertheless, InvestorGuide does offer a good mix of news, analysis, market research, and educational material, backed up with useful links.

IPO.com

http://www.ipo.com/

If you got a hankerin' for IPO news, this is where you can find it. The site lists IPOs scheduled for the week with the expected offering price and profiles of the companies going public. Throw in the latest IPO news, information on IPO underwriters, accountants, and venture capital firms, and you've got yourself an IPO party. Two other sites also offer very nearly the same information: IPO Central (http://www.hoovers.com/ipo/ AOL: IPO) and IPO Home (http://www.ipo-fund.com/).

iVillage Money Life

http://www.ivillagemoneylife.com/

Debt management and investment site targeted specifically at women. Information categories include Starting Out, Couples and Kids, Suddenly Single, and Retire Rich.

MoneyCentral

http://moneycentral.msn.com/home.asp

Microsoft essays the subject of money in all its various permutations on this site: Major content areas (most of which are very large sites in their own right) include Investing, Banking, Saving & Spending, Family & College, and Retirement & Wills. Lots of content, lots of tools, lots of stuff.

Money Minded

http://www.moneyminded.com/

The money area of Women.com offers some excellent articles on investing, finance, and real-world money issues, but then goes and puts up investment horoscopes. I mean, really.

Moneynet

http://www.moneynet.com/

Financial news Web site offered by Reuters, one of the largest news services in the world. Not especially well-designed, the site offers headlines on the front page and some market research underneath.

Moody's Investors Service

http://www.moodys.com/

Moody's rates bonds and other investment vehicles so you'll know whether to put your money into them. The site isn't especially user-friendly, but includes press releases on the latest ratings it has issued, as well as ratings for mutual funds.

Morningstar

http://www.morningstar.com/ AOL: Mornstar

A leading analyst of mutual funds, stocks, and other investments, Morningstar's Web site is stuffed with opinion and commentary on the state of the market, and also features good education and 401(k) advice areas. Solid information from a good, unbiased source.

✪ Motley Fool

http://www.fool.com/ AOL: Fool

One of the best finance sites in the business. The Fools are fearless in educating new investors on the ins and outs of the stock market, and equally fearless in their analysis of stocks and the companies behind them. Great content, vibrant message boards, smart commentary, and a fun but no-BS vibe. Investors should visit this site frequently.

Multex Investor

http://www.multexinvestor.com/ AOL: Multex Investor

"Research for serious investors." Well, okay, then. The site (free registration) features commentary, interviews with market analysts on the events of the day, and free research reports on selected companies.

The Mutual Fund Cafe

http://www.mfcafe.com/

Read mutual fund news and commentary over croissant and coffee (bring your own food and drink). The cutesy interface actually masks good content and reporting on mutual funds and those who run and invest in them.

Mutual Fund Investor's Center

http://www.mfea.com/

This home site of the Mutual Fund Education Alliance, a trade association for the industry, features fund information and data, and educational data.

NASDAQ Trader

http://www.nasdaqtrader.com/

Informational site provided by NASDAQ for those who buy and sell on the market. You can find out which stocks have trading halts, access NASDAQ-related news, and avail yourself of trading data.

Nightly Business Report

http://www.nbr.com/

When you've spent the business day hiding under a rock, this site will bring you up to speed on the events of the business day with news, streaming video, and financial tools. If you'd rather sleep, no problem, there's a Morning Business Report, too.

The Online Investor

http://www.theonlineinvestor.com/ AOL: OLI

This site provides excellent educational information for beginning investors on how to get up to speed buying, selling, and generally trading online. Not the zippiest looking site around, but the quality and friendliness of the writing make up for that.

Quicken.com

http://www.quicken.com/

Not a place to buy Quicken financial software (though you can do that), Quicken.com is actually one of the most comprehensive financial sites on the Web, with deep pockets of content and service covering investing, banking, mortgages, retirement, and more. A good one-stop source of information.

Quote.com

http://www.quote.com/quotecom/

The first provider of Internet-based equity research, Quote.com has quotes and market numbers coming pretty much out the wazoo. Track all major and minor indices, follow bond markets, and learn which mutual funds have been providing the greatest returns. Actually a very useful site.

Ric Edelman

http://www.ricedelman.com/ AOL: Ric Edelman

I like this site a lot: Ric Edelman's financial advice can be unconventional, but he backs it up logically, and his writing style is something that most folks can relate to. The site covers all aspects of one's financial life, from financial basics to retirement, with smart, readable articles. Clear a block of time, and come by for a read.

S&P Personal Wealth

http://www.personalwealth.com/

Nicely done financial information site from Standard & Poor, featuring news and analysis, charts of market indices, commentary on IPOs and the economy, and good articles on the basics.

Silicon Investor

http://www.siliconinvestor.com/index.gsp

Investor chat board that also provides latest market news, market tools, and links to annual reports and commentary on other sites.

TheStreet.com

http://www.thestreet.com/ AOL: TSC

One of the most controversial sites out there, thanks to theStreet's outspoken star commentator James Cramer. TheStreet's bread and butter is commentary from Cramer and others, but the site also provides news, message boards, educational articles, and tools and quotes. It is part free, part subscription.

TheWhiz.com

http://www.thewhiz.com AOL: The Whiz

Friendly and well-written site that covers the basics of everything relating to money and finance. Lots of how-to articles, quizzes, and "theWhiz 101" educational sections will walk novices through most of the financial events they'll have to face. Could be slightly better organized, but it's a minor quibble.

ThirdAge: Money

http://www.thirdage.com/money/ AOL: Third Age

Financial advice for boomers and their elders. (Yes, boomers, you're getting up there. Sorry.)

Women's Financial Network

http://www.wfn.com/

Women's site that provides financial advice and gives women a place to centralize their online financial accounts.

WorldlyInvestor.com

http://www.worldlyinvestor.com/

WorldlyInvestor provides a global perspective on stocks, focusing on stocks and companies that originate outside the borders of the United States.

✪ Xolia.com

http://www.xolia.com/

A really useful site that allows users to select the best online banks, brokerages, and credit cards by selecting criteria that are important to them. As additional criteria are added, the field narrows until a final list is created. A great help if you're overwhelmed with trying to find the right place online for your money.

Yahoo: Financial Newsletters

http://dir.yahoo.com/business_and_economy/shopping_and_services/financial_services/investment_services/market_information_and_research/newsletters/

A listing of various finance-related newsletters available on the Internet. Be advised that a newsletter's appearance on this list does not necessarily mean that either the provider of the newsletter or the information therein is entirely trustworthy—this is a case where caveat emptor ("let the buyer beware") certainly applies.

Yahoo Finance

http://finance.yahoo.com/

Web portal Yahoo! has put together an excellent collection of finance news, information, and services. This site isn't especially flashy, but it's loaded with useful stuff.

Zacks.com

http://my.zacks.com/

Zacks puts a lot of information on your screen: A portfolio into which you can place your own stocks, news headlines, a calendar for earnings, market reports, commentary and more. It's a lot to take in, but people who love market info will love it.

Tax

Tax Sites p.251

Tax Sites

Prices for tax-filing sites are current as of this writing.

1040.com

http://www.1040.com/

Tax information site that includes news, federal and state forms, and general tax advice. Pretty basic.

123 Tax Preparation

http://www.123taxprep.com/

Site offers online tax preparation for free—but charges $9.95 for filing your tax forms electronically.

1 800 Tax 1040

http://www.1800tax1040.com/

Online tax prep and filing for $9.95. Also includes links to state tax forms.

AmeriFile

http://www.amerifile.com/

This online site will process your 1040, 1040A, or 1040EZ starting at $20. It's an authorized IRS e-File provider, but it's got just about the cheesiest site design you ever saw.

CompleteTax

http://www.completetax.com/

One of the cheapest tax filing services, Complete Tax allows you to complete and file both your state and federal tax forms for $7.50. You can also choose to print the return and file it that way.

e1040.com

http://www.e1040.com/

This site gives you the option of preparing your own taxes online or using a human tax preparer to prepare and file your taxes within 48 hours. The site comes in exceptionally slow, however.

eSmart Tax Forms

http://www.etaxforms.com/

This has you prepare your taxes offline using Microsoft Word, and then files them online. The tax prep forms are free; the filing costs range from $5 to $10.

✪ H&R Block

http://www.hrblock.com/

Web site for the most famous tax preparation company around. Provides information on the company and local branch offices where you can bring your tax info and have someone else deal with it. You can also file online for $9.95.

H.D. Vest

http://www.hdvest.com/

In return for enduring constant advertisements for other H.D. Vest financial products, the company will allow you to prepare and file your taxes online with them.

Intelligent Taxes

http://www.intelligenttaxes.com/

One of the more useful and complete tax information sites around, Intelligent Taxes will walk you through the basics of tax planning and preparation, keep you up to date with the latest tax news and provide you with resources and forms you'll need to do your taxes right. The site even keeps track of deadlines you shouldn't miss.

The Internal Revenue Service

http://www.irs.gov/

It's the tax man, yeah, it's the tax man. The IRS has tried to make its site friendly and accessible, so as not to frighten and confuse taxpayers any more than they already have been. It works, but only on the surface; get below the campy Fifties of the front page, and you're awash in confusing IRS publications, forms, and regulations. Still, whatever you want from the IRS is here, including forms, schedules, information for personal and business taxes, and a search engine to find stuff you didn't even think you wanted to know about. Enjoy.

Jackson Hewitt

http://www.jacksonhewitt.com/

Number-two tax preparer after H&R Block. You can't file online through Jackson Hewitt, but you can get tax forms from the site, as well as find a local branch office to have them file for you (they'll file electronically from there). Jackson Hewitt offers refund anticipation loans if you just can't wait a couple of weeks to get your refund cash.

National Association of Tax Preparers

http://www.taxprofessionals.com/

Want someone local to help you wade through your taxes? This site will connect you to a NATP member near you.

Nolo.com: Tax Law

http://www.nolo.com/encyclopedia/tax_ency.html

Everything you wanted to know about your legal rights concerning the IRS, filing appeals, surviving audits, and (uh-oh) dealing with fraud, cheating, and other tax crimes (hint: don't).

Personal Finance: Taxes

http://www.compuserve.com/gateway/personal_finance/taxes.asp

Tax information site put together by online service provider CompuServe. Lots of useful links and some interesting tax-related content, but not the most complete site out there.

✪ Quicken.com: Taxes

http://www.quicken.com/taxes/

The home of TurboTax, the popular tax preparation software, as well as TurboTax for the Web, which you can use to prepare your taxes online for $9.95 each (or if you file the 1040EZ or make less than $20,000 a year, you can file for free). The site also contains useful articles and tips.

Quick-Tax.com

http://quick-tax.com

Files 1040EZ and 1040A forms online for $14.95.

Snap Tax Center

http://home.snap.com/LMOID/resource/0,566,-1355,00.html

Snap's tax center includes electronic tax filing and tax tools from H&R Block, and tax articles from theWhiz.

TaxAct.com

http://www.taxact.com/

TaxAct is tax software that you can use for free to prepare and file your federal taxes (the TaxAct people are hoping you'll actually shell out $10 for the deluxe version they also sell).

Tax Analysts Online

http://www.tax.org/

Web home of a non-profit tax organization, this site features tax-related news and catalogs for the organization's publications.

TaxAttack.com

http://www.taxattack.com/msie.htm

When you enter the site, the theme to "Jaws" plays (can't help but wonder if they got permission for that). The site offers online tax preparation that is then reviewed by an actual CPA, who will then contact you with any questions. Yes, it costs money.

Tax Cut

http://www.taxcut.com/

Downloadable tax software put out by Kiplinger's and H&R Block. You can buy it at the site in mailable or downloadable form, or you can link over to the online version, which allows you to prepare and file your taxes online.

Tax Foundation

http://www.taxfoundation.org/

These are the guys who tell us when "Tax Freedom Day" is every year—that being that day our income has paid for all our federal, state, and local taxes, and we start getting to keep what we earn. Beyond Tax Freedom Day updates, the site also features less dramatic tax information and commentary.

Tax Logic

http://www.taxlogic.com/

Another site that connects you online to a professional tax preparer, who will do all the heavy lifting as far as preparing your tax return is concerned.

Tax Planet

http://www.taxplanet.com/

The scariest planet in the solar system? No, an informational Web site on taxes. Nicely designed site has latest tax news, a year-round tax planner, updates on legislation and new tax laws, and lots of other tax goodies.

The Tax Prophet

http://www.taxprophet.com/tp.htm

Web site of Robert Sommers, a tax lawyer and columnist for the *San Francisco Examiner*. Site features his columns and other tax-related content, including a whole area on various tax scams you'll be wanting to avoid.

Taxes4Less

http://www.taxes4less.com/

Site doesn't offer software, it offers people—tax preparers who will help you with your return. There's even a "Shoe Box" option in which you simply mail in all your paperwork and let them handle the busy work.

United States Tax Code

http://www4.law.cornell.edu/uscode/26/

Here's a little light reading for you: The entire United States Tax Code. Share it with friends! Send it to loved ones! Read it to your children as a bedtime story!

WorldWideWeb Tax

http://www.wwwebtax.com/

Site offers online tax preparation and filing for $9.95, but another reason to visit the site is the truly impressive tax directory, which covers nearly 1000 specific tax issues, from Academic Scholarships to Worker's Compensation. An eye-popper and well worth a visit.

Yahoo: Tax Forms Online

http://dir.yahoo.com/Government/U_S__Government/Taxes/Online_Tax_Forms/

Can't find the tax forms you need? Look here—forms for federal and state governments can be linked to from this spot.

Part Three

Canada Sites Guide

Star Web Sites

A select number of Web sites in this Canada directory have been tagged with a star icon ✪. They are—at time of writing—the top recommendations in their respective categories, and even if they don't suit you personally, they should provide benchmarks for measuring your own final choices.

Canadian Finance Sites

Banks and Banking p.259, Credit Cards p.263,
Credit/Debt Problems p.264, Financial Sites and Magazines p.264,
Investing and Brokerages p.268,
Mortgages, Homes and Loans p.270, Taxes p.271

The sections following include URLs for Canadian banks, brokerages, loan companies, financial magazines and information, and more. While options for Canadian finance sites and information are not as varied as in the US, you can still do just about anything with your money online, from banking it to (hey!) paying your taxes.

Links detailed go to the English-language version of a Web site unless specifically noted otherwise; French versions (if any) are usually linked to the pages listed. Dollar information is Canadian dollars unless otherwise specified.

Banks and Banking

AAA Directory: Banks of Canada

http://www.aaadir.com/m_northamerica.html

This is a Web directory of banks (and credit unions) in Canada. The directory includes basic information concerning the banks, including location and phone numbers, and links to their Web sites.

The Bank of Canada

http://www.bank-banque-canada.ca/

The national bank of Canada; you won't be able to bank here unless you're actually a bank of some sort. Nevertheless, the site contains banking news, information on Canada's banking policy, monetary systems and securities, and exchange rates.

Bank of Montreal NetBanking

http://www.bmo.com/personal/banking/netbanking.html

Online banking service allows customers already cleared for telephone banking to pay bills, transfer money, and access account information. The Bank of Montreal also offers a more direct online bank option called mbanx.com (http://www.mbanx.com/)

Canadian Banking Ombudsman

http://bankingombudsman.com/

Got a beef with your bank? The Canadian Banking Ombudsman can help; it's an independent company devoted to resolving issues between banks and their customers before anybody goes to court. The service is free (and you can still sue if you're not happy).

The Canadian Bankers Association

http://www.cba.ca/

The online site of Canada's banking association, this site has the latest news involving Canada's banks, a media center, a "consumer kiosk" of basic information on Canada's banking community, and other bank-related material and information.

Canada Deposit Insurance Corporation

http://www.cdic.ca/

This is the Canadian national entity that insures your deposits up to $60,000 if your bank goes under. The site includes information on the CDIC, its member banks and institutions, plus the types of deposits and accounts covered.

Canada Trust

http://www.canadatrust.com/

Canada Trust's EasyWeb online banking site allows you to pay bills, check account balances, transfer funds, and reorder checks. It also contains corporate information.

CIBC PC Banking

http://www.pcbanking.cibc.com/

Bank online with the Canadian Imperial Bank of Commerce. This very sparse and simple-looking site provides account balance and transfers and Bill Pay, and also allows you to manage your CIBC credit cards and stop payments.

Citizen's Bank of Canada

http://www.citizensbank.ca/

This online-only bank claims to be the only bank in Canada with an ethical policy to guide investment decisions (no investing in companies that test cosmetics on animals, for example). It offers all its banking services online or through the phone, including mortgage loans and credit cards. You can make deposits by ATM.

ING Direct

http://www.ingdirect.ca/

ING is a funky-looking site that offers basic online money management: account access and money transfers. Interesting, but it could probably stand to be a little less groovy looking and a little more direct in telling you about products and services.

LBC Direct

http://www.lbcdirect.laurentianbank.ca/newcorpo/Retail/?UCLang=_en

The Laurentian Bank of Canada offers bill payment, account information, and transfers. The site also links to the bank's other services, including commercial banking and brokerage.

National Bank of Canada

http://www.nbc.ca/index_e.html

National Bank's site features a comprehensive profile of the bank, including a listing of financial products and services, and "Direct N@t", their online banking service, which offers Bill Pay, account balances and transfers, and a demo to get you going.

Pacific Coast Internet Banking

http://www.pacoast.com/banking/inetbanking/default.asp

Access your Pacific Coast Savings accounts from anywhere, pay bills, and transfer funds. At this writing, the site is in the process of adding significant features, including the ability to download financial information into Money or Quicken.

President's Choice Financial

http://www.preschoicefinancial.com/

Now here's an interesting idea: President's Choice Financial rewards transactions with "PC points" which are good for free groceries at various stores across Canada. The site also offers the usual account services, Bill Pay, and transfers, plus links to President's Choice's other financial services, including mortgages.

Royal Bank On-line Banking

http://www.royalbank.com/online/index.html

This online service lets Royal Bank customers access accounts, (including brokerage accounts), make transfers, and pay bills.

✪ TD Access Web Banking

http://www.tdbank.ca/tdaccess/tda-web.html

A whiz-bang of a site with a whole set of financial tools to complement its banking and other online financial services.

Yahoo: Canadian Credit Unions

http://ca.yahoo.com/Regional/Countries/Canada/Business_and_Economy/Shopping_and_Services/Financial_Services/Banking/Credit_Unions/

Prefer the personal touch of credit unions to that somewhat more impersonal bank experience? Here's a list of credit unions all over Canada.

Credit Cards

American Express Canada

http://home3.americanexpress.com/canada/index.html

The American Express Canada site will allow you to track current charges and examine previous bills. You can download applications for the various cards Amex offers, though at time of writing you can't actually apply for a card online.

Bank One International

http://www.bankone.ca/

This very large issuer of credit cards offers a variety of affinity cards for Canadian sport teams, universities, and other organizations. The site allows you to apply online, but does not at this writing allow online card management services.

Equifax Canada

http://www.equifax.ca/

The Canadian branch of one of the world's largest credit-reporting services, through which you can order credit reports for commercial companies online.

MasterCard International

http://www.mastercard.com/cgi-bin/apply/outsidetheus.cgi

This is where you need to go to apply for a MasterCard in Canada. Select "Canada" in the drop-down list, and the Web site will generate a linkable list of banks in Canada that issue MasterCards.

Visa Canada

http://www.visa.com/pd/cards/canada/main.html

The world's largest provider of credit cards is just itchin' to get you one, too. This site links you through to individual banks in Canada that offer Visa cards, and provides general information about Visa cards worldwide.

Credit/Debt Problems

Bankruptcy Canada

http://www.bankruptcycanada.com/

Facing bankruptcy? Bankruptcy Canada features information on how you might be able to avoid it, and can connect you to a trustee to help you figure out your affairs. The site also features information on bankruptcy itself, both for individuals and for small companies.

Consumer Help Desk: Credit Counseling Services

http://strategis.ic.gc.ca/SSG/ca00719e.html

This page, put together by the Canadian Office of Consumer Affairs, connects folks to the various consumer credit counseling services in their province.

Dealing With Debt: A Consumer's Guide

http://strategis.ic.gc.ca/SSG/br01035e.html

More information on debt and what it can do to you and your finances, this time from the Canadian Office of the Superintendent of Bankruptcy (now, there's a cheery job). The site outlines warning signs that you may have too much debt as well as the options you have for clearing up before it gets to be too late.

Financial Sites and Magazines

Brian Costello Presents Your Money

http://www.briancostelloyourmoney.com/main.html

Web site of the notable financial author and commentator features financial advice, links to Costello's books and software, and a referral service to help you find a local investment professional.

Canada.Com Finance

http://finance.canada.com/

This finance Web site features the latest financial headlines for Canada from the *Financial Post* and for stock markets around the world, Canadian and US stock indices, personalized stock portfolios, and other customizable features.

CBC Business

http://cbc.ca/business/

All the latest business news and information from the Canadian Broadcast Company. Includes links to personal finance stories, stock indices and quotes, and a program guide.

Canadian Business

http://www.canbus.com/index.shtml

Online version of the offline business magazine. The site features articles from the magazine, an archive of articles, and the option to order (or re-order) a subscription to the print magazine.

Canadian Earnings

http://www.newswire.ca/earnings/

Part of the Canada News Wire, this clean, simply done site provides basic earnings information in a daily earnings report, archived conference calls, and Canadian business news.

E News Services

http://www.isdnwire.com/en/today/

All Canadian business press releases, all the time.

✪ Financial Post

http://www.nationalpost.com/financialpost.asp

The online site for the business section of the National Post has lots of news, stock indices, and commentary on Canadian and global business.

Garth Turner

http://www.garth.ca/

Former Minister of Revenue turned financial commentator Garth Turner features on his site his latest columns, an archive of said columns, a bunch of links to his books, television and radio appearances, and a schedule of his financial seminars.

✪ Globe and Mail: Report on Business

http://www.globeandmail.com/hubs/rob.html

The online business section of the Toronto *Globe and Mail* features all the latest business news from staff writers, involved coverage of stocks, funds and markets, and special sections on small business and tech investing.

IE: Money

http://www.iemoney.com/

This online adjunct of the semi-monthly personal finance magazine features selections from the current issue, an archive of past articles, and subscription information.

iMoney

http://www.imoney.com/index_home.html

A comprehensive but cluttered financial site that features current headlines, tutorials on a range of financial subjects, online tools and calculators, and financial products to purchase online.

Investing Canada

http://investingcanada.about.com/money/investingcanada/

A really useful site that has over 700 links to sites online that feature information and services to Canadian investors. That's a lot of links, but the site is broken up into specific subjects and is pretty easy to move around.

Investment Executive

http://investmentexecutive.com/

This Web site of the investment professionals' newspaper is subscription only and features news and information for the pros. If you're in the Canadian investment industry, a subscription is free; otherwise it's $60 a year.

Investopedia.com

http://www.investopedia.com/

This Canadian-based site offers over 1500 definitions of various financial terms and phenomena, as well as a "university" area where you can learn the fund, stock, and bond basics. Definitions come with links to articles that illustrate the term in question.

Investor Canada

http://www.investorcanada.com/

The online offering of the financial radio show of the same name, this includes real audio sound files and transcripts of interviews conducted on the show, plus opinion polls and business news.

Investor Learning Centre of Canada

http://www.investorlearning.ca/

The ILC is an independent, non-profit organization that offers books and seminars to help novice investors get up to speed; their Web site features information on both, plus columns from financial experts, an online "money school," and a financial Question of the Week (with an answer, of course).

Merrill Lynch

http://www.canada.ml.com/

The Canadian site of this financial powerhouse features a lot of interesting articles about the markets and investing (with a lot of emphasis on Merrill Lynch products, of course). You have to be a member to read the articles, but the membership is free.

Q1234.com

http://www.q1234.com

Q1234 broadcasts and archives quarterly earnings conference calls online using the Real Player application. It also features a list of upcoming conference calls, so you can plan ahead.

RetireWeb.com

http://www.retireweb.com/

A site devoted to helping people plan, save, and otherwise prepare fiscally and emotionally for retirement. Lots of subjects, although some pages are less well-put-together than others.

StockHouse Canada

http://stockhouse.ca/index.asp

Canadian arm of the international financial news Web site. Lots of news stories from Canadian business news media and international news wires, plus message boards on hot Canadian and global stocks.

There's Something About Money

http://www.yourmoney.cba.ca/

Finding it hard to talk to teens about the important facts of life—like how to do anything with money other than spend it? This could be what you or they need—a quick financial education that's not entirely stuffy and square.

WorkdayTV.com

http://www.workdaytv.com/

Workday proudly claims to be "The world's first regularly scheduled television style Internet broadcast program." Well, that means you can view streaming audio of financial news and commentary for the site every weekday between 9 and 5. Try to have a lot of bandwidth at your disposal.

Yahoo! Canada Finance

http://ca.finance.yahoo.com/

This corner of Yahoo! is not very pretty but contains a truckload of info on Canadian and global markets, on-site research and reference, the latest financial news from Canada and abroad, and financial message boards and chat.

Investing and Brokerages

Action Direct Brokerage Services

http://www.actiondirect.com/

Action Direct's "PC Action" software allows you to make stock and option transactions in Canadian and US markets, get real-time quotes, and view your portfolio. Trades are $29 a shot.

BMO InvestorLine

http://www.bmoinvestorline.com/

Bank of Montreal's online brokerage allows you to buy and sell stocks, options, and funds online, and bonds and other government securities through a phone broker. $25 for market orders, $29 for limit orders.

E*Trade Canada

http://www.canada.etrade.com/

Not quite as fully featured as its southern sister site, E*Trade Canada offers a full range of online trading options for stocks and mutual funds, market research on Canadian and American companies, and a raft of planning tools. Trades begin at $27.

InvesNET

http://www.invesnet.com/pbnIndex.htm

National Bank of Canada's in-house brokerage. A decent but no-frills interface, a good range of stock execution options, and a $24.50 per trade price tag. Market information could be better, though currently the site seems to offer price quotes with only a 20-minute delay.

TD Waterhouse

http://www.tdwaterhouse.ca/

A nicely done site with a range of investor research and information available (including real-time quotes), and easy access to other parts of the TD Waterhouse Web site (including insurance, mutual fund, and education areas). Trades at $29 each.

✪ Schwab Canada

http://www.prioritybrokerage.com/english/index.html

Schwab's trading fees are on the high end ($39 flat fee), but the site lets you do just about anything: In addition to trading stocks and mutual funds, customers have access to IPO and over-the-counter stocks and government securities and bonds. Schwab also offers wireless trading for those wanting to get away from their PC.

Scotia Discount Brokerage

http://www.sdbi.com/

It may not sport the world's best Web design, but the Scotia Discount Brokerage site offers low trading fees ($25 a trade) and a nice range of tradables, including stocks, funds, bonds, and other government securities.

Mortgages, Homes, and Loans

Canada-wide City and County Real Estate Search

http://web.onramp.ca/jpearcy/

This rather basic site lists properties for sale in all the provinces and territories. Enter the information on the type of house you want, what you're willing to spend, and contact information, and a realty agent from that area will contact you.

Canada Mortgage

http://www.canmortgage.com/

This omnibus features a nice education area about mortgages and other real estate-oriented issues, mortgage news, calculators and glossaries, and of course you can apply for a mortgage online. It also has an element of humour: A little "hangman" game. Cute.

Carbanx.com

http://www.carbanx.com/

Carbanx is an online car loan site, sketchy on information and rates, although applying for a loan is easy enough online; after you have done so, you're contacted by a rep to talk over the specifics.

CIBC Mortgage Specialist

http://www.cibcmortgagespecialist.com/

CIBC offers information on the various types of mortgages available, and some very basic info on buying a house and moving your stuff into it. You can apply for a mortgage online, or select a CIBC mortgage specialist online to help you through the process.

✪ The Mortgage Centre

http://www.mortgages-canada.com/

The Mortgage Centre works to get you the best mortgage rate by allowing banks to compete to sell you a mortgage. Beyond the loan application, the site has a nice range of calculators, informational articles, news, and a list of Mortgage Centre franchises near you.

The Mortgage Group

http://www.mortgagegroup.ab.ca/

Another site that offers a range of lenders to bid on your mortgage. The site seems a little spare, offering only very basic educational and mortgage rate information.

TheMortgage.com

http://www.themortgage

This site presents information on ten Canadian lending institutions so that you can see at a glance which banks and lenders are offering the best rates, and then apply online. There are also some helpful educational materials and finance calculators.

Taxes

CoolTax

http://www.cooltax.com/

CoolTax is a tax preparation program offered free for personal taxes (it's offered to attract attention to maker FLS Research's professional tax suite); users can prepare and then file their taxes online through Canada Revenue's "Netfile" program. Mac users be warned: CoolTax is Windows only.

KMPG Canada: Tax Online

http://www.kpmg.ca/tax/home.htm

Interesting tax information site that offers detailed information on national and provincial taxation, as well as general tax tips and tax planning, and of course promotion of KMPG services.

NetFile

http://www.netfile.gc.ca/

Homepage for Revenue Canada's program to allow taxpayers to file online. At this writing, NetFile is still in a limited introduction phase, but it looks to be rolling out fairly rapidly. This site gives details of the program, links to software that works with NetFile, and other FAQs and information.

QuickTax

http://www.intuit.com/canada/quicktax/

Home site of Intuit's Canadian tax software package. You can purchase the software to be delivered by mail, or download it directly from the site. Site also provides product information, a help desk, and free software demos.

Revenue Canada

http://www.ccra-adrc.gc.ca/menu.html

This is where your money goes at the end of every April. The site features everything you wish you didn't have to know about taxes, including information on taxes for individuals and businesses, and the various benefits allowed. Comprehensive and business-like without being obtuse.

Tax Court of Canada

http://www.tcc-cci.gc.ca/

If you have a beef with Revenue Canada, this Web site lets you know how to appeal to the Tax Court, either as an individual or a businessperson, and what happens once you do.

The Tax Page

http://www.taxpage.com/

Lovingly presented by tax lawyers, these pages are stocked with informative tax articles, links to Canadian tax sites, "Top Ten Tax Tidbits" and a Tax Challenge game. And you thought taxes were boring?

Taxpayer.com

http://www.taxpayer.com/

Home site of the Canadian Taxpayer's Association, Taxpayer, as you may expect, wants to keep a close eye on who is doing what with Canadians' taxes. A feisty site, it is filled with rabble-rousing editorials, reports on tax issues, online petitions, and more.

Taxwiz

http://www.taxwiz.ca/

Tax software that comes in two flavors: the original version for your computer, which can be purchased and sent through the mail or downloaded onto your computer, or the new online version, which allows you to do your taxes over the Web and then file online for $7.95.

Index

Subject areas, and subjects or Web sites discussed in the main chapters, are listed below in plain type. Entries in italics refer to individual Web site reviews in Part Two (US Web sites) and Part Three (Canada Web sites).

B

C

M

N

U

V

W

Notes

Rough Guides on the Web

www.travel.roughguides.com

We keep getting bigger and better! The Rough Guide to Travel Online now covers more than 14,000 searchable locations. You're just a click away from access to the most in-depth travel content, weekly destination features, online reservation services, and an outspoken community of fellow travelers. Whether you're looking for ideas for your next holiday or you know exactly where you're going, join us online.

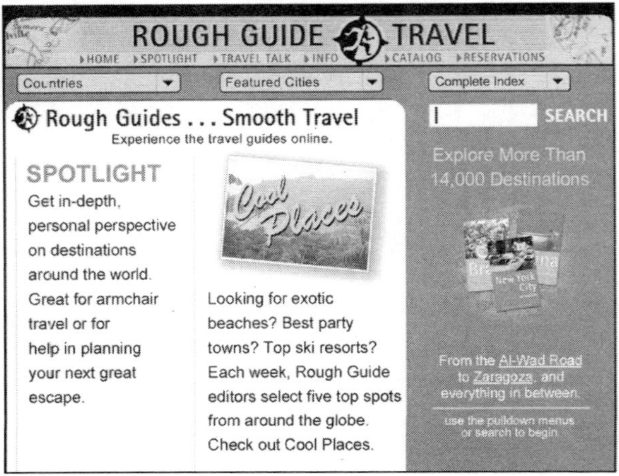

You can also find us on Yahoo!® Travel (http://travel.yahoo.com) and Microsoft Expedia® UK (http://www.expediauk.com).